Structures of Power in Modern France

Also by Gino G. Raymond

FRANCE DURING THE SOCIALIST YEARS (*editor*)
ANDRÉ MALRAUX: Politics and the Temptation of Myth
A HISTORICAL DICTIONARY OF FRANCE

Structures of Power in Modern France

Edited by

Gino G. Raymond
Senior Lecturer in French
University of Bristol

First published in Great Britain 2000 by
MACMILLAN PRESS LTD
Houndmills, Basingstoke, Hampshire RG21 6XS and London
Companies and representatives throughout the world

A catalogue record for this book is available from the British Library.

ISBN 0–333–67088–4

 First published in the United States of America 2000 by
ST. MARTIN'S PRESS, INC.,
Scholarly and Reference Division,
175 Fifth Avenue, New York, N.Y. 10010

ISBN 0–312–22558–X

Library of Congress Cataloging-in-Publication Data
Structures of power in modern France / edited by Gino G. Raymond.
p.   cm.
Includes bibliographical references and index.
ISBN 0–312–22558–X (cloth)
1. France—Politics and government—1995– 2. Power (Social
sciences)—France.   3. Decentralization in government—France.
I. Raymond, Gino.
JN2594.2.S78   1999
303.3'0944—dc21   99–32872
                                                                              CIP

This book is printed on paper suitable for recycling and made from fully managed and sustained
forest sources.

10   9   8   7   6   5   4   3   2   1
09   08   07   06   05   04   03   02   01   00

Printed and bound in Great Britain by
Antony Rowe Ltd, Chippenham, Wiltshire

To Phen, last of the old guard

Contents

Acknowledgements

This project grew out of a number of discussions with individuals and in institutions united by a common interest in France, ranging from colleagues in the Politics and History Departments of Bristol University, to the excellent forum provided for the analysis of French and British political culture by the *Centre de recherches sur les relations interculturelles anglophones et francophones* at its conference at l'Université de Paris XIII in 1996. I am much indebted to them all. My thanks also to all the contributors for their trust and forbearance, and the limitless resources of goodwill they displayed. Grants from the Bristol University Arts Faculty Research Fund and the research-leave afforded by the French Department were of immense help in the completion of this project, as was the support provided by my Departmental colleague John Parkin, and James Watson of the University of Bristol Computing Service. Last but not least, I am very grateful to Sunder Katwala at Macmillan for guiding this project to a successful conclusion.

Abbreviations and Acronyms

ANPE	Agence nationale pour l'emploi
ASSEDIC	Association pour l'emploi dans l'industrie et le commerce
BEP	Brevet d'études professionnelles
BNP	Banque nationale de Paris
BTP	Bâtiment et travaux publics
BTS	Brevet de technicien supérieur
CAP	Certificat d'aptitude professionnelle
CAPES	Certificat d'aptitude professionnelle à l'enseignement secondaire
CDS	Centre des démocrates sociaux
CECA	Communauté européenne du charbon et de l'acier
CEE	Communauté économique européenne
CEP	Certificat d'études primaires
CERC	Centre d'études des revenus et des coûts
CERES	Centre d'études, de recherches, et d'éducation socialistes
CES	Collège d'enseignement supérieur
CFDT	Confédération française démocratique du travail
CFI	Crédit formation individuelle
CFTC	Confédération française des travailleurs chrétiens
CGP	Commissariat général du plan
CGT	Confédération générale du travail
CNCL	Commission nationale de la communication et des libertés
CNPF	Conseil national du patronat français
CNRS	Centre national de recherches scientifiques
CREDOC	Centre de recherches pour l'étude et l'observation des conditions de vie
DATAR	Délégation à l'aménagement du territoire et à l'action régionale
DDE	Direction départementale de l'équipement
DEUG	Diplôme d'études universitaires générales
DGF	Dotation globale de fonctionnement
DL	Démocratie libérale

DRE	Direction régionale de l'équipement
DUT	Diplôme universitaire de technologie
EDF	Electricité de France
ENA	Ecole nationale d'administration
ENS	Ecole normale supérieure
FEN	Fédération de l'éducation nationale
FGDS	Fédération de la gauche démocratique et socialiste
FIS	Front islamique du salut
FN	Front national
FNSEA	Fédération nationale des syndicats d'exploitants agricoles
FO	Force ouvrière
GIA	Groupe islamique armé
HLM	Habitation à loyer modérée
IFOP	Institut français de l'opinion publique
IHEC	Institut des hautes études du cinéma
INED	Institut national des études démographiques
INSEE	Institut national de la statistique et des études économiques
IUT	Institut universitaire de technologie
MATIF	Marché à terme international de France
MDC	Mouvement des citoyens
MPF	Mouvement pour la France
MRP	Mouvement républicain populaire
OFCE	Observatoire français de la conjoncture économique
ORTF	Office de la radiodiffusion-télévision française
OS	Ouvrier spécialisé
OTAN	Organisation du traité de l'Atlantique Nord
PAC	Politique agricole commune
PAF	Paysage audiovisuel français
PCF	Parti communiste français
PME	Petites et moyennes entreprises
PRS	Parti des radicaux-socialistes
PS	Parti socialiste
PSU	Parti socialiste unifié
RATP	Régie autonome des transports parisiens
RER	Réseau express régional
RI	Républicains indépendants
RMI	Revenu minimum d'insertion
RPR	Rassemblement pour la république
SDF	Sans domicile fixe

SFIO	Section française de l'Internationale ouvrière
SICAV	Société d'investissement à capital variable
SME	Système monétaire européen
SMIC	Salaire minimum interprofessionnel de croissance
SMIG	Salaire minimum interprofessionnel garanti
SNCF	Société nationale des chemins de fer français
SOFRES	Société française d'études par sondages
TGV	Train à grande vitesse
TUC	Travaux d'utilité collective
UDF	Union pour la démocratie française
UNEF	Union nationale des étudiants de France
ZAC	Zone d'aménagement concerté
ZUP	Zone à urbaniser en priorité

Notes on Contributors

Dennis Ager is Professor of Modern Languages at Aston University and is the author of numerous major publications on the interface between language and society. His most recent published books are: *Francophonie in the 1990s. Problems and Opportunities* (1996), *Language Policy in Britain and France: the Processes of Policy* (1996), *Language, Community and the State* (1997), and *Identity, Insecurity and Image. France and Language* (1999).

Alistair Cole is Reader in the School of European Studies at Bradford University. He has published widely on the nature of party politics and the political system in France. His most recent books include, *François Mitterrand: A Study in Political Leadership* (1994), and *French Politics and Society* (1998).

Jill Forbes is Ashley Watkins Professor of French at the University of Bristol. She has authored a number of major works on French cinema, the media and the culture of contemporary France. Her most recent books include *French Cultural Studies* (1995) and *Contemporary France* (1994, 1999). She is currently completing a major project entitled *European Cinema*.

George Jones is Programme Tutor for the International Business and Modern Languages degree at Aston University. Trained in both modern languages and business studies, he is the author of a substantial body of articles on the business culture in France and the relationship between the business and the political elite.

Susan Milner is Senior Lecturer in European Studies at Bath University. Her research interests cover employment and training policies in Western Europe, and the political behaviour of working-class communities in France. Among her major publications, she co-edited *Workers' Rights in Europe* (1991), and authored *The Dilemmas of Internationalism: French Syndicalism and the International Labour Movement, 1900–1914* (1990).

Gino Raymond is Senior Lecturer in French at the University of Bristol. His research interests encompass both politics and literature, in partic-ular the impact of their relationship upon the cultural life of twentieth-century France. He is the editor of *France during the Socialist Years*

(1994), the author of *André Malraux: Politics and the Temptation of Myth* (1995), and most recently *A Historical Dictionary of France* (1998).

Georges Salemohamed is Lecturer in the Department of European Studies at Loughborough University. His publications include studies on postmodernism and politics, Levinas and ethics, and translations of Baudrillard and Durkheim. He is currently completing a book entitled *Management and Society in France*.

Introduction: A Centralized National Destiny

Dramatic representations of the destiny of the French people under the Fifth Republic are familiar and consistent features of political life in the Hexagon, from the banner headline in *l'Humanité* proclaiming the return of absolute monarchy after the constitution of the Fifth Republic was approved by referendum in September 1958, to more recent manifestos extolling the need for a democratic insurrection to overcome the immobilism of the Fifth Republic.[1] More seasoned observers with the benefit of a longer historical perspective credit the Fifth Republic with more robustness and prestige in the eyes of its citizenry, especially in comparison with the Fourth, the perception of which as a moribund system for a divided polity was acutely felt, especially at moments when its institutional deficiencies were cruelly exposed, such as the 13 ballots that were needed to elect René Coty President of the Republic in 1953.[2] In Europe as a whole, recent studies suggest that the legitimacy crisis theory can be exaggerated. While it is undoubtedly the case that individualism has grown, the argument that we are witnessing a backlash against the state, especially from the middle classes, is countered by surveys which illustrate that traditional beliefs in the vocation of the state, particularly in the field of social and economic equality, prevail consistently across the European states.[3]

Structural changes have occurred. In Europe generally, identification with parties has declined as citizens are quicker and more ready to use non-institutional forms of political action to express their dissatisfaction with the agents of representative democracy. However, the greater enthusiasm for criticizing parties and governments is not automatically synonymous with a crisis of democracy itself. Evidence collected across western Europe suggests that in spite of profound economic, social and cultural change, citizens continue to believe in their democracies.[4] But implicit in evocations of the crisis of representation in Europe is the notion that the long-established homologies between structures of authority and the constituencies that they represent have become distended, even severed, and now need to be rethought.[5] This is particularly pertinent in France where, as Cole illustrates, political parties cannot mobilize cohorts of partisan supporters as they used to, and as Raymond illustrates in the final essay, in France's relationship with Europe, where the relationship of its constituent regions with European institutions possesses the potential for diminishing the tutelary presence of the national government in Paris.

That the 'crise de représentation' should be felt, or at least commented on, so much more widely in France than in a comparable liberal democracy like Britain is attributable to the historical circumstances that fashioned, in a conscious and conspicuous manner, the relationship between the citizen and the state. Ager reminds us that the concept of the state as a uniformizing and homogenizing influence in shaping the nation goes back, linguistically, at least to the declaration of French as the nation's official language in 1539. However, it is the revolution of 1789 which, as Salemohamed underlines, gives the French polity its specificity vis-à-vis its European neighbours in the comprehensive way the establishment of the Jacobin state precedes and shapes the establishment of national identity through the understanding of cultural norms like *laïcité*. The Anglo-Saxon paradigm defined by Hobbes for the relationship between the citizen and the state, separating the civil from the civic by positing the silence of the sovereign as those aspects of life in civil society over which he has no sway,[6] survived both revolution and regicide – whereas in France, the Declaration of the Rights of Man and the Citizen resulted in an abstract conjoining of the person in his or her civil guise as a private individual with his or her persona as a civic entity, and part of a community of rights underscored by principles of intervention, egalitarianism and solidarity. This, allied to the transfer of sovereignty from the monarch to the nation – whose will, in theory, was expressed by the unitary voice of the state – meant that the citizen was defined primarily in relation to the national state, making the process of assimilation the key criterion for success, both for the individual with regard to his or her social ascent and for the state in the assumption of its republican vocation.

The notion of a crisis of representation existed, in a sense, straight from the outset of the rapid transition to a form of delegated authority that could be viewed by the citizens as having fallen into the hands of a self-serving oligarchy.[7] The potential for frustration became fixed by the hardening in republican ideology of the assumption that the national state was the overarching means for condensing and regulating social and political questions, and questions concerning the private and public individual, thereby conflating the civil and the civic.[8] The familiar plea for the 'retour du civil' in France expresses the idea that there should be a greater willingness by the state to recognize the need for more silence on its part, allowing the sphere of civil action to be oxygenated by prerogatives determined by citizens, in response to citizens' agenda. Some obituaries of republican statism have seen, in its diminishing ability to secure the confidence of the citizens, a return to the kind of communal allegiances that predated the fidelity to the national state conditioned after 1789[9] – while some defenders of the Republic's vocation have argued that the best way to restore its credibility must entail a readjustment where it, in effect, renounces its all-encompassing role and becomes an intermediary insulating minimum individual rights against the pressures of expanding and extraterritorial market forces.[10]

Beginning with the essay on the presidency, Raymond will argue that the sophistication of the electorate's reactions to the incumbent is indicative of a new hierarchy of distinctions in the public mind that the state's representatives have not sufficiently appreciated. Hence the rapid reversals of fortune in the opinion polls and the ballot-boxes of both 'présidentiables' and their parties, while the link between the elites in these spheres and those in the media and business, which sustains the perception of the tutelary vocation of the state, will be seen to have been overtaken by change, both technological and socioeconomic, and sometimes curtailed, as Jones shows, by the sovereignty transferred to European institutions. In the treatment of trade unions, Milner will shed light on the process by which the ambiguous nature of state tutelage can be problematized by conjunctural factors, thus allowing unions with a weak membership base in the workforce and dependent on the public sector to be invested with the expectations of a civil society frustrated by the apparent indifference of government policies. What the treatment of education and secularism will share is the idea that some of the classic reference points that set the ideological compass for the republican state may need to be remapped, if the republican state is to retain an effective inclusive principle. Finally, the evocation of the challenges to the power of language to structure a uniform perception of the nation, and the redefinition of the administrative structures that bind the polity together, will point to the way civil society and the realities of shared sovereignty are forcing the Republic to become a more 'modest' state.

It is the purpose of the following essays to give students, teachers and an informed public a sense of the way the hierarchy of structures that have determined the relationships between the state and its constituencies in France are engaged in an irreversible process of change;

and what they will suggest, in their diverse ways, is that the way forward for the Republic in a postmodern society is the adoption of adaptable structures that can accommodate change instead of trying to catch up with them. In short, the outline of a future Republic that emerges from this overview is one that, whether enthusiastically or not, will have to emancipate itself from the vocation to realize the citizen in pursuit of a national project, to embrace one which is constantly responding to individuals and groups seeking to realize themselves as citizen consumers of an expanding variety of products – ranging from education, as Raymond illustrates, to audiovisual output, as Forbes demonstrates, in a globalized community where communications and political alliances are making the pursuit of a singular, centralized national destiny highly problematical.

Notes

1. For example, Boccara, B. (1993), *L'Insurrection démocratique. Manifeste pour la VIe République*, Democratica, Paris.
2. Toinet, M.-F. (1996), 'The Limits of Malaise in France', in Keeler, John T.S. and Schain, Martin A., *Chirac's Challenge: Liberalization, Europeanization and Malaise in France*, Macmillan, Basingstoke, pp.279–298.
3. Kaase, M. and Newton, K. (1995), *Beliefs in Government*, OUP, Oxford.
4. Klingeman, H.-D. and Fuchs, D. (1995), *Citizens and the State*, OUP, Oxford.
5. Hayward, J. (1995), 'Preface: The Crisis of Representation in Europe', *West European Politics*, vol. 18, no. 3, pp.1–3.
6. Hobbes, T. (1975 ed.), *Leviathan*, Dent, London, p.115.
7. Furet, F. and Halévi, R. (1996), *La Monarchie républicaine: la constitution de 1791*, Fayard, Paris.
8. Wievorka, M. (1993), 'L'Etat et ses sujets', *Projet*, no. 233, spring, pp.17–25.
9. Minc, A. (1993), *Le nouveau moyen âge*, Gallimard, Paris.
10. Touraine, A. (1992), *Critique de la modernité*, Fayard, Paris.

1
The President: Still a 'Republican Monarch'?

Gino G. Raymond

Introduction: an ambiguous relationship

It is a commonplace observation that the presidential remit specifically defined and tacitly accommodated by the constitution of the Fifth Republic makes the President of France the most powerful leader of his nation in comparison with the other heads of state of the western world. And yet figures who seemed to preside imperiously over the French political system could be cruelly exposed as having feet of clay – figures who, once their presidential charisma had cracked under the weight of failure or scandal, proved to be as vulnerable as the figures of lesser stature they had previously dominated: most notably Charles de Gaulle, who during his mandate had defined the operation of presidential power, had barely seen his parliamentary majority secure an overwhelming victory in the legislative elections of June 1968, after the tumult of the previous month, before he gambled on the potency of his presidential charisma and lost. Having made approval of his plans for decentralization dependent on a direct consultation with the people by referendum, the prerogative which had significantly strengthened de Gaulle's presidency proved its undoing. The consequences of the vote on 27 April 1969 against the proposed reforms were terminal, prompting the announcement of de Gaulle's resignation on the following day.

The foregoing ambiguity stems from the expectations of the people whose interests the president is meant to pursue, above and beyond all factional loyalties, and to whose interests he must ultimately defer. Implicit in the mandate to exercise leadership while respecting the contract at its origin is the tension inherent in all the forms of representation Duverger calls 'republican monarchy'.[1] Indeed, as Duverger presciently pointed out before the advent of Thatcherism, even in a system with a constitutional monarch as head of state, the freedom of action available to a British prime minister means that his or her authority can be deployed with quasi-monarchical insouciance. But the tension between democratic egalitarianism and quasi-monarchical leadership assumes a particular pertinence in France, whose political culture in modern times is so shaped by an ideological commitment to the former at the expense of the latter. However, as Furet and Halévi have suggested,[2] the perception of the revolution of 1789 as the unleashing of a passion that would sweep down through the succeeding generations glosses over a more complex picture. Republican France's first revolutionary constitution was a monarchical one which, ironically, rather than marking the end of the revolutionary impetus, was swept away when that impetus really began to swell, and thus lasted barely a year, from September 1791 to August 1792. But that did not end the debate as to what would fill the vacuum left by the demise of the throne after fourteen hundred years. As commentators at the time noted (and would continue to observe subsequently), the Republic had at its core the rights of man, but simultaneously entrusted their safe-keeping to an oligarchy of representatives.[3]

The separation of powers between the legislature and the executive in the post-revolutionary period has focused, sometimes dramatically, the tension inherent in the act of delegation which both empowers an Assembly with the voice of the people and allows it the potential to supplant that voice. In spite of his picaresque political background and what some commentators regarded as his conspicuous inability to impress,[4] Napoleon Bonaparte's nephew, Louis Napoleon, ran successfully for office in the presidential election of December of 1848 by capitalizing to an important extent on his uncle's mythic reputation for leadership, allied to the fear in the conservative provinces of the Assembly in Paris. When the Second Empire which Louis Napoleon had imposed on France collapsed under the weight of defeat in the Franco-Prussian War, the period between the proclamation of the Third Republic in September 1870 and the voting of the laws framing its constitution in February and July 1875 signified the intense manoeuvring around the issue of monarchical leadership and the deep divisions this elicited. Ultimately, the compromise reached through the *amendement Wallon* – and passed by a majority of one – was aimed at enabling France to emerge from the provisional arrangements which had governed its affairs up to that point. Furthermore, the seven-year term accorded to the presidency, together with the power of dissolution over a Chamber of Deputies to which he was not personally accountable, was designed to reassure monarchist sentiment that the president was the next best thing to a king.[5]

The theoretical reversibility of the transition from monarchy to republic disappeared permanently with the attempted 'coup d'état' of 16 May 1877. Fearing the increasing rootedness of the Republic, as exemplified by the victory of its supporters in the legislative elections of 1876, the monarchists encouraged their presidential ally, Maurice de MacMahon, to dissolve the Chamber in the hope that the new elections would allow the gains of the republicans to be reversed. Although MacMahon was acting strictly within his constitutional powers, the partisan nature of his intention was blatant and prompted the accusation of a coup d'état from the republican camp. The concentration of republican forces provoked by this move swept to victory in the ensuing elections with 326 seats to the right's 207, and it was this verdict by the electorate which can be regarded as the real founding act of the Third Republic. The defeat for the executive power was irrefutable, MacMahon was forced to resign, and the much narrower margins for manoeuvre which were set for the presidency would endure, except for the interruptions of war, for another eighty years. Power had shifted to the floor of the Chamber, and the role of the president, although a key element in providing continuity in the transition from one ministry to the next due to his duty to nominate each new head, was limited essentially to oiling the political machinery as the Third Republic (and the Fourth Republic afterwards) became dominated by 'la politique des partis'.[6]

The presidency redefined: the Fifth Republic

As recent studies have implied, there is often a simplistic tendency to see the establishment of the Fifth Republic in 1958 as a clean break with the past that cut through the immobilism of the party system by establishing a strong presidency, with a vocation to lead France through the decisive exercise of executive power. In some respects, the advent of Charles de Gaulle and the Fifth Republic accelerated certain changes that were already under way. The mediatization of politics, particularly through the spread of television, was very soon to prove its inescapable importance across the Atlantic in bolstering the presidential credibility of John F. Kennedy in the debates with his republican rival in the race for the US presidency, Richard Nixon. With hindsight, it is safe to assume that the possibility of direct visual as well as verbal appeal to the people was bound to accentuate the importance of the presidential persona.[7] As for the dominance of presidential executive power, this was neither immediate nor predetermined. The original constitutional arrangements allowed for a 'two-headed' presidency which constitutional practice turned into one, where the president took command.[8] The irresistible pressure for change on a political system compressed between an ungovernable situation in the colonial territory of Algeria on the one hand and the disillusionment of the domestic populace on the other, resulted in the extrusion of a constitutional solution that has been described as a 'rag-bag'[9] containing the legacy of a framework of government which was centred on the prime minister's office, and nonetheless became powerfully presidentialized.

The fact that the old party leaders who had voted de Gaulle into office, effectively to wind up the Fourth Republic, insisted on their participation in the constitutional reform committee signalled their intention not to let him have it all his own way. But the four years covering the Algerian crisis, from the impasse in 1958 to its resolution in 1962, allowed de Gaulle the critical period in which to mould the presidency into the strong executive antidote to what he perceived as the drift and the sterile compromises characteristic of an Assembly-dominated system. In the new constitution approved by referendum in September 1958, De Gaulle inherited the traditional powers of the head of state exercised by his predecessors in the Third and Fourth Republics, in the judicial, legislative and diplomatic spheres, and in matters relating to appointments in the public and military service. While these powers were susceptible to a wider intepretation under the new constitution, the real departure came in the way the president's role as the supreme arbiter of the nation's interests was consecrated. Article 5 insists on the president's remit as the guarantor of France's independence, its territorial integrity and its fulfilment of treaty obligations. However, it is in the scope for action in the domestic sphere that the potential for the exercise of personalized power is the most marked in comparison with previous constitutions. Article 16 affords the president the emergency powers to take whatever measures may be required to counter what he deems a threat to the integrity of the Republic's institutions and the sovereignty of the state.[10] While the article stipulates consultation with the presidents of the Senate, the National Assembly and the Constitutional Council prior to the enactment of the emergency measures decided on by the president, he is not bound by the advice emanating from these bodies.

The granting of this exceptional power to the president was conditioned by the memory of the Republic's collapse in 1940 and the immediate need to deal with the convulsions of rapid decolonization.

The draconian powers accommodated by Article 16 were, appropriately, only deployed once, between April and September 1961, in response to the attempted 'putsch des généraux', namely those commanding French forces in Algeria (Challe, Salan, Jouhaud and Zeller) who wanted to prevent the slide to self-determination and thus the transfer of power to the indigenous majority. But this extraordinary prerogative of the president as the guarantor of the Republic's survival was cemented by an accretion of less dramatic powers: the appointment of three members of the Constitutional Council; the possibility of referring legislation to the Council for judgement as to its constitutionality; and the power of decision over whether a referendum desired by the government or parliament may be held.

In the four decades since the inception of the Fifth Republic, the counterweights to presidential power have proved their efficiency. With a few notable exceptions like the appointment of the prime minister, the calling of referenda, the dissolution of parliament and exceptionally, the invoking of special powers, presidential decisions require the countersignature of the prime minister. More significantly, by the 1990s the two bodies verifying the legality and constitutionality of presidential actions, the Council of State and the Constitutional Council, were proving their increasing value as checks on the untrammelled exercise of presidential authority. To place these presidential powers in a wider context, as Mrs Thatcher proved with the imposition of the universally disliked poll tax, a British Prime Minister with a solid majority in a uniquely sovereign parliament can act with considerably more impunity than a French president. This then throws the emphasis on the credibility of the presidential charisma, and the force with which the presidential persona seizes the opportunities provided by the conjunction of formal powers and temporal circumstances, in the manner established by de Gaulle for his successors.

As other commentators have observed, the crisis in Algeria fostered a sense of fear and deference which provided the parliamentary cohesion that substituted for a clear, party-based parliamentary majority supporting the president. Furthermore, in spite of the potential for the exercise of prime ministerial power in the fields of policy-making, the co-ordination of government activity and the management of the relationship with parliament, de Gaulle's choice of his faithful adept Michel Debré in 1959 meant that the latter was unlikely to flex his prime ministerial muscles in contravention of the president's wishes. However, the signature of the Accords d'Evian in 1962, bringing hostilities in Algeria to an end, forced de Gaulle to establish a more solid basis for the exercise of his presidential power. Already in April 1961 de Gaulle had rehearsed the argument that the election of the president by an electoral college of approximately 80,000 notables was an insufficient mandate for a national figure. But this did not neutralize the vigorous opposition when de Gaulle announced his intention, in September 1962, to use the provisions of the constitution – particularly article 11 – to call a referendum on the election of the president by universal suffrage. In addition to the outrage of the predictable champions of parliamentary power, other voices were raised, such as those of the ex-president and member of the Constitutional Council, René Coty, who called the move a 'constitutional coup d'état'.[11] Even more pointedly, Paul Reynaud, de Gaulle's former supporter, was instrumental in drafting the censure motion which the Assembly would adopt on October 5. In the debate Reynaud evoked the attempted coup of 16 May 1877 by President MacMahon, and taunted the prime minister by asking him to take to the Elysée the message that 'the Assembly is not so degenerate as to turn its back on the Republic'.[12]

For de Gaulle, the debate turned on the clash of two types of republic: the 'regime of misfortune'[13] of former times desired by the parliamentarians; or the new republic personified by him and whose perennity he would ensure. The personalized nature of the wager was expressed on 18 October, when de Gaulle weighted the outcome in his favour by alluding to the prospect of resignation should the referendum go against him, or should the majority in favour of the change prove too small. In the event, the result of the referendum on the 28 October 1962 was a victory, but not an emphatic endorsement of the proposal to elect the president by universal suffrage: six million of the 27.5 million citizens eligible to vote did not do so, which meant that the 13 million who voted in favour represented in the region of 46 per cent of the total electorate. But it was enough, and de Gaulle's broadcast on 7 November to the electorate who had 'sealed the condemnation of the disastrous party-based regime'[14] prepared the ground for the success of the Gaullist *Union pour la nouvelle république* in the legislative elections of 18 and 25 November. Thus, until 1986, such was the power of the presidency buttressed by a parliamentary majority that it was difficult to find a constitutional, institutional or political means of making a clear distinction between governmental and presidential decisions.

New robes for an imperial role

The situation de Gaulle had inherited in 1958 had enabled him to use the strength of his presidential persona to exploit the situation to the full and entrench the dominance of the president in the running of the government. For example, the government was not allowed to gather formally apart from the Wednesday morning Council of Ministers which he chaired. Although the prime minister was ostensibly its boss, the effective supervision of the General Secretariat of the Government, which organized its business, came under the president's control. This control was enhanced by the growth of a presidential staff at the Elysée which poached administrative talent from government ministries, and was verbalized by de Gaulle's willingness to usurp the prime ministerial function by articulating government policy through his dominant performances in the broadcast media.

The end of a sense of national emergency in 1962 and the establishment of a new electoral basis for the presidential mandate did, paradoxically, render the prime minister's position more secure, since the creation of a parliamentary majority behind the president's appointee meant that the latter could assume his responsibilities without the endless negotiations with other formations and factions in order to preserve a majority that had rendered the life of governments so precarious in the previous republics. Moreover, the providential leadership style which made de Gaulle's presidential voice so uniquely portentous was largely forsaken by successors for whom it would have been incongruous. In contrast to the war hero de Gaulle, the perception of Pompidou when he was elected president in June 1969 was that of the brilliant classicist with excellent managerial abilities that had been demonstrated following his appointment as prime minister in 1962. What distinguished Pompidou's presidency was the technocratic thrust of his ambition to achieve the phase of modernization that would successfully position France in global markets, and to achieve this as smoothly as possible, in keeping with his emollient presidential campaign slogan of 'continuity in change'. Pompidou's premature death in office from cancer in 1974 precipitated a presidential campaign that threw up a greater generational change, with a corresponding impact on the winning presidential style.

When Valéry Giscard d'Estaing ran for the presidency in 1974, his relative youth (48) and the fact that he stood outside the cohort of the Gaullist faithful as an independent republican underscored the less paternalistic implications of his campaigning ambition to help bring about an 'advanced liberal society'. In addition, the regular presidential contact with leading party politicians and the creation of a new formation in the Assembly in 1978 grouping radicals, centrists and Giscardians within the broad church of the *Union pour la démocratie française* (UDF) was perceived as a retreat from the disdain for parties exemplified by de

Gaulle and was interpreted by some commentators as adumbrating the
re-emergence of a 'partitocratic regime'. But in fact, these were minor
deviations from an agenda set firmly by de Gaulle. Even the purported
disdain for party politics was belied by the reality. As de Gaulle's interventions in the period between the referendum on the constitutional
amendment and the legislative elections of autumn 1962 demonstrated, he had in effect plunged into the fray on behalf of his supporters in the *Union pour la nouvelle république* (UNR) like the partisan party
political leader which he had refused to be for the *Rassemblement du
peuple français* (RPF) in 1958.[15]

As for the relationship between the president and his prime minister,
the disappearance of de Gaulle's giant shadow from the political scene
did not alter in any substantive sense the fact that the latter derived his
authority from the former. De Gaulle's election by universal suffrage in
1965 had established the presidency as the locus of power and the
leadership role above all others. Thus Pompidou did not hesitate in dis-
missing his prime minister, Jacques Chaban-Delmas, in May 1972 in
preference for someone more pliable to his wishes in the preparations
for the legislative elections of 1973. More surprisingly (due to appear-
ances to the contrary), the president's dissatisfaction with his prime
minister's failure to 'Giscardize' the Gaullist party forced Jacques
Chirac's resignation and led Giscard d'Estaing to appoint Raymond
Barre as his replacement in 1976. Ultimately, it may be argued that the
successor who emulated de Gaulle most ruthlessly in the presidential
relationship with the prime minister was the socialist François
Mitterrand. The end of Prime Minister Michel Rocard's tenure in 1991
was due in no small measure to the underlying friction in the relationship with Mitterrand, caused by the fact that his standing in the
opinion polls consistently placed him in higher public esteem that
the president. Conversely, his replacement, and France's first female
prime minister, Edith Cresson, lasted less than a year in office because
her deep unpopularity reflected badly on Mitterrand's decision to
appoint her.[16]

The determination expressed by de Gaulle to steer the nation's destiny in the 'domaine réservé' of foreign affairs and defence has been
adhered to by his successors with little deviation, especially in the field
of defence. During Mitterrand's second mandate, the half-hearted idea
emanating from the Elysée – in the aftermath of the collapse of the
Berlin wall – that the French nuclear umbrella might be transformed
into a European one was less a softening of the line on the independence of the French nuclear deterrent than an expression of one of the

key motivations for it in the first place under de Gaulle: the challenging of American hegemony in the determination of European defence policy. The presidential wilfulness in this domain was exemplified again by Jacques Chirac, who marked the months following his election to the presidency in 1995 with his refusal to yield to worldwide condemnation of his decision to proceed with nuclear tests in the waters of French Polynesia, even though there was little enthusiasm for it at home and in spite of the embarrassed silence from France's closest European ally, Germany. Chirac's overtly Gaullist refusal to compromise his presidential freedom of action in the 'domaine réservé' was no more autocratic than Mitterrand's covert determination in this area had been. The less acceptable face of Gaullist presidential practice, in creating a parallel team at the Elysée capable of circumventing the ministry of foreign affairs at the Quai d'Orsay, surfaced after Mitterrand's death. Assertions circulated, such as those repeated in *Le Figaro*,[17] that the advisory team on Africa at the Elysée (the 'cellule africaine') had been visited by leading Hutu extremists in May 1994 and that the policy of military as well as civil 'coopération' with the Francophone regime in Rwanda had continued even after the arms embargo imposed by the United Nations in May of that year. In short, the policy elaborated at the Elysée might have contributed to the genocide suffered by the Tutsis in Rwanda.

It is indeed one of the ironies of the Fifth Republic that one of its most eloquent critics, François Mitterrand,[18] should have come to incarnate, in a number of important respects, the archetypal Gaullist president. His candidature in the 1965 presidential race had enhanced his credibility as a *présidentiable* and this was borne out by the way he dominated the Federation of the Democratic and Socialist Left which had been formed to back his presidential bid, during its existence between 1965–68.[19] His future as the presidential leader of the left was secured when he acceded to the leadership of the new Socialist Party in 1971, turning the PS into a presidential party according to the pattern determined by de Gaulle.

In 1981 it was Mitterrand – pipped at the post in 1974 by Valéry Giscard d'Estaing, who polled a mere 400,000 more votes – who deployed the more believable presidential gravitas. Giscard d'Estaing's reputation had been damaged by the rumours which emerged in 1980 that he had abused his position by accepting diamonds from the Central African dictator Jean-Bedel Bokassa, and the perception of his monarchical disdain for the electorate was not dispelled by his patronizing performances on television in the build-up to the campaign or the dubious sincerity of his attempt to display the common touch through his tactic of securing invitations to dinner in the homes of French families selected to represent ordinary voters. However, the travails of Mitterrand's two presidential terms may be seen as justifying the argument that what has changed the relationship between the president and the people during the life of the Fifth Republic has been driven by the changing expectations of the latter rather than the peripheral changes brought about by the former. The paradox implied in Mitterrand's becoming the Republic's longest-serving president, coinciding with the dislocation of the presidential majority twice during that period and once again within two years of his departure from office, suggests that the familiar and useful criteria by which presidential power is assessed need to be nuanced.[20] As Peter Morris implies, the fact that cohabitation is no longer a phenomenon but a recurring fact is indicative of a situation where some prerogatives of leadership are less viable than others, and more dependent on the mood of the electorate.[21] The discussion initiated by Pompidou in 1973 on the possible shortening of the presidential mandate to five years, and revived again by Mitterrand in 1991 as a prospective remedy to the weakening of executive power brought about by cohabitation, appears to have been overtaken by the evolution of an electorate more inclined to clip the wings of the president rather than to strengthen them through mandates and majorities which are co-extensive.

What the French people have demonstrated is a diminishing sense of reserve in their willingness to turn the prerogatives of the presidency against it, when they deem fit. As the architect and chief exponent of the instrument of referendum as a means of popular endorsement in the Fifth Republic, de Gaulle discovered that it was a two-edged sword in the spring of 1969, when the electorate rejected his plans for decentralization. The paradox of an increasingly liberal electorate rejecting proposals aimed at decentralizing power, and designed to respond to the aspirations displayed in May 1968, is explained by the *ad hominem* nature of the verdict: the result expressed the desire to be freed from the tutelary presidential figure of de Gaulle. For, in some respects, the most Gaullist president after de Gaulle himself, François Mitterrand, the successful manner in which he pursued a national majority in favour of the Maastricht Treaty in the referendum of September 1992 (and in so doing enjoying the intended effect of dividing the centre-right), may be seen, on one hand, as reconfirming the pivotal role of the presidency in the exercise of French state power. But on the other hand, the result – 51.04 per cent in favour of the treaty and 48.95 per cent against – is indicative of how close the presidency came to a catastrophic loss of face. The gyrations in voting intentions were attenuated by Mitterrand's direct question and answer session with selected members of the public on the TF1 television channel on 3 September 1992. Before then the potential 'yes' vote had declined from 63 per cent at the beginning of June to 49 per cent in August.[22] Three days after Mitterrand's intervention on TF1 the potential 'yes' vote was nudged up to 52 per cent before subsiding again to the slim majority which, in view of Mitterrand's clearly partisan involvement in a project aimed at ensuring (European ideals aside) his posterity, so very nearly failed to preserve him from what would have amounted to a very personal rebuff.

A catastrophic loss of face is precisely what was inflicted on Jacques Chirac when he exploited his presidential power of dissolution to bring the legislative elections scheduled for 1998 forward by a year. His gamble that the presidential majority would be better able to absorb the consequences of public disaffection if that disaffection were not allowed to swell during a further year had clearly backfired when the results of the second round of the elections became known on 1 June 1997: while the seats held by the right declined from 484 in 1993 to 256, the left bounced back from 93 in 1993 to take 320 seats. And this pulverization of the presidential majority in the Assembly was not unconnected with the way the perception of the prime minister's subordination to the president rebounded to the cost of the latter. Chirac's determination to hang on to his prime minister, Alain Juppé, in spite of a massive wave of protests in the autumn of 1995 against government austerity measures (compounded by Juppé's inability to explain them persuasively), clearly did not enhance his chances of gambling successfully on early legislative elections.

What the voice of the electorate seems to be articulating, on every occasion that it is consulted, is the desire for a more modest kind of leadership, presidential or prime ministerial, for a more modest state. But therein lies the contradiction. A more 'modest' state does not mean a less providential one. What was evident in the criticism of the Gaullist prime minister Alain Juppé in the autumn of 1995, and also in the criticism of his Socialist successor Lionel Jospin at the beginning of 1998, was a reproach for their lofty incomprehension of their fellow-citizens: in the former case faced with the anxieties of millions of public sector workers about the security of their jobs in the light of the cuts to be made in the state's budget in order to qualify for inclusion in European Monetary Union; in the latter case faced with the demands of the unemployed in France not to be forgotten. However, at the same

time as this demand for greater closeness with the grassroots was articulated, the very existence of these movements testified to an abiding
desire for a kind of providential leadership guaranteeing the 'minima'
which would dominate political discussion in January 1998. But presidential distance from everyday political management led, in the age of
cohabitation, to the pursuit of subtler and sometimes paradoxical
means of restoring credibility when faced with a buffeting by public
opinion.

One could argue that the fact of habitual cohabitation, depriving the
presidency of the political clout afforded by a subservient majority in
the Assembly has, paradoxically, made the symbolic power of the president, in some instances, even more important. In the first cohabitation period of 1986–1988, Mitterrand redeemed himself as a leader
chastened by the defeat of his majority in the Assembly by projecting
his recognition of the limits of the market forces which the prime ministers previously chosen by him had unleashed, especially after the
stockmarket crash of October 1987. Significantly, there was no state of
grace for the president and his majority after Mitterrand's re-election in
1988. He had exploited presidential *hauteur*, which during the first
cohabitation had distinguished him vis-à-vis Prime Minister Chirac in
the field of foreign policy, to heighten the climate of *tontonmanie* –
a popular admiration for his avuncular reassurance – and thereby position himself clearly ahead of his rivals in the presidential race. But the
electorate had no sooner restored his mandate, underpinned by a relative majority in the Assembly, than it pushed the presidency onto the
back foot as Mitterrand was forced constantly to manoeuvre in order to
deflect from the presidency the discredit generated by the failures of
government and the stain of corruption that was attached to his party.

The defeat inflicted on the left in the legislative elections of 1993
was wholly predictable, even if the scale of it was not. Whereas before
1993 Mitterrand had still been able to play the card of heroic presidential leadership – as in his visit in the summer of 1992 to the besieged
city of Sarajevo, at the heart of the hostilities in the war in Yugoslavia –
after the change of majority in the Assembly this option was no longer
available as he faced attacks on his personal credibility. This came,
most dramatically, in the form of a book by Pierre Péan published in
1994 entitled *Une jeunesse française: François Mitterrand*, in which major
doubts were cast on Mitterrand's record as a *résistant* to the Vichy
regime in occupied France during the war. Mitterrand's counter-offensive
was to trade on humility rather than heroism and on his obvious
vulnerability as a terminally ill man. His televised dialogue with the

journalist Jean-Pierre Elkabbach on 12 September 1994 was a self-justification that was also a plea for clemency which, as the polls after the programme showed, was heeded by the French people. By the time Mitterrand had reached the final few weeks of his mandate, polling showed that the majority of voters judged his presidency to be 'globally positive'.[23] As Gérard Courtois has noted, one of the new and identifiable features of cohabitation is the resurrection of the president's popularity[24] – but with the difference that the sanction imposed by the people in divesting him of a majority in the legislature forces his transformation into a more benign and more modest republican monarch.

Conclusion: an ambiguous future

It has been argued that the 'imperial presidency' established by de Gaulle has now been superseded by a shared leadership pattern, with the prime minister as the key leadership figure in domestic politics.[25] But one could also argue that what now obtains in France is an 'alternance' within an 'alternance'. The great watershed represented by 1981 resulted from the fact that for the first time in the postwar years the dominance of the parliamentary and presidential centre-right would alternate with a left-wing majority in the National Assembly supporting a left-wing president in the Elysée. And whereas the scenario of a division between the foreign and the domestic in terms of presidential and prime ministerial leadership was sustainable when President Mitterrand faced Prime Minister Chirac or Balladur, it is no longer adequate to explain the situation following the exceptionally premature defeat of President Chirac's majority in 1997, in spite of his decision to bring the electoral calendar forward. The increasing breadth of the project to construct a European Union has inevitably diminished the individual profile of national players, even those as important as the French president or the German chancellor. Moreover, the construction of the Union has put in question the very notion of separate domestic and foreign, more specifically European, spheres.

By 1998 French domestic economic and social policy had become dominated by the fiscal disciplines imposed by the criteria to be met prior to the adoption of a single European currency. The obvious conjunction between European policy and national policy on tackling unemployment and welfare provision reversed the nature of the friction which had opposed prime minister and president during France's first period of cohabitation. Whereas in 1986 Jacques Chirac tried to assert the legitimacy of a prime ministerial voice in foreign affairs,[26] in November 1997 Jacques Chirac, while on a visit to Luxembourg, expressed presidential concern over the 'hazardous experiments' being conducted at home on employment issues. A thinly veiled rebuke came from Prime Minister Lionel Jospin, in a speech to the Socialist Party congress in Brest, when he alluded to his disinclination up to that point to criticize 'the other head of the executive', which had shown its own penchant for hazardous experiments such as the premature calling of legislative elections.[27]

In his first six months under the Chirac presidency, Prime Minister Jospin's performance suggested that the 'alternance' with the 'alternance' could be the transfer of leadership prestige from president to prime minister. Jospin's policy of 'écoute' – listening and dialogue with the different sections of society – proved popular with the public and notably defused the lorry drivers' strike which threatened to herald another winter of discontent in 1997. But Jospin's sensitivity to the pulse of society deserted him momentarily in January 1998 when a movement swept across France, articulating the frustrations of the unemployed and forcing media spotlight onto the issue through the occupation of government offices. However, Jospin's failure to register the depth of public anxiety on the issue of unemployment did not enhance the standing of the president. In fact, both leaders went down in the opinion polls. One is prompted to ask, therefore, whether the ultimate phase in the process of 'alternance' has now been reached, where the notion of the skeptron, the Homeric attribution of the right to speak, revived in Pierre Bourdieu's analysis of political representation,[28] is withdrawn by the voters, depriving presidential or prime ministerial discourse of its symbolic power, and is only restored by the electorate when it is confident that its voice will be heeded. As the outcome of the extraordinary congress of the RPR illustrated in January 1998, even a presidency like Jacques Chirac's, carrying the stigma of failure for having precipitated the premature demise of his parliamentary majority in 1997, can still deploy enough charisma to dominate his party. Plans by the party leader, Philippe Séguin, to initiate a renewal of the party by restoring the original Gaullist acronym it acquired in 1947, *Rassemblement du peuple français* (RPF), failed to materialize after the reception given to the President's message, read out by Séguin himself to the delegates. The twelve-minute ovation which ensued proved that Chirac remained the master of the party he had renewed and renamed the RPR in 1976.[29] Presidential court politics[30] had retained a potent appeal among the party faithful, even if its efficacy in dominating the structures of executive decision-making had waned.

As the IFOP poll conducted between 12–20 February 1998 covering the period from June 1997 to February 1998 illustrated,[31] trends in the popularity ratings of the president and prime minister have become increasingly short-term and less and less predictable. Whereas in the aftermath of the legislative elections Jospin's popularity seemed to climb at the expense of Chirac's, for most of the ensuing period the popularity of both figures rose and dipped concurrently. By the beginning of February 1998 the Jospin government's slowness to react to demonstrations by the unemployed in France at the beginning of the year had been effaced in the public mind by its determination to push through legislation aimed at tackling unemployment by shortening the working week, against the general background of a nascent feel-good factor due, finally, to a decline in unemployment according to statistics published at the end of the preceding month. As for Chirac, the endorsement for his presidency from his party's congress in the previous month was the prelude to his resumption of the presidential role as the embodiment of the nation's unity and integrity, at home and abroad. His articulation of the general outrage at the murder of the Prefect of Corsica on 6 February 1998 caught the public mood, and his classically Gaullist refusal to side with the American campaign to solicit international support for a resumption of hostilities against Iraq was also in line with French public opinion. But as the peaks and troughs in these polls suggest, both president and prime minister are caught in a succession of ever-shortening cycles characteristic of what has been called 'the routine of disillusionment'[32] – thus making it safe to assume that the reactions of the electorate are less constrained by an underlying regard for the prestige of these executive functions and increasingly liberated by judgements based on the short-term performance of the executive over single issues.[33] But as the chapter on decentralization will suggest, the decline in the prestige of the presidency, seen as symptomatic of the decline in the prestige of the Republic's institutions as a whole, has profound implications for the cohesion of the constituent parts of French society.

Notes

1. Duverger, M. (1974), *La monarchie républicaine*, Robert Laffont, Paris.
2. Furet, F. and Halévi, R. (1996), *La Monarchie républicaine: la constitution de 1791*, Fayard, Paris.
3. Ibid., p.245.

4. When Louis Napoleon came to the Assembly on 20 December 1848 to take the presidential oath, his choice of a blue suit with a white waistcoat led some hostile observers to liken him to a gymnasium attendant. In Postgate, R. (1955), *The Story of a Year, 1848*, Cassell, London, p.250.
5. Cobban, A. (1965), *A History of Modern France*, 3 vols., Penguin, Harmondsworth, vol. 3., p.18.
6. The phrase is taken from the title to François Goguel's classic study (1946), *La Politique des partis sous la IIIe République*, Seuil, Paris.
7. Hall, Peter A., Hayward, J. and Machin, H. (1994), *Developments in French Politics*, Macmillan, Basingstoke, p.95.
8. Morris, P. (1994), *French Politics Today*, Manchester University Press, Manchester, p.27.
9. Hall, Hayward and Machin, p.98.
10. For a clear and concise account of the key articles of the constitution of the Fifth Republic defining the powers of the president, see Stevens, A. (1996), *The Government and Politics of France*, Macmillan, Basingstoke, p.75.
11. Chevallier, J.-J. and Conac, G. (1991), *Histoires des institutions et des régimes politiques de la France de 1789 à nos jours*, Dalloz, Paris, p.677.
12. Ibid., p.680, my translation, and all subsequent translations from French.
13. Ibid., p.677.
14. Ibid., p.682.
15. Michel Debré commented on Radio Luxembourg at the time that one of the great services rendered to French political life by de Gaulle was to facilitate the emergence of large party formations capable of sustaining majorities in parliament. In Chevallier and Conac, p.685.
16. For an accessible and succinct account of these presidencies see Bezbakh, P. (1990), *Histoire de la France contemporaine*, Bordas, Paris.
17. de Saint-Exupéry, P., 'France-Rwanda: un génocide sans importance', *Le Figaro*, 12 January 1998.
18. In (1964), *Le Coup d'état permanent*, Plon, Paris, Mitterrand advanced the thesis that the Fifth Republic had been brought about by what amounted to a coup d'état in 1958, and that de Gaulle had sustained the regime by the systematic violation of the constitution and recourse to the arbitrary exercise of personalized power.
19. Cole, A. (1994), *François Mitterrand: A Study in Political Leadership*, Routledge, London, p.23.
20. Machin very helpfully enumerates the dimensions along which leadership operates as: symbolic representation, opinion formation, party organization, ideological production, agenda setting, decision-taking and co-ordination; in Hall, Hayward and Machin, p.95. And as Anne Stevens points out, the way these dimensions are exploited depends significantly on the priorities and perceptions of individual presidents; in Stevens p.98. But as the psephological trends in France since the mid-1980s suggest, the exploitation of the dimensions of presidential leadership is increasingly qualified by the way a less impressionable French electorate perceives the president.
21. Morris, p.40.
22. For a clear and informative overview of the referendum campaign, see Buffotot, P. (1993), 'Le Référendum sur l'union européenne', *Modern and Contemporary France*, no. 3, pp.277–286.

23. Amouroux, H., 'Nuancé! Les Français jugent l'ère Mitterrand', *Figaro Magazine*, 25 February 1995.
24. Courtois, G., 'Jacques Chirac, le retour', *Le Monde*, 1–2 March 1998.
25. Hall, Hayward and Machin, p.110.
26. The manoeuvrings that characterized Chirac's failed attempt to establish himself as the other head of the dyarchy serving France's interests in the field of foreign affairs are illustrated in his trip with Mitterrand to the G7 summit in Tokyo in 1986. See Favier P., and Martin-Roland, M. (1991), *La Décennie Mitterrand: Les épreuves*, Seuil, Paris, chapter 3.
27. Biffaud, O. 'Lionel Jospin veut mettre un terme aux critiques de Jacques Chirac', *Le Monde*, 25 November 1997.
28. Bourdieu, P. (1991), *Language and Symbolic Power*, Polity Press, Cambridge, p.193.
29. Saux, J.-L., 'Le RPR oppose à Philippe Séguin sa fidélité à Jacques Chirac', *Le Monde*, 3 February, 1998.
30. The term used by Jack Hayward (1993) for the concluding chapter of *De Gaulle to Mitterrand: Presidential Power in France*, Hurst & Co., London.
31. Published in *Le Journal du Dimanche*, 22 February 1998.
32. Georges, P., 'Charme brisé', *Le Monde*, 27 January 1998.
33. Courtois in 'Jacques Chirac, le retour' surveyed the findings by four polling organizations, IFOP, Ipsos, BVA and CSA, all of which indicated that for the first time since his election in May 1995, the president had regained the approval of more than 50 percent of his fellow-citizens. But, most significantly, the polls showed that two-thirds of the respondents still considered Chirac's performance over the longterm to be inadequate, and the majority still considered him to be 'superficial' and prone to 'frequent changes of opinion'. In short, the president seemed to have been placed on a form of permanent probation.

Bibliography

Bezbakh, P. (1990), *Histoire de la France contemporaine*, Bordas, Paris.
Bourdieu, P. (1991), *Language and Symbolic Power*, Polity Press, Cambridge.
Buffotot, P. (1993), 'Le Référendum sur l'union européenne', *Modern and Contemporary France*, no. 3.
Chagnollaud, D. and Quermonne, J.-L. (1996), *Le gouvernement de la France sous la Ve République*, Fayard, Paris.
Chevallier, J.-J. and Conac, G. (1991), *Histoires des institutions et des régimes politiques de la France de 1789 à nos jours*, Dalloz, Paris.
Cobban, A. (1965), *A History of Modern France*, 3 vols., Penguin, Harmondsworth.
Cole, A. (1994), *François Mitterrand: A Study in Political Leadership*, Routledge, London.
Duverger, M. (1974), *La monarchie républicaine*, Robert Laffont, Paris.
Favier P. and Martin-Roland, M. (1991), *La Décennie Mitterrand: Les épreuves*, Seuil, Paris.
Furet, F. and Halévi, R. (1996), *La Monarchie républicaine: la constitution de 1791*, Fayard, Paris.
Goguel, F. (1946), *La Politique des partis sous la IIIe République*, Seuil, Paris.

Guettier, C. (1995), *Le Président sous la Cinquième République*, Presses Universitaires de France.

Hall, Peter A., Hayward, J. and Machin, H. (1994), *Developments in French Politics*, Macmillan, Basingstoke.

Hayward, J. (ed.) (1993), *De Gaulle to Mitterrand: Presidential Power in France*, Hurst & Co., London.

Lacroix, B. (1992), *Le président de la république: usages et genèses d'une institution*, Presses de la Fondation nationale des sciences politiques, Paris.

Massot, J. (1987), *L'Arbitre et le capitaine: essai sur la responsabilité présidentielle*, Flammarion, Paris.

Mitterrand, F. (1964), *Le Coup d'état permanent*, Plon, Paris.

Morris, P. (1994), *French Politics Today*, Manchester University Press, Manchester.

Postgate, R. (1955), *The Story of a Year, 1848*, Cassell, London.

Stevens, A. (1996), *The Government and Politics of France* Macmillan, Basingstoke.

Zorgbibe, C. (1993), *De Gaulle, Mitterrand et l'esprit de la Constitution*, Hachette, Paris.

2
The Party System: the End of Old Certainties

Alistair Cole

Introduction

A system of competing political parties is generally held to be a key defining feature of a liberal democratic political system. Although the 1958 constitution recognizes the legitimacy of political parties as 'representative institutions', a powerful strand of Gaullism has denigrated political parties as divisive, fractious organizations, whose existence is barely tolerated, and even then on condition that they do not threaten the superior interests of the Republic. In the Gaullist tradition, parties have never been wholeheartedly accepted as instruments of democracy, reflecting a distrust of representative democracy in favour of a direct relationship between the providential leader and the nation. A suspicion of intermediary bodies between the citizens and the state (such as parties and pressure groups) is not limited to Gaullism. It is deeply embedded in the ideology of the unitary state itself. In the Rousseauite tradition, the state represents the general will, superior to the particularistic interests represented by parties, groups and regions. There is no natural sympathy for doctrines such as pluralism which emphasize the importance of the *corps intermédiaires* between the citizen and the state. In part, this is a natural consequence of France's historical development. The themes addressed in this chapter include a brief history of the origins and evolution of French parties, an overview of the development of party and electoral competition since 1958, and an evaluation of the state of the French party system in the aftermath of the 1997 parliamentary election.[1]

The origins of the French party system

What we might label as modern-day parliamentary factions first emerged in the course of the nineteenth century in Europe, in those liberal European regimes with representative Assemblies or Parliaments. Such factions existed initially at a parliamentary level. Only later did parliamentary factions organize throughout the nation as a whole. Within France, the moderate Republicans of the early Third Republic fitted this description well. Prior to the twentieth century, what passed for political parties were often little more than constellations of supporters based around political *notables*, whose power lay in their social, economic or political control over a local community. Centralized, coherent and disciplined parties were non-existent on the centre and right, and deficient – or fractious – on the left. In the Third Republic (1870–1940), the French party system reflected the profound divisions within French society. There were multiple lines of social cleavage which meant that no one party or even combination of parties had a natural majority of support within the country. France of the Third Republic was above all a localized society, divided into a multitude of different regions, each suspicious of each other and of the centralizing authority of Paris.

The localized bases of society had consequences for the organization of political parties. In Paris, the deputy was a fervent constituency ambassador before being a party representative. Indeed, many independent-minded deputies were not elected on any party label, or would be elected for one party but sit with another in the Chamber of Deputies. The significance of party labels varied in different parts of the country. In the Catholic west, a Radical would be a left-winger, fighting clerical reaction, and would be supported as such by Socialists. But in the anti-clerical south-west, a Radical would be primarily a conservative, supported by right-wing voters against a Socialist or Communist. For this reason, in the Third Republic it was somewhat misleading to talk of national parties. The obvious comparison was with the porkbarrel politics that still characterize elections to the US congress. Finally, policy divisions between parties were aggravated by the nature of the parliamentary-dominated system: small parties frequently changed coalitions in order to obtain temporary advantage. This exacerbated a situation of inherent governmental instability.

The French party system is marked by a measure of underlying continuity which belies the baffling array of party labels, the rise and fall of minor parties, and the emergence of new political movements such as

Gaullism. In Maurice Duverger's terminology, the earliest French parties were formed as cadre parties of the bourgeois variety.[2] They first developed within the Chamber of Deputies as parliamentary factions, and only gradually extended their coverage downwards and outwards towards the grassroots. These parties were forced to establish wider party organizations in order to cope with the need to organize elections, but they remained essentially parliamentary-dominated and centred. The moderate conservative factions (*modérés*) of the late 19th and early 20th century best corresponded to this model. In certain key respects, this heritage was carried over into the first half of the twentieth century by the Radical Party. In the early twentieth century, these elitist cadre parties were complemented by a series of 'outsider' or mass parties, which first developed as extra-parliamentary organizations in order to represent groups excluded from the political system, and only later became parliamentary groups as well. Within these 'outsider' parties, the extra-parliamentary organization has traditionally been more important vis-à-vis the parliamentary representatives than in the insider parties. The examples of the Communist Party (PCF) and, to a lesser extent, of the Socialist Party (the SFIO, later the PS) best fit the outsider model: party statutes in both parties subordinated parliamentary representatives to control by the party executive. In this respect, French parties continue to be differentiated according to their origins. Thus, the National Bureau of the French Communist Party exercises a tight supervision over the activities of its deputies, whereas centre-Right UDF deputies are not even certain of forming part of the same parliamentary group.

The origins of the French party system were laid in the Third Republic. The Radical Party was created at the turn of the century in order to defend the anticlerical Republic against the Catholic Church. From 1900 to 1940, the Radicals acted as the pivotal party of the Third Republic. Radical participation was often essential to enable government coalitions to survive. Initially a principled political movement formed to defend the Republic against the clerical threat, the Radical Party became highly opportunistic, prompt to change alliance partners when it served its interest. This was revealed with alacrity during the interwar period: on three occasions (1924, 1932, 1936), the Radicals allied with the Socialists during general elections only to desert their Socialist allies for the centre-right after two years. Politically republican, the Radicals were usually conservative in socio-economic matters, determined to support the cause of small anticlerical peasant farmers and artisans. The survival of Radicalism is limited to certain pockets of south-west and central France, where the movement articulates a republican, anticlerical and rural tradition.

The Socialist and Communist parties were the first powerfully organized mass parties. The SFIO (*Section Française de l'Internationale Ouvrière*) was created in 1905 as France's first unified Socialist Party, after the Second International had ordered France's six existing Socialist movements to fuse into a single organization. Under the impact of the Russian Revolution, the SFIO in turn split in 1920 into two parties: the French Communist Party (PCF), supporters of Lenin's '21 conditions' for joining the Third International, and the Socialist Party, which retained the party's existing title (SFIO), claimed to represent continuity with the old party, and resisted the Leninist model of socialism. The division of the left into two rival parties was a fundamental structuring feature of the French party system from 1920 onwards. Relations between these two parties oscillated between long periods of fratricidal strife, punctuated by brief spells of unity (such as during the 1936 Popular Front election campaign). The Communist and Socialist parties have survived intact since 1920, despite a period of illegality for the PCF, and a change of name for the Socialists in 1969.

On the centre and right of the French party spectrum, it would be fruitless to try to differentiate the myriad factions that existed during the Third Republic. A distinction might, nonetheless, be drawn between the *modérés*, conservative, parliamentary Republicans, and the *ultras*, opposed to all forms of parliamentary regime. The former category prevailed for most of the 1870–1940 period, especially after the Third Republic had overcome the early challenges to its legitimacy. The *ultras* adopted different guises, but never completely disappeared. The proliferation of reactionary, antiparliamentary leagues during the 1930s represented a real challenge to the legitimacy of the Third Republic and contributed to its collapse under the impact of German invasion in 1940.

A pattern of party fragmentation was carried through into the Fourth Republic (1946–58). This occurred in spite of the efforts of the founding fathers of the Fourth Republic at the Liberation to stimulate the emergence of a few large, disciplined parties. Legitimized by their role in the French resistance, three large parties initially dominated the political landscape: the PCF, the SFIO and the new Christian-democratic party, – the Popular Republican Movement (MRP) whose creation represented the final rallying of Catholics to the republican form of government. The three resistance parties served under de Gaulle in the postwar provisional government of 1944–46. After de Gaulle's departure in January 1946, PCF, SFIO and MRP formed the tripartite government of 1946–47, a government which enacted many landmark social reforms. The disciplined tripartite coalition broke down in May 1947, with the expulsion of the PCF from government, and the party system reverted to type: the early discipline of the Fourth Republic revealed itself to be illusory faced with the onset of severe domestic and international pressures. The rivalry between Socialists and Communists in particular postponed any prospect of renewed left-wing co-operation for a generation. The departure of de Gaulle from office in 1946 was a prelude to the formation of the *Rassemblement du Peuple Français* (RPF), a tough Gaullist organization campaigning for a presidential-style regime which prefigured the Fifth Republic.

By the mid-1950s, a pattern of party proliferation had reappeared. Many of these parties were tiny, with only a few deputies. But in the parliamentary-dominated regime of the Fourth Republic small parties were often able to exercise a political influence far greater than their numbers merited. This was especially the case for parties in the centre of the political spectrum. For much of the Fourth Republic, the Radicals continued to perform this function, although they were greatly weakened by comparison with the Third Republic, and they split into left- and right-wing components in the early 1950s.

It was undeniable that the major parties were more disciplined in the Fourth Republic. This was especially the case on the left (Communists and Socialists), but held true also for de Gaulle's RPF and the early MRP. But even strong parties fell victim to the decaying effects of the political system: notably, the tensions caused by participation in coalition governments; the ability of issues (such as the European Defence Community, or decolonization) to divide parties; and the short duration of governments, preventing parties from being judged on the basis of their performance in office. Ultimately, political parties were scarcely more cohesive during the Fourth Republic than under its predecessor.

However disingenuously, General de Gaulle was able to attract overwhelming support in May 1958 by condemning the instability induced by the *régime des partis* of the Fourth Republic, a regime he had actively sabotaged. At the beginning of the Fifth Republic, the term 'party' was hurled as one of abuse. It was instructive in this respect that the *Union pour la Nouvelle République* (UNR), the movement formed to support de Gaulle in 1958, refused to call itself a party, but preferred to think of itself as a rally behind a charismatic leader.

The evolving party system in the Fifth Republic: from confusion to bipolarity, 1958–83

In the preceding section, we addressed the divided and fragmented nature of political parties during the Third and Fourth Republics. No single party, or coalition of parties could muster a lasting majority of support either within the country, or within Parliament. This pattern changed abruptly with the creation of the Fifth Republic. After an initial period of confusion from 1958 to 1962, the party system became enormously simplified throughout the 1960s, 1970s and early 1980s on account of the process known as bipolarization, by which we mean the streamlining of parties into rival coalitions of the left and of the right. This electoral bipolarization between left and right reached its height in the 1978 National Assembly election, when RPR–UDF and PS–PCF coalitions divided the vote almost evenly between them. Since the mid-1980s, the structure of the French party system has become less neatly balanced. This has resulted from the emergence of new parties, and from the ability of political issues (such as European integration) to divide existing parties.

In order to understand the bipolar French party system, such as it existed in 1978, it is necessary briefly to enumerate the reasons most frequently cited for the development of left-right bipolarization during the 1960s and 1970s. Varying explanations have been put forward, the most common relating to the political, constitutional and institutional structure of the Fifth Republic; the historical role performed by Gaullism; sociological explanations, in particular the return of class politics; and the role of the second-ballot electoral system.

Those commentators who stress the importance of 'politico-institutional factors' in explaining left-right bipolarization point in particular to the enhanced prestige of the presidency as modelled by de Gaulle between 1958 and 1969; to the bipolarizing pressures of the direct election of the president after 1962 (only two candidates go through to the decisive second ballot), and to the strengthening of executive government in the constitution of the Fifth Republic. With the emergence of strong, stable governments encouraged by the 1958 constitution, parties were deprived of their former capacity for Byzantine political manoeuvre in an Assembly-dominated regime. The key contenders for office gradually refocused their attentions upon the presidential election. These various pressures combined to stimulate the emergence of stable government coalitions, and in turn more purposeful oppositions. One of the paradoxes of direct election was that the actual development of the Fifth Republic (partisan and bipolar until the mid-1980s) was in contradiction to de Gaulle's conception of the presidency and the Republic as being above parties.

A second explanation commonly put forward to explain left–right bipolarization relates to the 'historical role performed by Gaullism' and the development of party strategies on the non-Gaullist right, the left and the centre to respond to this. The progressive emergence after 1958 of Gaullism as a federating force of the right and eventually of most of the centre forced the disunited left to react in order to secure its own survival. Greater electoral co-operation between Socialists and Communists occurred from 1962 onwards against the common threat represented by Gaullism. In turn, the so-called independent centre (in fact composed mainly of conservative and centrist politicians left over from the old Fourth Republic), which maintained the pretence of autonomy from both Gaullism and the left throughout the 1960s, ultimately rallied in stages to the Gaullist-led majority from 1969 onwards. By 1978, the independent centre had completely disappeared and had been subsumed into Giscard d'Estaing's *Union pour la démocratie française* (UDF). The continuing survival of the centre-Right UDF confederation twenty years later testifies to the structural need to organize the various small parties of the centre and non-Gaullist right to prevent domination by the RPR.

A third explanation for left–right bipolarization was more 'sociological' in character. This pointed to the emergence of social class as the central political cleavage during the 1970s, which gave a structural basis to left–right bipolarization artificially created by the institutions and electoral system of the Fifth Republic. The capacity of Gaullism to attract a core working-class electorate during the 1960s had blurred natural class divisions. During the 1970s the increasingly stark division between the left and right reflected a genuine class division. It was contended that unemployment and the onset of sustained economic crisis (especially after the 1973 oil crisis) had revived latent class divisions.

This explanation appeared superficially attractive during the 1970s: the proportion of industrial workers voting for left-wing parties, for instance, increased dramatically from 1968 to 78. Within the left, the PCF claimed to be *the* party of the industrial working classes: as late as 1978, the Communists (36 per cent) still obtained more support from industrial workers than the revitalized Socialists (33 per cent).[3] François Mitterrand's Parti socialiste (PS) attracted support from many of the new social groups produced by post-war socio-economic change: clerical workers, middle management, and the new expanded professions (such as teaching and social work). It also proved remarkably successful at poaching the support of a traditional left-wing electoral clientèle (industrial and clerical workers) at the expense of the Communist Party. With the decline of Gaullism after 1973, the right-wing parties represented a more classic conservative electoral base: traditional elites, a fraction of the managers, the traditional professions, farmers, the lower middle-classes in the private sector, and a diminished proportion of industrial workers. This neo-Marxist class thesis hardly stood up to developments in the 1980s, however: a decade marked by extreme electoral volatility, by a marked decline in working-class support for the PCF and the PS, by a collapse of the Socialist electoral coalition, and by the emergence of new political parties such as the Front National and the Greens. In fact, in a decade of electoral instability, the political cleavage based around religious identity remained by far the most predictive indicator of voting choice, as it had since surveys were first carried out in the 1965 presidential election.[4] In the 1995 presidential election run-off, Chirac obtained the votes of 74 per cent of regularly practising Catholics, as against only 31 per cent of those declaring themselves to have 'no religion'.[5]

The 'electoral system' provides a fourth explanation for left–right bipolarization. Certain French political scientists consider it to be a self-evident truth that the structure of the party system in the Fifth Republic can be attributed primarily to the electoral system. For Jean-Luc Parodi, for instance, writing in 1978, the single-member constituency, second-ballot electoral system was destined to produce a *quadrille bipolaire*, a system with four main parties and two electoral coalitions.[6] Parodi was guilty of constructing a general model by observing the contours of the party system at that particular time: there is no political reason why this (or any other) electoral system should produce four major parties. But, in practice, it was undoubtedly the case that the use of the second-ballot system in legislative elections since 1958 had a salutary effect in stimulating electoral co-operation on left and right. The bipolarizing effects were enhanced by the fact that a similar electoral system was used for the presidential election.

The practical effect of the system was to provide an additional stimulus for coalition-building on the left and the right. Under the second-ballot system in use in parliamentary elections, a candidate must obtain an absolute majority of votes (and at least 25 per cent of registered electors) on the first round to be elected, failing which a second round is held, at which the candidate with the most votes wins. A five per cent voting threshold was introduced in 1958 to bar small minorities from contesting the second-round. This was raised to 12.5 per cent of registered electors in 1976.[7] The effect of the 12.5 per cent threshold has been to exclude candidates from significant minority parties contesting the second round, especially where they lack great regional concentrations of strength. The performance of the Greens in the 1993 legislative elections was an adequate testament to this: with 7.6 per cent of the first round vote, only two Green candidates managed to obtain more than the 12.5 per cent threshold and contest the second-ballot. Neither was elected. The electoral system has helped to preserve, rather artificially, a bipolar, left–right outcome to elections, notwithstanding the clear existence of a multi-party reality since the mid-1980s.

The parties' reactions to the new electoral rules of the game were variable. Initially inspired by the discipline and unity of the Gaullist movement, the main formations of the French right have generally agreed since 1962 to support only one candidate from the first ballot. Only in 1978 was there a general practice of competing RPR and UDF candidates on the first round. The presentation of a single candidate minimizes the problem of vote transfers on the second round that has classically afflicted the left-wing parties. The pattern of electoral co-operation was somewhat different on the left. In 1958 Socialists and Communists fought each other throughout France, effectively can-celling out the left-wing vote and allowing the election of numerous Gaullists on a minority of the vote. In 1962 the two parties formed the first of many second-ballot withdrawal agreements. Under the rules of such agreements, the left-wing parties each agree to stand down if their rival obtains more first-round votes in a particular constituency. Thus, if a Communist candidate arrives ahead on the first round, the Socialist withdraws and calls on his supporters to back the Communist, and vice versa. From 1967 to 1993, with the exception of the 1986 election (fought under proportional representation), the Communists and Socialists have agreed national withdrawal pacts in legislative elections fought under the second ballot. In 1993, the Socialists also unilaterally declared their intention to withdraw for better-placed Ecologist candi-dates, a gesture not reciprocated by the Greens. PS–PCF electoral pacts have historically been necessary for each party to maximize the num-ber of its deputies, but they have also greatly increased tensions within the left, as each party competes for first-round supremacy. During the 1970s and 1980s, this arrangement appeared to discriminate against the number of Communist deputies, since a significant fraction of Socialist first-round voters would always refuse to back the Communist candidate on the second, whereas Communist voters were far more disciplined. In 1962, Communists arrived ahead of Socialists in three-fifths of constituencies, reflecting the parties' respective electoral strengths. By 1988, however, Socialists came in front in 95 per cent of constituencies. By 1988, the once great Communist Party had become reduced to a reservoir of left-wing votes for electing Socialist candidates.

It has become increasingly apparent that traditional bipolar electoral alliances, for instance between Socialists and Communists, no longer accurately reflect the real divisions between France's political parties but are a legacy of what are perceived to be the dictates of the electoral system. Socialists and Communists continue to ally with each other in elections for the National Assembly, but violently disagree at all other times. In terms of economic policy, for instance, the Socialist record from 1981 to 1993 had more in common with monetarist norms espoused elsewhere in Europe than with the expansionary policies advocated by the French Communist Party. This disassociation between electoral alliances and political coalitions has increased the electorate's distrust felt towards the party system as a whole.

The influence of the electoral system must not be discounted. At a given period, the electoral system encouraged the parties of the left and right to form coalitions to fight the common enemy. By its discriminatory effects against smaller parties, the second-ballot system forced the centre parties to choose between the Gaullist-led majority, or the left in order to survive. The electoral system has also hindered political movements such as the Greens at an early stage in their development. The structure of the bipolar French party system of the late 1970s must not be reduced to the electoral system alone, however, but must incorporate all other elements mentioned above.

The evolution of the party system: from bipolarity to confusion, 1983–97

The height of left–right bipolarization occurred in 1978. In that year's National Assembly election, the four leading parties (PCF, PS, RPR, and UDF) obtained over 90 per cent of the vote, with each party polling between 20 and 25 per cent. In 1978, the structure of the party system was that of a *quadrille bipolaire*: four parties of roughly equal political strength divided voter preferences evenly between left (PCF–PS) and right (RPR–UDF) coalitions. The French party system was transformed beyond recognition during the twenty years separating the 1978 and 1997 National Assembly elections. As expressed in the 1997 parliamentary election, the French party system consisted of five main political families, of unequal importance. These are: the extreme left (principally the PCF and *Lutte ouvrière*); the centre-left (the PS and its allies – the *Parti des radicaux-socialistes*-PRS, and the *Mouvement des citoyens*-MDC; the various ecologist movements, especially *Les Verts*); the mainstream right (ranging from the neo-liberals in *Démocratie libérale*-DL to the statist centralizers in the RPR) and extreme Right (the *Front national*, also the *Mouvement pour la France* led by Philippe de Villiers).

No single explanation ought to be put forward to interpret the breakdown of the *quadrille bipolaire*. In part, the weakening of left–right bipolarization stems from features peculiar to each party. The decline of the PCF is clearly a central theme. Any attempt to chart this decline must combine an appraisal of the mistakes committed by the Communist Party leadership with longer-term sociological and ideological trends and the impact of the new post-Communist world order. The breakthrough of the *Front national* is equally, if not more important; the FN's presence has had a destabilizing impact, both on the structure of the party system (mainly to the detriment of the mainstream right), and on the nature of the policy issues processed by the political system (the security–immigration pairing). A comprehensive overview would require a similar approach to be applied to each single party. Apart from party-specific explanations, several more general themes emerge.

After the economic miracle of *les trente glorieuses* (1945–74), political parties in government have proved incapable of dealing with the perception of prolonged economic crisis since 1974. In a comparative European perspective, the reality of the French crisis is highly debatable, but the perception of economic *malaise* (combined with a marked French cultural pessimism) has had a destabilizing effect on all incumbent governments since 1974. Mitterrand's election as President in 1981 was regarded by many as fortuitous, an unforeseen consequence of Premier Barre's inability to master the economy. For this school, Mitterrand was carried to power on a wave of negative dissatisfaction with Giscard d'Estaing rather than positive endorsement. By January 1992, a series of by-elections had revealed the Socialists to be in a clear minority. In elections from 1982 to 1986, the PS was consistently defeated, culminating in the right-wing victory in the 1986 election. The swing to the right registered in 1986 ought to have ensured the presidential victory of a conservative candidate, and yet Mitterrand was comfortably re-elected in 1988. Mitterrand's re-election was facilitated by a catalogue of errors made by Chirac's conservative government, but it was also greatly aided by right-wing divisions, especially the emergence of Le Pen's far-right National Front. Mitterrand was re-elected in 1988 due to crucial centre-Right support, but betrayed this trust almost immediately. The Socialists' resounding electoral defeat in 1993 was inescapably linked to perceived poor economic performance and the misuse of political authority. In turn, the image of a government in permanent retreat augured ill for Premier Balladur's prospects of being elected President. To the surprise of many commentators, the anti-incumbent reaction was repeated in the 1995 presidential election, with the election of Chirac. Even more surprising to many observers was President's Chirac's massive April 1997 gamble in dissolving the National Assembly, leading ultimately to humiliating electoral defeat for the presidential majority and the election of the Socialist-led government of Lionel Jospin. Since 1981, key elections have tended to go against incumbent governments, in a manner which suggests the electorate's dissatisfaction with the performance of successive governments.

By the end of the 1980s, there was clear evidence from opinion polls that many French voters had grown tired of older ideological divisions and programmes, which had structured French party competition until the early 1980s and Mitterrand's election. This disillusionment was heightened especially after the high expectations and subsequent disappointments created by the 'dual alternation' of 1981–82, when the left took power, and 1986–87, when a Thatcherite-style government led by Chirac attempted to roll back the frontiers of the state. The limitations of party performance in office were exacerbated by exaggerated claims made by parties while in opposition. This had a particularly damaging effect upon the Socialist party. The Socialists in power (1981–86, 1988–93) were unable to satisfy the party's rhetorical demands made while in opposition. The reaction against the left was all the more keenly felt because these illusions had been maintained for so long. The myth of *l'autre politique* was exploded by the Socialist experience of 1981–82, which revealed Socialism in one country to be an illusion. The RPR–UDF government of 1986–88 suffered from a similar inability to match theoretical claims with practical results: what it defined as liberalism did not have the positive effects its supporters had claimed, such as a rapid reduction in unemployment, or an immediate economic recovery. In both cases, opposition parties had created false expectations, disappointed once these parties obtained power. The return of the Socialists in 1997 was predicated upon a careful balance between restoring the belief that politics matters, and that left and right do make a difference, while promising only what can be delivered.

Beneath the clash of rival political programmes between left and right lay a de facto convergence on many areas of public policy. This was particularly acute in relation to economic policy. With the left's abandonment of Keynesian-style reflationary policies in 1982, and its modification of its traditional statism, the dividing line between left and right became blurred, if not extinct as some commentators argued. The monetarist policies employed by the French Socialists after 1983 were at least as rigorous as those undertaken in other European countries. Developments in the European Community further blurred the economic distinction between left and right: the key elites in the three leading parties (PS, UDF, RPR) firmly supported moves towards closer European economic and political integration initiated at the Maastricht summit in 1991. The constraint represented by the European Community, and then the European Union, on the autonomy of party policy weighed increasingly heavily throughout the 1980s and 1990s.

There is some evidence of the return of a certain tradition of mobilizing, voluntaristic political action. The key to Chirac's presidential campaign in 1995 lay in protesting against *la pensée unique*, the notion that there was only one economic path (the strong franc policy) if France was to meet the convergence criteria for a single European currency. Chirac's campaign combined in a rather paradoxical alchemy of themes more normally associated with the political left, with the desire for an end to '14 years of socialism'. Influenced by the theses of French sociologist Emmanuel Todd, Chirac diagnosed a 'social fracture' within French society, based on the exclusion of minorities, bad housing, low salaries, and – crucially – unemployment. Given the lyricism of Chirac's campaign promises and the near-monopoly of power held by the right, high expectations were raised in the 1995 campaign, but these were soon disappointed.

The French party system and the 1997 National Assembly elections

More than any of its predecessors, the 1997 parliamentary election produced a differentiated party system. On the one hand, there is a formal, structured party system of enduring bipolar contours, characterized by the centrality of the left-right cleavage. On the other, there is a messy electoral reality which corresponds only imperfectly with the parliamentary party system.

Though the 1997 election witnessed a change of government shortly after the 1995 presidential election, and though the fortunes of individual parties changed greatly (both in seats and in votes), the structure of the formal party system did not change radically. Encouraged by the bipolarizing effects of the second-ballot electoral system, most seats continued to be fought between coalitions of the left and right. Only two deputies were elected outside of the left and right coalitions (Phillippe de Villiers in the Vendée, and the FN mayor of Toulon, Jean-Marie Chevallier). As in previous elections, movements of votes were greatly exaggerated by the amplifying effects of the electoral system; moving from 19 per cent to 25 per cent, the PS increased its parliamentary representation from 58 to 246 seats. The RPR-UDF and various right group declined by 8 percentage points (44 per cent to 36 per cent) but lost almost half of their parliamentary seats. (476 to 255). Most deputies continued to belong to the PS, the RPR, or one of the UDF parties. This is demonstrated below.

The Socialists demonstrated their domination of the left more comprehensively than in 1993. A resurgent PS (25.71 per cent with PRS) was flanked by several minor allies: the PCF (9.98 per cent), the Greens (3.68 per cent), and the MDC (1.07 per cent). The good performance of the smaller left parties was almost entirely due to an intelligent PS electoral strategy. Under the leadership of Lionel Jospin, the PS came to first-round agreements with a range of minor parties: the Greens, the MDC, and the Radicals (PRS). Though the Socialists ran candidates in

Table 1   Parliamentary seats, 1993 and 1997

Party	Seats '93	Seats '97
PCF	24	37
PS	56	246
Ecologists	0	8
PRS	5	13
MDC	4	7
Various left	10	9
UDF	206	109
RPR	258	139
MPF	0	1
FN	0	1
Other right	13	7

most constituencies (479 of 577), in around 100 seats the PS supported candidates of smaller parties (the Greens, the PRS, the MDC, certain left-wing personalities) offering the latter unprecedented electoral success. Thus, the Greens won 8 seats (0 in 1993) on a lower percentage of the vote than in 1993. This clever tactic prevented the left parties from dissipating their votes on the first round of the election. The left's traditional 'republican discipline' strategy came into play on the second round; whichever left-wing candidate (PS, PS allies or PCF) arrived ahead on the first round represented all left parties on the second. This benefited the PCF greatly. Though its electorate increased only marginally (9.18 to 9.98 per cent), the PCF increased its seats from 24 to 37. With their 37 deputies, the Communists hold the balance of power within the new Assembly.[8]

There was a steep decline in overall total support for the parties of the mainstream right. The RPR–UDF – various right total was 36.16 per cent, down from 44.1 per cent in 1993. For the first time, the FN (15.06 per cent) came ahead of one of the main pro-system right-wing parties, the UDF (14.34 per cent). The RPR–UDF total was the lowest polled by the mainstream right since the beginning of the Fifth Republic. But a major paradox in the functioning of the French party system was again highlighted by the 1997 parliamentary election. Defined in its largest sense (UDF, RPR, various right and FN), the French right is electorally majoritarian, even with a reduced combined total of 51.5 per cent in 1997 (compared with 56.9 per cent in 1993). Yet it is once again in a political and parliamentary minority. The tripartite structure of the French Right has been its undoing ever since the breakthrough of the *Front national*.

The UDF–RPR electoral coalition suffered in 1997 from the highest vote ever for the *Front national* in a parliamentary election, and the determination of the *Front* leader Jean-Marie Le Pen to defeat the Juppé government by fair means or foul. Wherever it could, the FN maintained its candidates in the second ballot. The FN succeeded in holding onto most of its first-round voters where the party put up candidates in the second round. This damaged the RPR/UDF. There were 76 left–right–FN triangular contests; the left won 47, the right 29.[9] The success of the FN demonstrated the persistence of a movement that certain analysts had initially linked to being a short-term reaction against the left. With mayors in local government, an active European parliamentary delegation and one deputy, the FN had taken root in French political life, though it remained an anti-establishment party. Above all, with over 15 per cent of the electorate in two successive elections, the

FN affirmed its troubling presence on the edges of France's liberal democratic system.

As the FN example testified, the 'electoral' party system thus corresponded rather crudely with the parliamentary one. Apart from the success of the FN, the 1997 election demonstrated a continuing fragmentation of electoral choice, to the detriment of the mainstream parties of all persuasions; as well as an enduring sense of anti-political feeling amongst important sections of the French electorate. Abstentions reached their second highest level in any parliamentary election since 1958; small and extreme parties increased their share of the vote; the proportion of the vote captured by the four parties of the bipolar quadrille (PS, PCF, RPR, UDF) was under 65 per cent, as opposed to over 90 per cent in 1978. The 1997 result added to evidence provided from other recent elections of a disaffection with mainstream political supply. In the 1994 European election the two leading lists were reduced to a combined total of 40 per cent. On the first round of the 1995 presidential election the two leading candidates (Jospin and Chirac) polled just over 40 per cent of the vote, a far weaker proportion than in any other presidential election. The 1995 presidential election also witnessed an usually strong showing of anti-system candidates, with the combined totals of far-left (14 per cent) and far-right candidates (20 per cent) exceeding one-third of the electorate, in addition to a higher than average abstention rate and number of spoilt votes.

Conclusion

Viewed as a whole, the party system of the Fifth Republic has underpinned a political regime which, in French terms, provides a model of political stability. The emergence of cohesive majorities to support governments (albeit with assistance from the 1958 constitution and a majoritarian electoral system) represented a novel departure in French politics. Initial Gaullist hegemony incited opposition parties to increase co-operation in order to survive. Right-wing domination of the party system from 1958 to 1981 gradually produced its antibody in the form of a resurgent left which finally achieved power in 1981. A decade of Socialist-led government (1981–86, 1988–93) proved that the regime could withstand an alternation-in-power. With the return of Gaullism in 1995, in the form of the election of Jacques Chirac as President, the Fifth Republic seemingly reverted to its initial inspiration. This illusion proved short-lived. The severe political reversal of 1997 inflicted upon Jacques Chirac demonstrated that the French President is no longer the undisputed master of the political game. The weakening relationship between presidentialism and the party system forcibly modifies interpretations of the Fifth Republic. A presidentialized party system has now breached the systemic disciplines that once anchored it, both from above, in terms of presidential control over the party system, and from below, in the form of the French electorate's willingness to place its trust in the President. The 1997 election revealed a French electorate no longer willing to respond positively to the call to elect a 'majority for the President'. This might be interpreted either as a sign of political maturity, or as further evidence of a crisis of representation. Both interpretations are consistent with observing a weakening of presidential control over the presidential party or coalition, even in periods of presidential ascendancy. President Chirac's loss of control over the RPR shortly after the 1997 election demonstrated this. Repeated incidences of *cohabitation* have fatally weakened the 'myth of the President' and impaired the presidential ability to control the structure of the party system.

A presidentialized party system has fallen victim to the inherent electoral volatility that has ensured electoral defeat for each incumbent government since 1978. The *bipolar quadrille* no longer accurately describes the structure of the French party system. The challenge of new parties, the decline of certain older parties (notably the PCF) and the limited capacity of existing parties to master new political issues has called the effective functioning of the party system into question.[10] And the humiliating rebuff for Jacques Chirac's parliamentary majority when he called the legislative elections earlier than scheduled revealed a new depth of public dissatisfaction so shortly after a presidential election.

Notes

1. This chapter is a revised and updated version of Chapter Nine of Alistair Cole's *French Politics and Society*, reprinted by kind permission of Prentice Hall, Hemel Hempstead, 1998.
2. Duverger, M. (1964), *Political Parties*, Methuen, London.
3. Capdeveille, J. (ed.) (1981), *France de Gauche vote à droite*, Presses de la FNSP, Paris.
4. Michelat, G. and Simon, M. (1977), *Classe, religion et comportement politique*, Presses de la FNSP, Paris.
5. *Le Monde* (1995), *L'Election présidentielle de 1995*, Le Monde: dossiers et documents, Paris.
6. Parodi, J-L. (1978), 'Les règles du scrutin majoritaire', *Revue française de science politique*, vol. 28, no. 1, pp.21–27.

7. Bartolini, S. (1984), 'Institutional Constraints and Party Competition in the French Party System', *West European Politics*, vol. 7, no. 4, pp.103–128.
8. This 'plural' electoral alliance is represented within the Jospin government. The PCF has two Ministers: J-C Gayssot (*Equipement*, Transport, Housing), and M.C. Buffet (Youth and Sports); the Greens one (D. Voynet, Environment), the MDC one (J-P Chevènement, Interior) and the PRS one (E. Zuccarelli, civil service and decentralization).
9. *Le Monde* (1997), *Le Président désavoué. Elections législatives 25 mai – 1 juin 1997*, Le Monde dossiers et documents, Paris.
10. See Appleton, A. (1995) 'Parties under pressure: challenges to established French parties', *West European Politics*, vol. 18, no. 1, pp.52–77.

Bibliography

Appleton, A. (1995), 'Parties under pressure: challenges to established French parties', *West European Politics*, vol. 18, no. 1.
Bartolini, S. (1984), 'Institutional Constraints and Party Competition in the French Party System', *West European Politics*, vol. 7, no. 4.
Bell, D. S. and Criddle, B. (1994), *The French Communist Party*, OUP, Oxford.
—— (1988) *The French Socialist Party: the Emergence of a Party of Government*, OUP, Oxford.
Birenbaum, G. (1992), *Le Front national en politique*, Balland, Paris.
Bréchon, P. (1993), *La France aux urnes*, Documentation Française, Paris.
Cole, A. (ed.) (1990), *French Political Parties in Transition*, Dartmouth Aldershot.
Dupin, E. (1991), *L'Après-Mitterrand: le Parti Socialiste à la dérive*, Calmann-Levy, Paris.
Duverger, M. (1964), *Political Parties*, Methuen, London.
Frears, J. (1990), *Parties and Voters in France*, Hurst, London.
Gaffney, J. (1989), *The French Left and the Fifth Republic*, Macmillan, London.
Knapp, A. (1994), *Gaullism since de Gaulle*, Dartmouth, Aldershot.
Le Monde (1995), *L'Election présidentielle de 1995*, Le Monde: dossiers et documents, Paris.
Le Monde (1997), *Le Président désavoué. Elections législatives 25 mai – 1 juin 1997*, Le Monde: dossiers et documents, Paris.
Machin, H. (1989), 'Stages and Dynamics in the Evolution of the French Party System', *West European Politics*, vol. 12, no. 4.
Marcus, J. (1995), *The National Front and French Politics: the resistible rise of Jean-Marie Le Pen*, Macmillan, London.
Mayer, N. and Perrineau, P. (eds.) (1989), *Le Front National à découvert*, Presses de la FNSP, Paris.
—— (1992), 'Why do they vote for Le Pen?', *European Journal of Political Research*, vol. 22, no. 1.
Milne, L. and Gaffney, J. (1997), *The French Presidential Election of 1995*, Avebury, Aldershot.
Ysmal, C. (1989), *Les Partis Politiques sous La Ve République*, Montchrestien Paris.

3
Trade Unions: a New Civil Agenda?
Susan Milner

Introduction

The place of trade unions within the national power structures – specifically, the relationship between the unions and the state – has been at the heart of activity and policy since labour organization was permitted in 1884. By legalizing union activity (albeit within strict limits) the republican government sought to channel working-class protest and marginalize radical activists. The state's reponse was conditioned by a fear of unrest fuelled by memories of France's revolutionary past and the fragility of its own institutions. The strategic dilemmas created by the state's approach for the already politicized syndicalist movement have never disappeared, and they go a long way towards explaining the notorious divisions which continue to plague the French labour movement.

'Divided, weakened and quarrelsome',[1] the French trade unions have never (except at very rare moments such as the Popular Front and Liberation) managed to organize more than a quarter of the national workforce. Today, it is estimated that trade union membership stands well below ten per cent of the workforce, and as low as five per cent in the private sector. However, although the unions are numerically weak, they are not without resources. As Reynaud points out,[2] the image of French trade unions as rich in individual activism and lacking in money and power is far from the whole picture. On the contrary, he states, they are 'an institution, firmly established in [French] society, a major power in the balance of political powers, an integral part of this institutional equilibrium'.

The issue of trade union power is complex and controversial, not least because it has at least four main targets: employers, government or other public decision-makers, public opinion, and other unions or other factions within the same union.[3] It will be helpful briefly to examine the concepts of 'power' and 'influence' in the context of labour organization before outlining the main issues in the debate about trade union power.

Trade union power and corporatism

It is notoriously difficult to separate the concepts of 'power' and 'influence' in political science. Mokken and Stokman's definition gives us a useful start: 'The characteristic feature of power is given by the possibility to restrict or expand freedom of action, or the capacity to preserve that freedom to a given degree'.[4] Freedom of action is determined by the action and choice alternatives which the actor has at his/her disposal. Many other authors similarly link 'power' with will and purpose, and with outcomes. Influence can be seen as 'the possibility to determine the outcomes of the behaviour of others, without the restriction or expansion of their freedom of action'.[5] Thus, influence is a more restricted notion than 'power', which can also include a coercive notion of 'power over' others.

Some actors in the political process, as well as observers, argue that trade union power and influence should be limited. One critic of trade union power in 1980s Britain, for example, contended that the legitimate role of trade unions was to provide certain types of service to their members (insurance and welfare), and that 'when trade unions seek to interfere in contracts in the labour market, and to influence the attitudes and behaviour or employees at work, they cease to be voluntary associations and become coercive groups and private monopolies'.[6] This criticism of trade unions focuses on their impact on the functioning of capitalist economies. Others query the legitimacy of trade unions (as voluntary, non-elected bodies, and as representatives of sectional interests) in their dealings with elected political bodies.

On the other hand, it can be argued that the entire raison d'être of trade unions is to acquire influence (with employers and with public bodies)[7] and that to deny voluntary groupings this role in the economy and in the polity would in itself be a denial of social pluralism. Trade unions may possess an array of mechanisms which legitimate their action, as we shall see. Problems arise because, whilst originally trade unions were looking for a very modest amount of power (or a tiny reduction in the power of employers over their members), they have become power centres in their own right. At the same time, the role of the state has expanded and blurred the distinction between public and private, with trade unions becoming drawn into the inter-face between the two.

Political scientists have used the term 'neocorporatism' to conceptu-alize this new relationship between the state, the market and certain interest groups. This new strain of corporatism (the prefix 'neo' serving to distinguish it from earlier, authoritarian versions of corporatism such as the Vichy regime) is characterized by hierarchical ordering of interest groups which are given special recognition from the state and access to decision-making in return for observing certain controls on their selection of leaders and articulation of demands and supports.[8] More generally, the term is used to denote an important degree of highly stable 'concertation of major economic interests'.[9] However, the use of 'neocorporatism' has also proved problematic. It is heavily dependent on the type of arrangements common in the 1970s, notably incomes policies, and therefore current investigations tend to neglect the complex, changing relationship between centralized and decentral-ized bargaining.[10] Moreover, the neocorporatist model applies only to a handful of states, mainly in northern Europe. Once it is applied to other countries, its validity is questionable. This is particularly true when attempts are made to fit France into the model. In 1982, Lehmbruch and Schmitter mapped out European countries on a scale ranging from strong (Austria, Sweden and the Netherlands) through medium (Denmark and West Germany, with Britain in the early throes of Thatcherism as a borderline case) to weak (France).[11] When Lehmbruch revised this model a little later, France did not appear on the scale but was treated separately as a case of 'concertation without labour', where (ironically, as he notes, since the term 'concer-tation' was invented in France!) weak trade unions play a minor role and the corporatist arrangements are overwhelmingly state-led.[12]

In the French case, corporatism was originally a syndicalist idea, a plea for autonomy in the face of a repressive state. A more statist view of corporatism emerged with the spread of Saint-Simonian ideas advo-cating the representation of distinct groups in parliament. This notion was later taken up by the influential thinker Emile Dürkheim, who argued that the state was not competent to carry out economic deci-sion-making, which should therefore be devolved to socio-economic actors, allowing the state to act as an independent 'arbiter'.[13] An authoritarian version of corporatism emerged under the Vichy regime, with the support of a fraction of the labour movement under Belin (a close associate of the CGT leader Léon Jouhaux), but this project failed to take root. It was an instrumental policy rather than a real corporatist vision: more *dirigisme* than corporatism.[14] In this sense, Vichy reinforced the French tradition of state-led corporatism. Gaullist 'concertation', based on national-level bargaining and incorporation of sectional interest groups into the institutional life of the Fifth Republic, continued this trend, but differed markedly from Vichy proto-fascism in that groups were allowed to organize freely.[15]

If the first characteristic of the French model of interest intermediation is state-led, technocratic policy-making, the second is its fragmentation or sectionalism, which the all-embracing term 'social partners' unsuccessfully tries to hide. According to some analysts, this 'segment and partial mode of concertation' which forms the basis of the French model is the direct result of the state's legitimation strategies as it extended its role further into the private (market) sphere.[16] It is an inevitable consequence of the growing indifferentiation between political and economic matters. We will return to this argument later, as it suggests that French-style corporatism is here to stay. It is important, though, to note the implications of this analysis. Unlike the north-European (social-democratic) form of neocorporatism, based on a diffuse social consensus and involving well-organized employer and trade union bodies, the French model is extremely difficult to manage in times of economic crisis because the narrow sectional interests fostered by state-led corporatism militate against any sense of shared goals and rule out constructive bargaining over change. Crozier's 1970 critique of the 'stalled society'[17] seems to have lost none of its relevance, particularly in the light of the massive strike movement at the end of 1995, which we shall examine towards the end of this chapter.

Sources of trade union influence in France

At this stage it is useful to return to the idea of 'trade union power', particularly in comparison with Britain. In both Britain and France there was a debate about trade union power, in Britain in the 1970s and in France in the 1980s. The timing of these debates suggests a link with periods of left government in office, but much wider questions were raised about the role of trade unions in contemporary society and politics. In the British case, trade union power was much greater and the debate was at the heart of policy-making. In the decade 1970–80, three successive governments were prevented by union power from pursuing their economic strategy, and all lost the elections which followed the defeat of their policies. Trade unions were also able to resist two attempts by government to force them to change their ways, by introducing a 'conciliation pause' during strikes, strike ballots and opening unions to fines for strike action, and (in the Industrial Relations Act of 1971) by setting up an industrial court to make unions answerable for alleged unfair industrial practices.[18] Trade union power resulted from their legal immunities which made it possible to strike and picket without facing legal action. This lack of regulation, in line with the British tradition of 'voluntarism' and free collective bargaining, was regarded as imposing unnecessary costs on British businesses. Trade unions' economic power also gave them considerable political leverage, whilst the influence they had acquired within the corporatist structures of the state and with the Labour Party now in office further boosted their ability to determine policy outcomes.

Successive Conservative governments under Margaret Thatcher gradually but decisively reversed this situation, beginning with trade unions' role in decision-making. By 1983, the incomes policy had been scrapped and the Price Commission abolished. One by one, the structures of concerted decision-making (wage councils, the National Economic Development Council, the tripartite Manpower Services Commission) disappeared. In the wake of the government's defeat of the 1984–85 miners' strike, trade unions' legal immunities were lifted and strike ballots made compulsory. Finally, the monetarist economic policies which the government was now free to pursue further eroded trade unions' power and to some extent their membership base; regulation at the workplace level was not necessary.

In France, the 1980s debate on trade union power was less central to policy-making, and it engendered no consensus on how to tackle the problems identified. It focused on the civil service, where journalists accused trade unions (the 'syndicracy') of controlling recruitment and promotions.[19] (It is noteworthy that the closed shop is illegal in France.) In the private sector, it was argued, unrepresentative trade unions remained wedded to long-dead class antagonisms and prevented the development of a more consensual style of industrial relations. Both of these criticisms hit a chord with a French public which regards civil servants as 'privileged' because they enjoy job security and which regularly expresses dissatisfaction with 'politicized' trade unions.

Undoubtedly, the sizeable public sector in France has created pockets of trade union power. Union membership is much higher in the public sector, and some public companies (particularly those with a long-standing tradition of public service, notably the gas and electricity company EDF–GDF) constitute veritable 'bastions', particularly of the

CGT. This helps to finance union staff and activities. Union militancy in key sectors (particularly public transport and energy) effectively drives the movement and keeps it in the public eye: most of the major strikes in the 1980s and 1990s have taken place in the public or semi-public sector (transport, shipbuilding, steel, air traffic, customs and finance, hospitals). Moreover, by increasing union leverage in national bargaining (through the use of 'showcase' public sector agreements and the ripple effect of bargaining in the nationalized companies), public sector presence has gone some way towards compensating for the chronic weakness of labour organization in the private sector. Undoubtedly, the strong trade union presence in the public sector has at least delayed policy change, and the left government's return to a policy of public sector recruitment in 1997 shows that the shift to marketization is far from complete. However, in the longer term privatization will spell the end of many trade union privileges.

Other accounts of trade union power were more sympathetic to the unions, although in general observers saw the case for a fundamental change in their ideology and organization. Thus, Adam[20] stressed the democratic legitimacy given to French unions by the system of elected bodies which exist to regulate workplace relations: in particular, works committees (*comités d'entreprise*) in companies with more than fifty employees and bipartite (since 1979) industrial tribunals (*conseils de prud'hommes*), which exist in each French *département*. However, this legitimacy has been severely eroded in recent years as the participation rate continues to drop and the proportion of non-union-affiliated delegates grows: 72.1 per cent of workers voted in works committee elections in 1970–71, but only 64.4 per cent in 1990–91. Non-participation has particularly hit the *prud'hommes* elections: just over half of workers (59.4 per cent) voted in 1992, but only around a third of workers took part in the 1997 elections. In the public sector, where unions are stronger, turnout at the first elections to administration boards of social security funds in 1983 was so disappointing that further elections were not repeated. Non-union affiliates accounted for only 13.8 per cent of those elected to works committees in 1970–71, but 28.7 per cent in 1990–91.[21] The argument that French trade unions are more representative than their membership figures suggest, because of the electoral support they receive through such bodies, holds less water than it did when Adam's book appeared. Moreover, by making them compete for votes, professional elections exacerbate divisions between unions and therefore weaken them further.

Nevertheless, 'professional' elections give the unions some institutional support and allow them to maintain a network of activists who are paid by their employer and by the state, so in this sense they bolster their power. Access to industrial jurisprudence is also secured through the *prud'hommes*, and this is potentially significant since the gradual retreat of the state since the 1980s has led to a regulatory shift towards the judiciary: for example, the removal in 1986 of the requirement for prior administrative authorization of mass redundancies opened the floodgates for individual appeals against employer decisions. The workload of the *prud'hommes* continues to rise: they deal with around 150,000 cases a year. However, trade union input is constrained by labour legislation, so there is little opportunity to shape jurisprudence. The move away from active bargaining to defence of individual cases appears to be shaping trade union activity in all advanced economies, and whilst it can help to boost unions' image (particularly in the French context of competition between unions) it puts them in a defensive and therefore relatively weak position.

More generally, Adam's argument about democratic legitimacy reveals a political culture organized around the republican model, which gives unions a further source of legitimization. The republican tradition in France provides trade unions with a set of values (democratic freedoms, equality, fraternity) justifying their appeal on behalf of a much wider audience than their membership and their intervention in public life. By posing as the defenders of the republican tradition they can call government to account, forge alliances with citizens and even intervene in the electoral process.[22] Thus, countless opinion surveys which show that, whilst French people may criticize unions as incapable of representing them adequately, they want them to play an important role in public life and see their presence as indispensable to the functioning of a democratic system. This powerful legitimization mechanism also allows the unions to make links with public service users in campaigns for jobs (for example, postal services or energy provision to rural areas) and against privatization plans which would threaten the unions' position.[23]

Let us now examine the two main areas in which trade unions' institutional power lies: access to decision-making through public committees, and in the 'family community' with left parties.

Access to public decision-making

We have seen that trade union influence originates to a large extent from the state: it reflects state regulation of matters which in some

countries are left in the private sphere (individual contract or free collective bargaining) and a partial incorporation of interest groups by the
state into the decision-making process. After the 1884 law legalizing
labour unions, there were some attempts to set up compulsory arbitra-
tion and conciliation procedures and state-run social security schemes,
although this happened later and less coherently than in Germany, for
example. However, it was in the post-1945 period, within a technocratic policy framework, that the unions gained a foothold in state
institutions. The Gaullist Fifth Republic continued this technocratic
incorporation of sectional interests. Official consultation and subven-
tion of labour unions takes place through a plethora of committees
and regulatory bodies.

The most important of these bodies is the Economic and Social
Council[24]. Its 231 members, elected for five years, represent specific
socio- economic categories: employers, employees, farmers, co-operatives
and mutual societies, family, tenants and savers, public companies, artisans, various cultural and economic associations. Of these, 69 represent
wage-earners (essentially, trade union delegates): 17 CGT, 17 CFDT, 17
CGT–FO, 7 CGC, 6 CFTC, 4 *Fédération Nationale de l'Enseignement* and
1 farmworkers' representative. The ESC's role is to bring the different
interest groups together and encourage their participation in economic
and social decision-making. But its function is merely consultative.

The government must consult the ESC before presenting bills of an
economic and social nature, but the Committee has no say in the state
budget. In addition, the ESC can discuss other matters as it sees fit and
call on expert opinion to draw up reports, and this has helped it to
raise contentious issues and have a significant impact on opinion and
policy formation: the most obvious example is the debate on 'new
poverty' in the 1980s, which was launched through the ESC's reports.
In general terms, though, it is hard to see any cases of direct ESC influence on government policy, particularly in areas of interest to trade
unions. Rather, participation in the ESC adds to the wider sense of
union legitimacy and gives them access to resources (payment of official representatives, and information and expertise).

Access to economic policy-making is provided by the various committees attached to the five-year Plan, on which trade union representatives sit and to which they are ritually invited to give evidence.
However, the importance of the Plan in achieving economic objectives
has reduced sharply in a period of very low growth. Moreover, it
was always the case that trade unions were under-represented in the
planning committees, which followed an employer-oriented logic.[25]

For the unions, the main advantages of participation are information and access to expertise, and also simply 'claim-staking': to some extent the unions are there because they assert their right not to be left out. This aspect of integration into networks of power, not only national but also regional (through the regional modernization committees) should not be underestimated, however. Formal decision-making is only one dimension of the daily exercise of power which, particularly since the 1981–82 decentralization laws, is quite diffuse, particularly in the grey area between public and private activities.

Other public bodies which include trade union representation are the National Commission on Employment Relations, which has helped to maintain links between unions, employers and the labour and social affairs ministry, and the Wages Commission which makes recommendations on the minimum wage. But direct influence on government policy is hard to discern. Social security funds are administered by the state, with input from trade unions and employers, and the unemployment benefit funds are run jointly by employers and trade unions; however, in practice, state contributions are crucial and this gives the state the final say in social security spending.

In addition, there are various advisory committees attached to ministers, many of which were revived by the incoming Socialist government in 1981. Trade union input to ministerial plans was especially visible after 1981, when officials from the CFDT in particular took up appointments within ministries or public agencies.[26] One of the most important ways in which interest groups influence policy within corporatist politics is through their specialist expertise, and the CFDT sees itself as a 'laboratory for ideas'. The CFDT's interests in political decentralization and workplace reform undoubtedly influenced the legislative programme in 1981–82.

In general terms, direct contact with ministers seems to constitute a more immediate channel of influence than participation in bipartite or tripartite consultative bodies, whose role in decision-making remains marginal. Trade unions make much of their meetings with politicians, particularly with the President of the Republic. One-to-one meetings on the steps in front of the Elysée Palace ('les consultations du perron') between the President and the leaders of the main union confederations have become a ritual of political life. Their importance is largely symbolic but far from negligible. Presidents of both left and right make a point of organizing such meetings within days of reaching office, and their frequency is commented upon in the national press as an indicator of economic policy goals as well as policy style.

Clearly, trade union influence cannot just be measured by their participation in formal committees, nor is influence necessarily the main reason for unions' 'policy of presence'. As well as the material benefits which prop up a membership-poor union movement, unions gain legitimacy for their campaigns and for their leaders. Access to information and expertise also supports their campaigning. An analogy with workplace structures is instructive: Parsons has shown how the CGT can use the information obtained through such committees, and even the fact of the committees' impotence in the face of employer plans, to its own advantage in mobilizing workers.[27] Similarly, unions can publicize their stance in state committees and, should the government fail to take heed, use this fact to win public support.

Apart from trade union access to state decision-making through such committees, it should further be noted that the unions and employers' organizations have a role in social policy-making within the social security system (health, old age, disability, housing, family allowances), which is organized on a tripartite basis at regional and national level, and within social insurance schemes which, strictly speaking, fall outside the state's competence (notably unemployment insurance). Here the situation is different in that, theoretically, the 'social partners' control the funds – which their members contribute – and their allocation. However, in practice the state's role, and hence its power, has increased significantly as the contributions-based funding mechanism is inadequate to cover spending. At the same time, state spending is squeezed by budgetary constraints, resulting in tensions between government on one hand, and employers' organizations and unions on the other. Nonetheless, as trade unions, they are given a stake in social policy through the administration of social expenditure and hence social legitimization, as well as considerable material benefits to the organizations themselves. Welfare policy represents a powerful mobilizing issue for unions and gives them a universal role over and above the work-related interests of their members.

Trade unions and political parties

A necessary condition of neocorporatism, or simply sustained relations between state and interest groups, is the existence of more or less formal links with the government in office; in particular, osmosis between trade unions and left parties acts as a guarantor of neocorporatist bargaining. It is commonly noted that one of the more important characteristics of the French labour movement is its links with political parties. This is not, of course, a phenomenon peculiar to France, but its specific configuration reflects the particular conditions in which the political and economic arms of the labour movement grew up. In Britain, labour organization developed after the failure of the Chartist movement, and trade unions later set up the Labour Party in order to gain independent representation in Parliament. In Germany, trade unions were banned from involvement in any kind of political activity, so the labour movement developed two separate but mutually supporting branches, which paved the way for the SPD's early electoral successes. In France, however, trade unions struggled to organize independently of a divided and quarrelsome socialist movement. Nevertheless, employer hostility and growing union awareness of the potential gains to be made from nationalization pushed the labour movement into counting increasingly on the possibility of a left government. The ambivalence resulting from this stance – on one hand fear of subordination, on the other fear of isolation – prevented the development of relations based on mutual trust, whilst apparently condemning the unions to partnership with left parties. Moreover, in the postwar period, the dominance of the French Communist Party (PCF) on the left ensured that deep ideological splits would remain. This difficult relationship has not proved conducive to the development of neocorporatism in France: Maier suggests that nations in which social-democratic arrangements have been able to sustain and benefit from corporatist arrangements have been those where the industrial and political branches of the labour movement developed side by side, rather than those where unions developed ahead of the party (especially Britain) or vice versa (as in the case of France).[28]

Nevertheless, at critical junctures collective action worked in tandem with the political forces of the left to form a powerful force for change. In 1936, a huge strike wave accompanied the arrival of a centre-left coalition (including the PCF) led by the first Socialist prime minister, Léon Blum. Significantly, all the left parties had worked together for victory in the face of the external fascist threat and internal far-right extremism. The Popular Front government signalled major change in the power structures. It marked the beginning of a more interventionist role for the state in key sectors of the economy. It also showed the main union confederation, the *Confédération Générale du Travail* (CGT), the advantages of working with a friendly government: the unionists were at a stroke able to achieve many of the demands (notably on working time) for which they had been struggling to campaign through workplace agitation. Although some of these gains were reversed after the fall of the Popular Front government, the lesson that change could be initiated only through the state had been learnt. In the postwar period, this relationship between the major union confederations and the left (particularly between the CGT and the PCF, based on an ideology of 'mass and class unionism') politicized labour activity and forced the state to take notice. The left union of the late 1970s was mirrored by a 'united action' pact between the CGT and the CFDT, with the aim of mobilizing workers to achieve an electoral victory for the left.

In 1981, the coming to power of a left coalition (including the PCF) promised to usher in a new shift in the structures of power, as in 1936. However, after an initial honeymoon period, the government's austerity policies after 1983, accompanied by steel plant and dockyard closures, made clashes between the socialists and labour leaders inevitable. A new split developed within the trade union movement, with a leading fraction of the ex-Catholic, 'new' left CFDT pursuing an unorthodox line of 'thinking the unthinkable', supporting austerity plans and urging politicians to go beyond traditional defensive policies. After 1993, under right-wing governments, the CFDT under Nicole Notat pushed this strategy to the extreme. Her public support for Prime Minister Alain Juppé's health reform plan in 1995 earned her extreme unpopularity in some union circles, but she became the first union leader to be invited to speak at a UDF party conference, and the main employers' organization (*Conseil National du Patronat Français*, or CNPF) supported CFDT candidates for nomination to the chair of social security and unemployment administration boards.

The 1980s may thus be seen as a period of readjustment after the political mobilization which had dominated the French labour movement in the 1970s and which came to a definitive end with the CFDT's overtures to right governments after 1993. Significantly, the unions stood aside from the 1995 presidential election campaign and, unlike in 1981 and 1988, refrained from issuing voting instructions. Similarly, it was noted that not only did the major unions (with the exception of the CGT) keep quiet about their preferences during the 1997 legislative election campaign, but there was no 'social truce': public sector unrest continued during the campaign period. Trade unions appeared uncertain how to act: as government lobbyists, or as autonomous agents.[29]

In any case, it is unlikely that direct instructions from the unions would have significantly altered workers' voting patterns. Alignment between union members and political parties has weakened, although a pattern of support emerges from pre-election and exit polls. In the run-up to the legislative elections of 1986, 60 per cent of CGT members favoured the PCF, 22 per cent the PS, and 8 per cent the RPR-UDF; 12 per cent of CFDT members declared their intention to vote for the PCF, 63 per cent for the PS, and 19 per cent the RPR-UDF; 6 per cent of FO members opted for the PCF, 34 per cent for the PCF, and 54 per cent for the RPR-UDF.[30] Presidential elections show a similar pattern: 50 per cent of CGT members voted for the PCF candidate, André Lajoinie, in 1988, and 38 per cent for François Mitterrand; 70 per cent of CFDT members voted for Mitterrand; 35 per cent of FO members chose Mitterrand, 26 per cent Raymond Barre (UDF), 20 per cent Jean-Marie Le Pen and 8 per cent Jacques Chirac.[31] Communist support among CGT members had dropped by 1995, however: 35 per cent voted for the PCF candidate, Robert Hue, and 39 per cent for Lionel Jospin (PS). In the CFDT, 45 per cent of members voted for Jospin, 14 per cent for Edouard Balladur and 16 per cent for Jacques Chirac; 25 per cent of FO members voted for Chirac, 20 per cent for Balladur, 16 per cent for Le Pen and 15 per cent for Jospin.[32] Undoubtedly, trade union membership is strongly linked to the political left: by way of comparison, around a third of British trade union members voted for the Labour Party in the 1980s. But the PCF's hold on trade unionists has weakened significantly.

The decline in CGT members' support for Communist candidates has been accompanied by changes in the relationship between the party and the union confederation. Traditionally, the CGT leadership has had formal links with the PCF's organizational structure, and even in the 1970s many observers saw the CGT as the 'transmission belt' of the Communist Party, in line with the Marxist-Leninist model. The CGT leader has always been a member of the PCF's 'political bureau' (renamed 'national bureau' in 1994), and the party played a major role in filling the key posts in the union. However, the practice of 'cumul des mandats' (simultaneous party and union leadership roles) proved a heavy burden, restricting the CGT's freedom of action, creating internal dissent and severely damaging its image and credibility among potential members.[33] The relationship between party and union has slowly evolved, and at the 1996 congress of the PCF a new era began, when the two CGT leaders sitting on the party's *bureau national* did not put themselves forward for renewal.

Force Ouvrière, on the other hand, has always made great play of its political independence, not least because, as the voting patterns reviewed above show, its members are split across the whole political spectrum. Any leader foolish enough to court one political party or politician over another would soon be called to account. Such ideological diversity makes the union too unpredictable a partner for any government to favour FO over the larger CGT and CFDT; moreover, FO's strength in the public sector would bring it sooner or later into conflict with the state as employer. FO's pretensions to being a 'privileged partner' of both left and right governments therefore sound rather hollow.

In the 1970s and 1980s, FO was able to capitalize on the perceived 'politicization' of the two leading confederations to woo members more interested in workplace issues. However, changes in the CGT and especially the CFDT since then have reduced this relative advantage. A measure of this change was the reaction of trade unions to the election of a left coalition in 1997: they looked forward to friendlier policies and policy style after their antagonistic dealings with Juppé, but caution rather than expectation characterized their approach.

The debate about reduction of working time reveals the fragility of relationships between the left, employers' organizations and trade unions. In the early 1990s, both left and right-wing politicians (including President Mitterrand) expressed exasperation with the 'social partners' and their failure to enter into meaningful dialogue, but could not find a way of stimulating discussions. When Jean Gandois, the new president of the CNPF, launched talks with the union confederations in January 1995, there was a feeling that a new 'social pact' might emerge, around the key themes of youth employment and working time. Both employers and unions insisted that dialogue depended on freedom from state interference. A series of historic national-level meetings took place and led to some significant agreements, notably on early retirement schemes for those aged 57 with a full contributions record, and on reduction and reorganization of working time. The latter agreement showed that, despite a relatively united trade union front, the employers held the balance of power as they secured their key demand of linking working time reduction with annualization of hours and shifted the locus of bargaining from branch level to company level (where unions are weaker). However, despite the apparent satisfaction of the CNPF's demands, employers' organizations were slow to reach agreement at sub-national level. The logjam on working time bargaining was broken not by this bipartite bargaining but by the Robien law which came into effect in Autumn 1996. This law, offering financial incentives to firms which reduced working time in order to preserve or create jobs, attracted business interest whilst the bargaining process set off by the October 1995 agreement between the CNPF and some of the union confederations stalled. This situation seemed to confirm the state's pre-eminent role and the weakness of collective bargaining, due largely to the unions' inability to force employers to the negotiating table, much less into significant concessions.

In 1997, a 'pluralist' left (including Green and PCF ministers) came into government with an explicit commitment to a 35-hour week. Rather than legislate, the government fixed a date for a national-level 'summit' to decide on how to proceed. Despite Gandois's close links with the administration, this initiative placed the CNPF on the defensive and led to a head-on clash between the employers and the government. As the deadline for the summit approached, the pressure on the government increased, and on the day of the summit Lionel Jospin announced that a law would be presented to oblige companies to reduce the working week to 35 hours within five years. Although the impact was later softened with the inclusion of financial incentives and exemptions for small businesses, the employers reacted with outright hostility and Gandois resigned. However, although the trade unions' power had been boosted by the state's intervention, they reacted with some suspicion to the proposed law and criticized its content. The left government had not acted as the political arm of the labour movement; it had acted independently. In a real sense, the unions' dependence on legislative back-up demonstrated their lack of bargaining muscle rather than political power. The unions themselves had not dictated this course of events; rather, the employers' actions determined it.

Power in the workplace

Trade unions' economic power is limited. They do not possess the membership networks, infrastructure or resources to have a significant say in business decisions. Formal representation structures – works committees (*comités d'entreprise* and *comités d'établissement*, dating from 1946) and employee delegates (*délégués du personnel* – akin to shop stewards – introduced in 1919) – were boosted by the 1981–82 Auroux laws, but they still function patchily. A sizeable proportion (over a quarter) of those companies legally obliged to set up works committees (those with fifty or more employees) do not have one. The activities of the various bodies overlap, often with overstretched delegates sitting on several at once; representatives lack training and employers can manipulate the information provided.[34]

Unions' capacity to resist economic change and impose costs on businesses through strike activity is, however, spectacularly demonstrated from time to time. Many strikes originate in grass-roots militancy, with the unions struggling (and often competing with each other) to gain control of the movement and channel workers' demands. This worker 'combativeness' is the envy of trade unions in other countries (such as Britain) and gives French unions an important lever in their dealings with employers and public authorities. On the other hand, the unions' ability to guarantee social peace is fragile and therefore their seat at the negotiating table always provisional. In the 1980s, the emergence of new structures of representation during public sector strikes drew attention to the major confederations' inability to control strike movements: some commentators saw these *coordinations* (ad hoc groupings independent of existing unions) as a major threat to the existing unions and the precursors of a new type of labour organization.[35] It was no accident, they noted, that the *coordinations* sprang up outside the industrial plants which formed the bedrock of traditional unionism, and in professions such as nursing with a large proportion of women workers. However, on the whole *coordinations* have not developed as a serious alternative to mainstream trade unions.

It is true that new, autonomous unions have become a force to be reckoned with, particularly in the public sector. The CFDT's drift away from left politics created pockets of radical activists who left or were expelled from their unions and set up rival organizations: the best known of these is Sud (*Solidaires, Unitaires, Démocratiques*), which makes up for its small numbers (it claims around 9,000 members, although the real figure may be nearer 6,000) with determined campaigning around issues such as support for immigrants, the homeless and the unemployed. Five years after its creation, Sud came second in workplace elections at France Télécom (with 22 per cent of the vote). A survey of Sud members showed that nearly all of them worked in the public sector, and 20 per cent had previously been CFDT members, with 40 per cent having no trade union experience.[36] Along with other non-affiliated public-sector unions, in 1981 Sud formed a 'Group of Ten' (which has now grown to include 23 unions). Claiming a combined membership of 60,000 (and 160,000 votes in workplace elections), the 'Group of Ten' in 1997 announced plans to obtain full representative status in collective bargaining. The small autonomous unions similarly formed an umbrella federation which seeks full bargaining rights alongside the established unions, and in the long term, they pose a serious threat to the established trade unions' hold over public sector workers.

There is also evidence to suggest that worker militancy has declined, as might be expected in a climate of mass unemployment (over 10 per cent since the early 1980s). The number of days lost through disputes fell from an annual average of 217,000 in 1975–79 to 41,000 in 1985 and 25,000 in 1992, placing France among the group of European Union countries with the lowest strike rate (along with the UK and Denmark).[37] Nonetheless, public sector strikes can be costly and have a huge impact on public opinion and policy-makers.

A further source of influence is large companies (public and private sector). In France's fragmented economic structure, with its large number of small and medium-sized firms, large companies have occupied a dominant role. In the early 1990s, SMEs of between ten and 499 employees accounted for nearly 50 per cent of France's total wageforce, while around 40 per cent worked in companies with a staff of over 500.[38] The larger companies, which in the latter half of the 1990s shed employees at an alarming rate, account for the lion's share of the country's turnover, exports and investments. Their directors, usually sharing similar social and educational backgrounds with the country's political leaders, form an important part of France's elite, with privileged access to policy decisions. Many of these large companies have been at the forefront of industrial relations modernization, and some (such as BSN, now Danone) have traditionally been known as 'labour-friendly' companies. Whatever the company's approach to labour relations, the prominence of large companies has given those unions present a strategic role in the French economy and a public relations platform. According to Labbé, it helped to foster a particular model of French unionism based on company activism.[39] Labour legislation and more recently the 1981–82 Auroux laws on workplace representation and company-level collective bargaining reinforced this concentration of union activities in a handful of very large companies. On the other hand, union activism is in decline even in large companies and may well have been further pressurized by the extra commitments resulting from the laws.

Trade union organization

Some observers place the blame for falling membership squarely on the unions themselves, for failing to take adequate account of workers' needs and aspirations and becoming organizationally rigid, bureaucratic institutions.[40] Certainly, the appearance of the *coordinations* and widespread dissatisfaction with existing trade unions among French employees would seem to confirm this criticism.

Any examination of the place of trade unions within national power structures must consider the question of democracy. As noted earlier, critics of trade union power point to the lack of an electoral mandate as a reason for limiting the influence of such bodies within democratic systems. Moreover, trade unions themselves are open to accusations of undemocratic practices in their internal organization. Partridge speaks of 'double moralities': 'Many trade unionists [...] support forms of organization and procedure in trade unions which they would strongly oppose if applied within the state'.[41] French trade unions respond to this criticism by emphasizing their role as expressions of pluralism (a role guaranteed in the constitution) and the electoral mandate given in workplace elections. But this sidesteps the issue of centralization and bureaucratization.

French trade unions have a dual structure, based on industrial/professional federations and local (*département*) groupings. The relationship between federations, departmental unions and confederations varies. As regards finances, for example, the CFDT collects union dues centrally and sends back a proportion to federations and departmental unions, whereas in the CGT and FO it is the federation which collects subscriptions. Often the federations keep money for themselves, which is one reason why it is notoriously difficult to obtain reliable statistics on trade union membership. In terms of internal structures, there are important differences. *Force Ouvrière's* structure depends heavily on federations and the confederal level has less importance. The CFDT's complex organizational structure allows the confederal leadership considerable power to determine strategy. The CGT, too, modified its statutes in 1969 to give more weight to the confederal level.[42]

In all cases, leadership tends to be very stable, not to say self-perpetuating. Congress is a ritualistic affair, with voting on leadership reports acting as a kind of plebiscite; reports presented by the confederal executive rarely receive less than 75 per cent support. Unions' federalist ideology is thus mitigated in practice by an increase in powers given to the confederal leadership (except FO) and the plebiscitary, rather than deliberative role of congress. It is further undermined by 'the personal role of the great leaders'.[43] French magazines publish popularity polls of union leaders alongside those of politicians, and it is normal to refer to 'Mr. Viannet's union' rather than the CGT, for example.

Without doubt, the bureaucratization of French trade unions reflects the prioritization of activities in relation to the state. If the state provides money for training and employment of full-time union officials, as in the French case, it pays the unions to invest in activities organized by the state rather than to recruit voluntary members in the workplace. In turn, bureaucratization accentuates the divide between officials and members and perpetuates the circle. Thus, some observers see the state's central role as a major factor explaining trade union weakness in the workplace.

The 1995 strike movement and beyond

In Autumn 1995, the most unpopular government in the history of the Fifth Republic took on the trade unions – and lost. After 24 days of strike action, Juppé shelved his welfare spending reform and withdrew plans to overhaul the loss-making state railway system. Given the points made above about the weakness of trade unions in the power structures of contemporary France, this apparent victory deserves comment.

Civil servants were the first to protest against the wage freeze imposed by the government. Significantly, their strike was the first united action of this kind since 1990. Employees of the state-owned railway company SNCF took part in the 10 October strike, and the movement later took hold in the railways in response to Alain Juppé's plan to reorganize the company. The public-sector employees were joined by university students, who began a protest movement for more funding after the start of the new term on October 9, adding to the mood of unrest and evoking once more the spectre of May–June 1968. The movement absorbed specific demands relating to wages and working conditions in the public sector, but focused on the Juppé health spending plan (particularly the threat to complementary health and pension schemes). By the end of November, the public transport system was paralyzed in Paris and several other urban centres, and by early December the strike had spread throughout the public administration. Paris in particular resembled a city under siege.

The government was at first caught off guard and attempted to dismiss the strike as insignificant. But once it became clear that the strike was effective and set to continue, Juppé quickly sought to make concessions. Extra funds were found for the universities, the SNCF plan was shelved and most of the railway workers' demands met, and the Prime Minister quietly put away his health plan. The government then courted the trade union leaderships in order to persuade them to bring their members back to work, by promising a major debate on public services and proposing a 'jobs summit'.[44]

The movement showed the effectiveness of public-sector strikes (particularly in the key sector of transport) and their ability to affect the whole economy, as well as their wider impact on daily life (and therefore on public opinion, to which French governments are acutely sensitive). The movement also demonstrated the power of unity. The trade union leaderships were divided: CFDT leader Nicole Notat took the bold step of defending the new health plan, but her intervention had the result of uniting her opponents against her. Opposition to the health plan and to the government's pay policy acted as a vehicle for a more diffuse sense of outrage at the downgrading and marketization of public services, mobilizing public sector workers and creating a huge grass-roots movement which seemed to take the union leaderships by surprise. Significantly, the strike movement did not see the emergence of *coordinations* as in earlier public-sector unrest; rather, action was organized through *assemblées générales* which brought together the local delegates from the major unions, and the 'stars' of the movement tended to be union representatives.

A further crucial factor in the movement's success was the weight of public opinion. Despite the inconvenience to themselves, three-quarters of French people declared their support for the strikers in opinion polls. Many private-sector workers, unwilling or unable to participate themselves because of fears of dismissal or loss of income, considered themselves to be taking part in the strike 'by proxy'. As well as the general climate marked by unemployment and insecurity, the government's unpopularity was clearly reflected in the public's response to the strikes. Indeed, the government itself helped to fuel the movement by its own clumsy response and apparent disdain for ordinary workers. Some commentators interpreted the strike first and foremost as a sign of the French state's failure to establish a peaceful social dialogue.[45]

But for others, the strike movement of autumn 1995 served only to reveal the last throes of a privileged core of workers and a union oligarchy dependent on a centralized state.[46] The movement itself petered out over the Christmas break, although many participants felt that the wider issues had not been satisfactorily resolved. Moreover, the divisions within the trade union movement prevented them from building on the movement. FO saw internal dissent targeted at its aggressive leader, Marc Blondel (whose attitude towards the strikers had oscillated), whilst Notat's defiant non-conformism split the CFDT into two camps. Meanwhile, increasing numbers of disgruntled CFDT activists left to set up new Sud unions or join other autonomous organizations.

Union divisions were further exacerbated by an unprecedented protest movement of the unemployed in December 1996–January 1997, which began with the illegal occupation of job centres (ANPE: *Agence Nationale pour l'Emploi*) in Marseille. With the exception of the CGT, which took a leadership role in the movement through its 'Defence committee of those deprived of work', and various Sud groupings associated with other unemployed organizations, the major confederations were left behind by this protest. Nicole Notat, as president of the tripartite organization which administers unemployment insurance (UNEDIC), found herself in a particularly awkward position, and she misjudged the movement in her hasty dismissal of it. The movement revealed the ideological and tactical disarray of large sections of the union movement and its difficult relationship both with wider society and with the left government.

Significantly, the trade unions focus their policy interventions and mass actions increasingly on issues concerning the welfare state. Notwithstanding the new lines of division between the unions that have emerged on these issues, Dufour and Hege argue that 'the issue of social protection could prove effective [...] in compensating for the difficulties [unions] face at company level; it is an issue which could promote strong cohesion among workers',[47] particularly as ideological forces for cohesion have declined dramatically.

More generally, the strike and protest movements of the mid-1990s continued a tradition of popular revolt against unpopular policies and governments which, it could be argued, give trade unions a powerful weapon in its dealings with the state. But the weapon is double-edged. Just as May–June 1968 has been interpreted as a sign that the access of unions and other interest groups to public authorities was either too undeveloped or too insecure to influence political decisions,[48] the 1995 movement shows that, for trade unions, pressure on government has to be exercised through public opinion rather than through privileged action. The unions thus act as a channel for popular discontent but they seem unable to capitalize on this role. The state uses the unions as a channel to end the conflict, but as there is no durable or adequate negotiation conflicts will arise again.

Conclusion

Trade unions do not enjoy a great deal of power in France: their power depends on certain rights which are given to them by the state (and which may therefore be taken away) and on their ability to mobilize. They therefore seem rather weak in relation to the state. Mobilization on issues of widespread public concern can give the unions important leverage in their dealings with the state. But it can also trap them in a logic of contestation at the expense of strategies aimed at gaining real influence. In terms of policy-making, power based on militancy tends to produce an essentially negative or blocking reaction, with obvious consequences for reform.

Trade union influence is widespread, because of the unions' claim to speak on behalf of society as a whole and all wage-earners in particular, and because of their involvement with the administration of social protection. To some extent, this influence denotes incorporation of labour interests into state bodies, but as we have seen this incorporation is undermined by the state's pre-eminence. Thus France's structures of power are neither neocorporatistic nor pluralistic, but possess elements of both. They are characterized by a plethora of sectional interests which umbrella organizations and official bodies can only mitigate but not fully overcome.

The place of trade unions within the power structures reveals as much about the nature of the French state as about trade unions. The state is highly centralized but unevenly diffuse in that there are multiple points of access (especially local/regional networks). Indeed, the justification for centralization is precisely to counteract the negative consequences of localization. Because of the density of the state, there are many opportunities to acquire influence, and it pays non-governmental organizations to seek influence. Also, the existence of a sizeable interface between the public and private sectors gives space to non-elected agents.

As the state redefines its role, particularly in the sphere of social protection, many questions are raised about the trade unions' future role. Dufour and Hege suggest that, 'rather than trade unionism losing its political identity, one might diagnose a stronger involvement of trade unions in defining macro-social compromises which the political parties and organs of government lack the capacity to carry through on their own'.[49] Certainly there are as yet few signs that the unions are moving away from macro-level campaigning towards 'micro-corporatism' based on workplace bargaining. On the other hand, the unions' capacity to take on social protection issues which have so far proved intractable seems doubtful.

Notes

1.   Validire, J.-L. (1995), 'Un syndicalisme divisé, affaibli et querelleur', *Le Figaro*, 15 February. There are no less than five major union confederations

which are recognized by the state, as well as public sector unions which are recognized for bargaining purposes. The major confederations are the *Confédération Générale du Travail* (CGT: around 500,000 members), the *Confédération Française Démocratique du Travail* (CFDT: also around 500,000 members), the *CGT-Force Ouvrière* (FO: fewer than 400,000 members), the *Confédération Française des Travailleurs Chrétiens* (CFTC) and the *Confédération Générale des Cadres* (CGC), with barely 100,000 members each. There is no umbrella organization like the British Trades Union Congress or the German Deutscher Gewerkschaftsbund.

2. In his preface to Adam, G. (1985), *Le pouvoir syndical*, Dunod, Paris, p.v.
3. Macbeath, I. (1979), *Votes, Virtues and Vices. Trade Union Power*, Associated Business Press, London, pp.xiii–xiv.
4. Mokken, R.J. and Stokman, F.N. (1976), 'Power and influence as political phenomena', in Barry, B. (ed.), *Power and Political Theory*, John Wiley, New York, pp.33–54, p.33.
5. Ibid., p.37.
6. Gamble, A. (1985), *Britain in decline*, Macmillan, Basingstoke, p.149.
7. See, for example, Macbeath, *Votes, Virtues and Vices*, p.xi: 'If [trade unions] do not influence the behaviour of other people in the interests of their members, they are not achieving anything'.
8. Based on Schmitter's classic definition (1979), in 'Still the century of corporatism?', Schmitter, P. and Lehmbruch, G. (eds), *Trends towards corporatist intermediation*, Sage, London, pp.7–52, p.13.
9. Lehmbruch, G. (1984), 'Concertation and the structure of corporatist networks', in Goldthorpe, J. (ed.), *Order and Conflict in Contemporary Capitalism*, Oxford University Press, Oxford, pp.60–80, p.66.
10. On this, see Thelen, K. (1994), 'Beyond corporatism. Towards a new framework for the study of labor in advanced capitalism', *Comparative Politics*, vol. 27, no.1, October, pp.107–24.
11. Lehmbruch, G. and Schmitter, P. (eds) (1982), *Patterns of Corporatist Policy-Making*, Sage, London.
12. Lehmbruch, 'Concertation and the structure of corporatist networks'.
13. See Rumillat, C. (1988), 'L'idée professionnaliste aux origines du corporatisme républicain', in Colas, D., *L'Etat et les corporatismes. Travaux de la mission sur la modernisation de l'Etat*, Presses Universitaires de France, Paris, pp.47–65.
14. See Marou, J. (1988), 'Le corporatisme contre le corporatisme. Etude des stratégies corporatistes sous Vichy', ibid., pp.67–87.
15. This point is made by Safran, W. (1995), *The French Polity*, Longman, New York, p.145.
16. Jobert, B. (1988), 'La version française du corporatisme: définition et implications pour la modernisation de l'Etat dans une économie en crise', in Colas, D., *L'Etat et les corporatismes*, pp.3–18, p.4.
17. Crozier, M. (1970), *La société bloquée*, Paris, Seuil. Published in English (1973), as *The Stalled Society*, Viking Press, New York.
18. See Phelps Brown, H. (1983), *The Origins of Trade Union Power*, Clarendon Press, Oxford.
19. François de Closets' (1985) account, though sensationalist, hit close to home: *Tous ensemble (pour en finir avec la syndicratie)*, Seuil, Paris. See also

Montaldo, J. (1981), *La mafia des syndicats*, Albin Michel, Paris, although this even more sensationalist diatribe was taken less seriously.
20. Adam, *Le pouvoir syndical*.
21. Labour Ministry figures.
22. See Milner, S. (1989), 'Guardians of the republican tradition? The trade unions', in Gaffney, J. (ed.), *The French Presidential Elections of 1988*, Dartmouth, Aldershot, pp.211–39.
23. See Parsons, N. (1997), *Employee Participation in Europe. A Case Study in the British and French Gas Industries*, Avebury, Aldershot.
24. Originally set up in 1925 as the National Economic Council, its basis was modified in 1936. It was re-established after the War as the Economic Council, then included in the new constitutional order after 1958 as the Economic and Social Council. The first chair of the NEC in 1925 was CGT leader Léon Jouhaux.
25. Hall, P. (1986), *Governing the Economy. The Politics of State Intervention in Britain and France*, Polity Press, Cambridge, p.158; Safran, *The French Polity*, pp.149–50.
26. See Wilson, F. (1985), 'Trade unions and economic policy', in Machin, H. and Wright, V. (eds), *Economic Policy and Policy-Making under the Mitterrand Presidency (1981–1984)*, Pinter, London, pp. 255–278. 21 per cent of the new Socialist ministerial *cabinets*, and one third of *cabinet* directors, were CFDT members.
27. Parsons, *Employee Participation in Europe*.
28. See Maier, C.S. (1984), 'Preconditions for corporatism', in Goldthorpe, *Order and Conflict in Contemporary Capitalism*, pp.39–59.
29. Favilla, 'Cordon ombilical', *Les Echos*, 4 June 1997.
30. Mouriaux, R. (1986), *Le syndicalisme face à la crise*, La Découverte, Paris, p.65.
31. CSA exit poll conducted after the first round: Bouguereau, J.-M. (1988), 'Radioscopie du séisme', *L'Evénement du Jeudi*, 28 April, pp.11–15, p.13.
32. CSA-SSU exit poll conducted after the first round, published in *La Tribune-Desfossés*, 25 April 1995.
33. See Lydia Brovelli (CGT treasurer, not a member of the PCF), quoted in *Le Figaro*, 17 February 1994: 'Double office-holding [*le cumul des mandats*] is completely disadvantageous, particularly in terms of image'.
34. See Le Maître, A. and Tchobanian, R. (1991), *Les institutions représentatives du personnel dans l'entreprise*, La Documentation Française, Paris.
35. See Noblecourt, M. (1990), *Les syndicats en questions*, Editions Ouvrières, Paris.
36. Vidalie, A. (1996), 'Comment Sud glisse entre la CFDT et la CGT', *Le Nouvel Economiste*, 4 October, pp.82–3.
37. Lecher, W. (ed.) (1994), *Trade Unions in the European Union*, Lawrence & Wishart, London, p.95. The figures are collected and standardized by the International Labour Organization.
38. Coriat, B. and Taddéi, D. (1993), *Entreprise France*, Librairie Générale Française, Paris.
39. Labbé, D. (1995), 'La crise du syndicalisme français', *La Revue de l'IRES*, no.16, Autumn, pp.75–101.
40. See Bevort, A. and Labbé, D. (1992), *La CFDT: organisation et audience depuis 1945*, La Documentation Française, Paris.

41. Partridge, P.H. (1971), *Consent and Consensus*, Praeger, New York, p.55.
42. For a fuller discussion of trade union structures, see Adam, *Le pouvoir syndical*, chapter 1.
43. Mouriaux, R. (1983), *Les syndicats dans la société française*, Presses de la Fondation Nationale des Sciences Politiques, Paris, p.44.
44. This chronology is based on Mouriaux, R. and Subileau, F. (1996), 'Les grèves françaises de l'automne 1995: défense des acquis ou mouvement social?', *Modern and Contemporary France*, IV/3, pp.299–306.
45. See especially Le Goff, J.-P. and Caillé, A. (1996), *Le Tournant de Décembre*, La Découverte, Paris.
46. See Touraine, A. et al (1996), *Le Grand Refus. Réflexions sur la grève de décembre 1995*, Fayard, Paris.
47. Dufour, C. and Hege, A. (1997), 'The transformation of French industrial relations: glorification of the enterprise and disaffection on the streets', *European Journal of Industrial Relations*, II/3, November, pp.333–356, p.350.
48. Safran, W. (1993), 'France', in Hancock, M.D. et al, *Politics in Western Europe*, Basingstoke, Macmillan, pp.95–182
49. Dufour and Hege, 'The transformation of French industrial relations', p.350.

Bibliography

Adam, G. (1985), *Le pouvoir syndical*, Dunod, Paris.
Barry, B. (ed.) (1976), *Power and Political Theory*, John Wiley, New York.
Bevort, A. and Labbé, D. (1992), *La CFDT: organisation et audience depuis 1945*, La Documentation Française, Paris.
Colas, D. (1988), *L'Etat et les corporatismes. Travaux de la mission sur la modernisation de l'Etat*, PUF, Paris.
Coriat, B. and Taddéi, D. (1993), *Entreprise France*, Librairie Générale Française, Paris.
Crozier, M. (1973), *The Stalled Society*, Viking Press, New York.
Gamble, A. (1985), *Britain in decline*, Macmillan, Basingstoke.
Labbé, D. (1995), 'La crise du syndicalisme français', *La Revue de l'IRES*, no. 16, Autumn.
Goldthorpe, J. (ed.) (1984), *Order and Conflict in Contemporary Capitalism*, Oxford University Press, Oxford.
Hall, P. (1986), *Governing the Economy. The Politics of State Intervention in Britain and France*, Cambridge, Polity Press.
Hancock, M. D. et al. (1993), *Politics in Western Europe*, Basingstoke, Macmillan.
Le Goff, J.-P. and Caillé, A. (1996), *Le Tournant de décembre*, La Découverte, Paris.
Lehmbruch, G. and Schmitter, P. (eds) (1982), *Patterns of Corporatist Policy-Making*, Sage London.
Le Maître, A. and Tchobanian, R. (1991), *Les institutions représentatives du personnel dans l'entreprise*, La Documentation Française, Paris.
Macbeath, I. (1979), *Votes, Virtues and Vices. Trade Union Power*, Associated Business Press, London.
Machin, H. and Wright, V. (eds) (1985), *Economic Policy and Policy-Making under the Mitterrand Presidency 1981–1984*, Frances Pinter Publishing, London.

Milner, S. (1989), 'Guardians of the republican tradition? The trade unions', in Gaffney, J. (ed.), *The French Presidential Elections of 1988*, Dartmouth, Aldershot.

Mouriaux, R. (1983), *Les syndicats dans la société française*, Presses de la Fondation Nationale des Sciences Politiques, Paris.

—— (1988), *Le syndicalisme face à la crise*, Armand Colin, Paris.

—— and Subileau, F. (1996), 'Les grèves françaises de l'automne 1995: défense des acquis ou mouvement social?', *Modern and Contemporary France*, IV/3.

Noblecourt, M. (1990), *Les syndicats en questions*, Editions Ouvrières, Paris.

Parsons, N. (1997), *Employee Participation in Europe. A Case Study in the British and French Gas Industries*, Avebury, Aldershot.

Phelps Brown, H. (1983), *The Origins of Trade Union Power*, Clarendon Press, Oxford.

Schmitter, P. and Lehmbruch, G. (eds) (1979), *Trends towards corporatist intermediation*, Sage, London.

Thelen, K. (1994), 'Beyond corporatism. Towards a new framework for the study of labor in advanced capitalism', *Comparative Politics*, vol. 27, no. 1, October.

Tilley, C. (1986), *The Contentious French*, Harvard University Press, Cambridge, Mass.

Validire, J.-L., 'Un syndicalisme divisé, affaibli et querelleur', *Le Figaro*, 15 February 1995.

4
The Limits of Economic *Dirigisme* and Collusion

George Jones

Introduction

Within a few weeks of the invention of the electric telegraph in 1837, the French government banned its use by the public. Thirteen years later, the government relented under pressure from French industrialists, who had observed the effect on British and American firms of this new method of doing business, and permitted it to be used, under strict conditions. The *rapporteur* who presented to parliament the bill permitting private use of the telegraph indicated how useful the device had become to the state itself:

> Telegraphy has become the most powerful tool at the disposal of our government. [It makes it possible] to foresee and control (*diriger*) great events before the masses have heard of them and become alarmed by them ... and to avoid upheavals, protect the frontiers, and give administrative and diplomatic reports the urgent attention of the authorities [*de la volonté dirigeante* – literally 'of the guiding will'].[1]

It was a long-standing principle that the *volonté dirigeante* should extend its guidance to business. The high point of the policy which came to be known as *dirigisme* was in the years following World War II, in which France became, for the first time, one of the world's leading industrial countries. But government guidance and planning will achieve their targets most easily when the government itself is the customer – for great public works projects, or defence – or when a foreign government is the customer and the French government can use its influence on behalf of its chosen French firm. *Dirigisme* when applied to a mass consumer market may be as effective as pushing on a piece of string. We shall see that the tradition of state guidance means that consumers' needs have been comparatively little regarded; the decline of *dirigisme* is in part explained by the rise of consumerism. Whether many different firms are able to attempt to satisfy consumers' wants will depend in part on the degree of business competition, and the rules governing it. We shall study some of the changes in those rules.

One of the sources of such rules is the European Union. The European Union is not, or is not solely, an experiment in international co-operation. It is a system of law, which can alter the business environment to the detriment of some interests and to the advantage of others. We shall see how various producer interests in France have suffered commercially motivated legal challenges to their privileges. We shall examine, in particular the market for air travel, where it is, overwhelmingly, European rules which have shifted the balance of advantage against French carriers.

Finally, we shall see how the need to compete for investment funds, both French and foreign, has started to chip away at the structures by which those in control of French firms have traditionally maintained their power.

'Dirigisme', prices, and competition

The France of the late 1940s was never a 'command' economy, unlike the Soviet Union. But the authorities had powerful weapons available to them to influence economic development and the behaviour of firms. Above all, they had control of the funds needed for investment. The state could make outright grants to firms to pay for new equipment; it could sell bonds to savers and re-lend the proceeds to business at a low rate of interest; it could channel money from publicly-owned financial institutions for loans to business. Millions of French people had accounts with the Post Office; these funds could be tapped for loans to industry. As for the banks, the four largest had been nationalized in 1945 and the State could 'lean' on them to adapt their lending policy to its wishes.

The French authorities could pursue these policies because they were operating behind a barrier of legal and regulatory controls which, partially at least, isolated the country from the outside world. There were of course high tariffs (taxes on imports). Tariff-free trade had always been the exception and not the rule in France. However, in the 1940s and 1950s imports were limited far more directly, by quotas. This meant that only prescribed quantities could be imported. If consumers' demand for, say, Italian shoes exceeded the quota, the importer would be unable to get a licence to bring in more.

Of the restrictions in force at this time, it is impossible to overestimate the importance of exchange controls. First introduced on the outbreak of war in 1939, they remained in force, with varying degrees of severity, until 1990. One of the features of what we now call 'globalization' is that there is world-wide competition for savings. This has only been possible with the gradual dismantling of exchange controls in many countries. The franc remained unconvertible until 1958, and so French foreign trade had to be financed from a pool of convertible currency (chiefly dollars) which was increased by the proceeds of export sales and diminished by payment for imports. Even when the convertibility of the franc was restored in 1958, firm exchange controls remained in place. For instance, investment abroad was discouraged by requiring the would-be investor to convert from the franc at a special, and punitively unfavourable, rate of exchange.

The Marshall Aid given by the United States between 1948 and 1952 to France and other European countries consisted, essentially, in adding, by gift or loan, to the pool of dollars from which they could finance their foreign trade, and in particular their imports from the United States. Imports of machinery from the USA were an important part of the Modernization Plan drawn up under Jean Monnet's chairmanship after the war. Monnet's Planning Commission was essentially a network of committees, bringing together employers, civil servants and trade unionists (including, prominently, the Communist CGT) in key industries. What is noteworthy is that these committees became the advocates of their industries in a competition for the allocation of public resources. The system reinforced solidarity between firms producing the same type of goods rather than rivalry between them.

The agreements for the grant of Marshall Aid contained a clause providing that the beneficiary should foster competition between businesses. It was understandable that the United States, as the home of 'anti-trust', should want to see a vigorous competition policy, and equally understandable that France should resist it. Competition disperses power: that is precisely why the United States, during the occupation of Germany, imposed competition on that country, breaking up the cartels which it saw as having been a powerful support to the Hitler state. But there was no reason why the French state should wish to disperse power: it was engaged in an act of state power, namely building up French industry behind protectionist barriers. So there was a muted response from France to the American idea, as we shall see.

One of the great engines of competition is, of course, price, but the price mechanism could not function freely in 1945. Prices were under state control. The legal basis of price control consisted of two *Ordonnances* of June 1945[2] which were intended to fight black marketeering and hoarding. The two *Ordonnances* in fact rolled forward much of the Vichy mechanism of price control, with the addition, in the 1945 version of the legislation, of 'popular committees' of *anciens combattants* and *résistants* who were to help the authorities detect profiteers and fraudsters. The minister was given the power to control the prices and profit margins of all goods and services.

Most wartime economies had had price controls, but in France the idea that inflation was caused by speculators and hoarders, and that the standard of living of working people could be protected by legislation, had become established well before the war. In 1936, the Popular Front government had put through parliament a law 'prohibiting unjustified price rises' in the case of basic necessities.[3]

The postwar price controls were not very effective. There was strong underlying inflationary pressure, caused in part by the restrictions on the imports which would otherwise have helped to meet the rapidly recovering demand. The governments of the Fourth Republic had inherited from the Third the power to control not only prices but wages. This had been introduced as a temporary measure in 1939 but was still in force five years after the war. The labour unions had pressed for its abolition, which they obtained in 1950. Wages could now be negotiated freely. The unions were not perhaps as confident of their negotiating power as they seemed, for at their instigation a 'floor' was put on wages by the introduction of a national minimum wage, the SMIG.[4] The level of the SMIG was at first fixed by ministerial decree, but from 1952 it was indexed to the cost of living.

Governments were now strongly tempted to use their powers over prices to block an increase in the price of one of the 213 items which made up the index, especially if the index was just reaching the point which would trigger an increase in the SMIG. Businesses, on the one hand, were only too happy to encourage the government in its efforts to keep down the cost-of-living index, which in turn helped to keep down the cost of wages. On the other, they were vigorous lobbyists, begging the minister to approve an increase in the price of their own product.

Price controls varied in their scope and their severity, but they were not finally lifted until 1986. Forty years of price controls had an important influence on business behaviour: they encouraged a culture of collusion between firms rather than competition. Firms would jointly make their case to the minister for a price rise.

Did *modernisation* have a place for competition between firms? There was a minority of civil servants in the Ministry of Economic Affairs who thought so, and in 1952 and 1953, they had, briefly, their opportunity. In March 1952, the composition of the government moved sharply to the right. The support of dissident Gaullists led to the formation of a new coalition headed by Antoine Pinay. Under the Pinay government, the argument gained ground that competition might have a role to play in keeping down price rises. The law of 18 July 1952 reflects this current of thinking by outlawing *barèmes syndicaux*, a version of resale price maintenance imposed by trade associations (*syndicats professionnels*). The association published price lists and members agreed not to sell their goods for less than the approved price.

Resale price maintenance (*prix imposés* in French) is the right of (usually) a manufacturer to insist that his goods are sold at a certain minimum price by those, such as retailers, who handle them further down the distribution chain. Resale price maintenance is popular with small retailers and, indeed, many manufacturers: the reason is that it limits the bargaining power of the large retailers who can otherwise negotiate substantial discounts from the manufacturers and then undercut the selling prices of the small traders. This advantage is negated if the manufacturer can put a 'floor' under the selling price.

There was confusion and indecision within the Ministry of Economic Affairs about what the text of the 1952 law should actually say. The bill reached the parliamentary committee charged with examining it only a few hours before the debate at which the committee was supposed to report. The bill had been expected to outlaw all forms of resale price maintenance but in the event was limited to collective discrimination: in other words, *individual* manufacturers could continue to fix prices (and refuse to supply retailers who did not stick to them); only resale price maintenance resulting from agreements between firms, or from the decisions of trade associations, were forbidden. The government had drawn back at the last minute from a confrontation with the small retailers who were amongst its strongest supporters.

The parliamentary reactions to the bill illustrate the confusion, in the France of 1952, with regard to business competition. Some members deplored the watering down of the prohibition on resale price maintenance. The Communists purported to make common cause with small business by presenting the bill as an attack on the latter, but which left the 'big capitalists' untouched. The way to reduce prices, according to them, was to reduce the charges for public services such as electricity or transport.[5] Other deputies merely wanted to know what would be the effect on the various vested interests they were pledged to defend. The Communists also said that the bill served the interests of chain stores, whereas, for the Christian Democratic MRP, it did not tackle the 'abuse' committed by firms which refused to supply known price cutters. Both these observations were true, and were the reflection of a battle of interests between modern and traditional forms of retailing which had its origin even before the war, and has continued to this day.

In 1930, two of the large Paris department stores, Galeries Lafayette and Printemps, sought to imitate the success of the Woolworths format in the USA and Britain by creating subsidiaries which would operate chains of shops. These would sell a range of mass-produced, basic items. The commercial strategy depended on a very fast turnover of stock and a very simple price structure: every item would be sold at one of only three or four prices, not in fact the single price which was suggested by the shop-names: Monoprix and Prisunic.

The idea was a huge success. By the mid-1930s, virtually every town with over 40,000 inhabitants had a Monoprix or a Prisunic or both. The reaction of the small shopkeepers and their political defenders was furious. The Chamber of Deputies twice debated restrictions on the opening of chain stores, in 1934 and in 1936. Speakers of all parties, from Communist to extreme right, denounced the new form of retailing, which, with its emphasis on standardization, would lead to de-skilling. The 1934 bill was rejected in the Senate, but that of 1936 passed both houses and banned the opening of further chain stores for one year, a period several times extended. In the 1936 debate, one speaker claimed that not only was the format foreign, but the 'obsession with low prices to which chain stores pander will throw open wide our frontiers to cheap goods from a certain Far Eastern country'.[6]

The language of these parliamentary debates is astonishingly modern (or astonishingly old-fashioned, depending on one's point of view). Sixty years later, the Minister of Commerce, Jean-Pierre Raffarin, justified a further round of restrictions on supermarkets and hypermarkets as follows:

> They have a destructive logic which leads them to sell products which are more and more foreign, in larger and larger sheds... French society should show penitence. For the last twenty years it has been abandoning its towns and its countryside to an American

logic, for the logic of the hypermarket surrounded by car parks runs on an American operating system.[7]

Or as the mercantilist author Montchrestien put it, almost four centuries ago:

> Are we blind or mad? Foreigners...sell their merchandise, rotten and poorly made as it is, in the stores and public markets, and the sound and honest French goods are relegated to the little shops. They are always inventing some new fraud to trap us, while our faithful manufacture is dying in front of us.[8]

In 1948, a certain Edouard Leclerc opened his first supermarket and began his policy of aggressive price-cutting. The response to Leclerc was, not for the last time, the collusion of manufacturers and small retailers. Leclerc and other supermarkets were often boycotted by manufacturers, throughout the 1950s and 1960s, and it was these tactics, applauded by some and deplored by others, which lay behind the debate on Pinay's law of 1952.[9]

Pinay's successor, Laniel, replaced Pinay's law by a more ambitious measure which included a surveillance authority, the *Commission technique des ententes*. The latter was supposed to enquire into anticompetitive practices and report on them to the minister for economic affairs. However, the real sting in the measure was the power of prosecution for collective boycotts. Aggrieved retailers in the electrical trade mounted a successful challenge, on a legal technicality, against this power. Although the power was re-introduced in 1958, no use was ever made of it. As for the *Commission technique des ententes*,[10] it conducted enquiries into this and that but had no power of sanction. In 1977, Raymond Barre, as prime minister, scrapped it and replaced it by a *Commission de la concurrence*; the minister for economic affairs was now given power to fine firms which the enquiries of the *Commission* had shown to be guilty of anti-competitive conduct. However, gradually the delays between the Commission's report and the minister's decision grew longer and longer, as contradictory pressures were put on him.

The big change came in 1986, as part of the brief flowering of *libéralisme* during the first *cohabitation*. The celebrated *Ordonnance* of December 1 firstly scrapped price controls and secondly set up a competition authority with real powers, the *Conseil de la Concurrence*. These are powers not only of investigation but of punishment. The minister for economic affairs may decide to refer a case to the *Conseil* (or it can decide for itself what to investigate) but he has no part in its decisions, and in particular the power of punishment has been taken away from the minister and given to the *Conseil* itself.

The key provision of the *Ordonnance* is the power to investigate and punish by fines 'agreements and concerted practices... which have the object or effect of preventing, restricting or distorting competition'.[11] The wording is borrowed from Article 85 of the Rome Treaty, as we shall see below. The collective boycotts by manufacturers directed against Leclerc in the 1950s and 1960s would be impossible today, as both the French and the European legislation would treat them as 'agreements... preventing, restricting, or distorting competition'.

For governments, the battles over retailing have not provided a discernible 'business interest' which they could support (or oppose) but rather a succession of clashing interests. In the 1950s, they began by rather timidly supporting the newer forms of retailing as part of the fight against inflation. Thereafter, they reverted to the behaviour of the 1930s and surrendered to the small trader interest group. In 1963, the government outlawed the practice of 'loss-leading',[12] as the small traders had requested. In 1973 it made the opening of new supermarkets subject to approval by committees of which nine out of twenty members were themselves small retailers.[13] It mattered little whether left or right was in power. The Socialists toughened up the restrictions in 1991. More restrictions were introduced in 1996, when the presidency and the government were both in the hands of the right. The fine for loss-leading was raised to 500,000 F even for a first offence. In reporting this the headline in *Le Monde* was, 'Large retailers helpless in the face of the government's hostility'.[14]

And yet, all the state could offer its client interest-group, the small traders, was a parachute to slow their descent – no more than that. The proportion of all retail sales represented by the small shops fell below 50 per cent for the first time in 1989, and has carried on declining at a rate of about one per cent or two per cent per year. For it is an area in which decisions are made not by the few but by the many: the consumers.

France and Europe

The formation of the European Economic Community in 1958 involved much more than an elimination of tariff barriers. Tariffs had indeed been abolished by 1967, though of course only between the member states themselves. A high external tariff was put in place against the rest of the world. The Community was not a free trade area but a customs union.

What had come into being was a system of law, modelled on that of the Coal and Steel Community, but much wider-ranging in scope. It is this system of law, enforced by the Commission and the European Court of Justice, which marks the Community out from other international organizations and has had a significant impact on business practice. Moreover, the scope and direction of the law are not readily predictable and cannot be controlled by member states. The role of the Court is to interpret and apply the Treaties and to assert their supremacy over national law. The latter point is not provided for explicitly in the Treaties themselves. It is a legal principle expounded by the judges, beginning with a case heard in 1963, when the Court said:

> ... the Community constitutes a new legal order ... for the benefit of which the states have limited their sovereign rights, albeit within limited fields, and the subjects of which comprise not only member states but also their nationals.[15]

In 1991, the Court went further and spoke of:

> ... a new legal order for the benefit of which the states have limited their rights *in ever wider fields* (my italics) ... The essential characteristics of the Community legal order ... are in particular its primacy over the law of the member states and the direct effect of a whole series of provisions which are applicable to their nationals and to member states themselves.[16]

The Court has been criticized by some observers for going beyond or even contradicting the text of the Treaties.[17] But be that as it may, the Court has shown itself willing to strike down (or, in its parlance, 'disapply') laws of member states which it believes to be in conflict with the Treaty. This has given a powerful new weapon to those who believe their business interests are damaged by those laws. This was what Michel-Edouard Leclerc, son of the founder and now managing director of the retail chain, meant when he told an interviewer:

> At Leclerc, we have always believed that the best way to bring down prices in France is to play the European card. That is why we went to the European Court of Justice in the cases of petrol, pharmaceuticals,

books, tobacco ... We have used the myth of the Single Market to smash the vested interests in France.[18]

In France, traditionally a producer-dominated society, as we have seen, many of the cases begin when someone is put on trial for selling something too cheap. Too cheap, that is, under the terms of a French regulation made to protect the national, or as some would see it, a sectional interest.

A classic type: the case of petrol

Petrol was until 1985 subject not only to a maximum but also to a minimum price, both at the retail and at the wholesale level. Under a law dating back to 1928, the government fixed a minimum price, based on the price at which the French refineries were able to supply. This made it less attractive to import, as cheaper supplies obtained abroad had to be sold to the consumer at the French price level.

The small independent garages which dominated the retail trade were also happy with the minimum price. Not only did they not have to compete with each other, but the price floor offered protection against a new and thoroughly unwelcome source of competition: the garages which, from the early 1980s onwards, were opened by the big chains of supermarkets. The latter had purchasing power; they could drive a hard bargain with the oil companies, and they had their own fleets of road tankers which could be used if necessary to bring in supplies from abroad. But they could not maximize these advantages so long as the law placed a floor on the price they could charge to the customer.

The first to move was Leclerc. He ignored the minimum price and challenged his opponents to do their worst. Some of the outraged garage proprietors responded in a way not unfamiliar in France – by a wave of hijackings and burnings of tankers belonging to Leclerc and other supermarkets. A more measured response came from a M. Henri Cullet, a garage proprietor near Toulouse, who was put up by his trade association to sue Leclerc. In the commercial court in Toulouse he sought an order requiring Leclerc to obey the law and raise his prices to the legal minimum and pay compensation for the damage caused to his own business by Leclerc selling petrol too cheaply.

Leclerc's lawyers argued that the French law of 1928 and the orders made under it in 1982 were incompatible with Article 30 of the Rome Treaty. It will be recalled that France had abolished quotas on imports as part of the 'opening of the frontiers' in 1958. However, Art 30 provides that 'quantitative restrictions on imports and *all measures having equivalent effect* shall ... be prohibited between Member States' (my italics). The French court now had to suspend the proceedings and request a ruling from the European Court of Justice on the compatibility of the French legislation with the Treaty.[19]

The right to appear before the Court is not limited to the parties (in this instance, Cullet and Leclerc); member states are entitled to submit 'observations' to the Court about how it should deal with a case. France was supported in its 'observations' by Italy and Greece, two other member states of strong protectionist tradition. The French government sought to argue that the system favoured imports. A firm which imported cheap fuel could allow its distributors a higher profit and the volume of imports had in fact risen. (So it had, the importers being the new supermarket garages.) This argument was dismissed by the Court: the system might give an advantage to certain distributors, but it gave none to *consumers*, who at the pumps had to be charged the French minimum price.

Next, the French government argued that, even if the minimum-price system was a 'measure having an effect equivalent to a quota', it should be a permitted exception under Article 36, on the grounds that it was public policy in France to maintain a nationwide coverage of garages. When this was dismissed by the Court the French government deployed its last argument, that to change the law would be a threat to public order and public security due to the reactions of outraged retailers. However, the Court was unmoved and found that the French legislation conflicted with Article 30 of the Treaty, because the minimum price was based on the price at which French refineries could supply and was a disguised means of protecting them. Thus the case against Leclerc collapsed.

His victory accelerated the dramatic changes in the trade. Between 1981 and 1995 the number of retail petrol outlets fell from 42,500 to 19,000 and is still falling at the rate of about 1,000 a year. The oil companies' own petrol stations have 52 per cent of sales, the supermarkets 44 per cent and rising, and the independents only 4 per cent.[20]

The case of brandy

Similar attempts to use Article 30 to strike down French regulations have occurred in the case of books, pharmaceuticals, and more notably, brandy. The trade in brandy is in the hands of one of the 'interprofessional' bodies which can trace their origins to the corporations of

Vichy. In its present form, the *Bureau national interprofessionnel du cognac* (BNIC) has existed since 1975. It is 'interprofessional' in the sense that it brings together representatives of the growers and the distillers, as well as a delegate supposedly representing the vineyard workers and another delegate representing the wineshed workers, along with civil servants and a president appointed by the government.

The BNIC has the power to fix minimum prices both for the wine from which the brandy will be distilled and for the finished product. The decisions of the BNIC are given legal effect by the process of *extension*. If the minister of agriculture approves the proposed prices, he incorporates them into a ministerial order (*arrêté*) by which the decisions of the meeting become binding on all firms in the trade. Anyone who sells below the minimum price finds that the law treats his contracts as null and void and that he can be sued by the BNIC for damaging its members' businesses. Or at least, that was the situation before the case brought against a certain M. Guy Clair.

In a slight variant on the situation to which we have become accustomed, M. Clair was accused of *buying* something too cheaply. He was a dealer in brandy who had bought from distillers at a price below the approved minimum. When sued, M. Clair turned the tables on those who were trying to declare his contracts void. It was the agreement by the BNIC's members to fix prices which was void, he said, under Article 85[21] of the Rome Treaty. On a reference from the French court, the European Court of Justice upheld this view; the case against Clair collapsed, and with it the price-fixing system for brandy.[22]

Three years later, the BNIC tried again. This time it was trying to enforce not a minimum price but a production quota. Each grower was required to pay a penalty if he produced too much. (The object of the quotas was of course to sustain the price in the face of excess supply and falling demand.) The difficulties of managing a large cartel, even with state backing, are shown by the fact that 463 growers refused to pay the penalty. The BNIC began enforcement proceedings against one of them, a certain M. Yves Aubert, claiming unpaid penalties of 7,916 francs (and two centimes).

Like M. Clair, M. Aubert argued that the rulings of the BNIC were in conflict with Article 85 of the Treaty. When the case was referred to the European Court of Justice,[23] the French government argued, as it had against Clair, that the decisions of BNIC could not be reviewed under Article 85 because they were those of a state authority. (Article 85 deals with the behaviour, basically, of firms,[24] not of governments). In Clair's case, the Court had said that the prices were in reality fixed by the participating firms and only approved by the minister, so the BNIC was not a state authority but was really just an association of firms fixing prices. But in *Aubert* the Court went further and attacked head-on the imposition of trading terms by ministerial extensions of the acts of trade associations: it restated the principle that member states must not make laws or regulations which have the effect of frustrating the operation of the competition provisions of the Treaty.

The application of this principle to a case brought against a travel agency precipitated the chain of events which has led British Airways to become the second largest air carrier in France.

Opening the skies

The Nouvelles Frontières agency and its director were on trial for (of course) selling something too cheaply, namely air tickets. They had sold tickets at prices below those fixed by the French Ministry of Aviation, and had been prosecuted. In fact, they were acquitted by the French Tribunal de Police, but in the course of the proceedings the European Court of Justice was asked to rule on the compatibility of the regime of fixed ticket prices with the competition provisions of the Treaty.[25] The French government had argued that neither Article 85 (forbidding anti-competitive agreements, such as price-fixing) nor Article 86 (forbidding abuse of a dominant position) applied to air transport.

In the late 1980s, international air traffic to and from France was governed by bilateral agreements between France and the other country involved. These stipulated which airlines were to operate on the route (usually one French and one foreign carrier) and what prices were to be charged. (In such a system, the fares will be set at a level high enough to permit the less efficient of the two operators to make a profit; the more efficient will be rewarded with a higher profit margin but will not be able to undercut the other carrier's prices.)

The system started to unravel in the 1980s under the impact of deregulation in the United States and the abolition of government control of fares on the air routes between Britain and the United States. This diverted some traffic from other European airlines onto carriers operating out of the UK.[26] In most cases the carrier designated by France for international routes was the state-owned Air France. Not always, however. There was another French airline, UTA, a private airline, which had operated some of the routes within the French Empire. With the ending of the colonial period, the French government decided in 1963 to divide the traffic geographically between the two carriers. UTA became the approved French carrier on routes to West Africa and to the South Pacific; other routes were reserved for Air France.

Internal air traffic was handled neither by Air France nor by UTA, but a third company, Air Inter. The majority of its shareholders were nationalized corporations (the state had made Air France a shareholder, when Air Inter was created in 1954) but UTA had a minority stake. On each internal air service the state had awarded a monopoly: to Air Inter on the busiest routes, to various regional carriers, both public and private, on the others.

In 1989, UTA was owned by a conglomerate, Les Chargeurs Réunis. In that year, UTA was put up for sale, and in a classic stroke of *dirigiste* policy, Bernard Attali, president of Air France, arranged with his minister that Air France would buy UTA. In so doing it had acquired a controlling interest in Air Inter too. Attali claims that a 'furious' Sir Leon Brittan told him that the European Commission would never permit the merger of Air France with UTA and Air Inter.[27] Armed with the Nouvelles Frontières judgement, the Commission threatened to treat the merger as being itself an abuse of Air France's dominant position, and to start legal proceedings to block it.

After an intense round of politico-commercial bargaining, the Commission agreed to drop its opposition to the Air France takeover of UTA and Air Inter, but on certain conditions: France must agree to open up its most important internal air routes to other carriers, who would therefore be competitors of Air Inter, and Air France must divest itself of its stake in the internal air carrier TAT, which operated a number of the routes not reserved for Air Inter.

The Commission, it will be noted, had no power to insist that France open up internal air transport to competition, for the European regulations on air transport which would require this had not yet been made. Nor did it have any power to require Air France to sell TAT. What it did have was the threat of legal action, based on Article 86 of the Treaty, which the Court of Justice had said did apply to air transport, to block the merger if the French refused to co-operate. So Air France's stake in TAT was transferred to a state-owned financial institution, the Caisse de Dépôts et Consignations, which put it up for sale. The highest bidder was British Airways.

Attali was outraged that a foreign rival had been allowed to buy TAT. But worse was to come. The Nouvelles Frontières judgement meant that the Commission could now start to attack the airlines for their price fixing and other restrictions of competition. Legally, this would have been a very complex business, but the protectionist countries of southern Europe could see the writing on the wall, and abandoned their longstanding opposition to the making of regulations which would spell out what the new European regime for air transport was to be. In July 1992, the Council of Ministers, with Britain holding the rotating presidency, adopted a series of regulations which provided that by 1997 airlines were to be free to operate services not only to and from their own state but between third countries.

Air France had been running at a loss for years, the losses being met by state subsidies. The root of the difficulty was that the airline was grossly overstaffed. In this it was not alone: the same was true of the Spanish and Italian national carriers. In the mid-1990s the endless subsidies began to be examined much more critically by the European Commission, partly in response to complaints from British Airways. The Commission has the task of vetting state aids and can block or order the repayment of any which in its view distort competition. In 1994 the French government was proposing to inject a further 20 billion francs of subsidy into Air France, demurely called 'recapitalization'. A further round of politico-commercial bargaining ensued before the Commission approved the aid, which was subject to conditions: this package had to be the last, it should be used to restructure the airline rather than to subsidize ticket prices, the French had to open up their internal air routes to international competition before the 1997 deadline laid down in the European regulation, and Air France had to make no acquisitions of other airlines.

The competition between French airlines on internal routes, which had begun in 1990, had led to an unprecedented price war. One new entrant, Air Liberté, had relied on its very low prices to build a substantial market share (imprudently, however, for it was the state-owned loss-making Air Inter which had the deeper pockets). Down went Air Liberté, bankrupt in 1996. A vintage *dirigiste* solution would have been to incorporate Air Liberté into the Air France/Air Inter group, but France had had to promise that the group would make no further acquisitions. So the French authorities had to sit on their hands and watch as the collapsed airline was bought up, by British Airways.

The account which Attali wrote of his presidency of Air France is a fascinating insight into the *dirigiste* mind as it tries to get to grips with modern business conditions (Attali has followed the classic career of the *énarque* administrator: education at the Institut d'Etudes Politiques in Paris, followed by ENA, and jobs in the elite corps of the civil service). The main arguments of the book may be summed up as follows: competition begins abroad, not at home; what matters is to be big; the world is an unfair place – or to France, at any rate.

Dirigiste bureaucracy has always associated competition with disorder. For Attali, in the field of air transport, it was by no means clear whether Europe was a threat or an opportunity:

> To insist, as some do, that on every European route, three or four airlines should be in competition seems to me to be full of danger. It can only lead the European carriers to pointless mutual destruction [*entre-déchirement stérile*], while others look on and laugh – especially the Americans.[28]

But Europe was certainly unfair:

> Let us hope that the European Commission will look at the disparities in social charges which firms have to bear and which depend on the country where they have their base. This disparity distorts competition. Every year British Airways saves three thousand million francs that way, compared with the Air France Group.[29]

The point here is that European 'harmonization' would offer a means of altering the environment of business to Britain's disadvantage. It was European rules and Court judgements which had altered the environment of business to the detriment of Air France. Yet Attali, the *dirigiste*, had the task of leading the airline into the new world of competition. He found it a frustrating and ultimately futile experience.

In September 1991 and October 1992 Air France had published plans which were supposed to bring the airline back into profitability. When the Socialists lost office in 1993 and the second cohabitation began, the incoming right-wing government initially told Attali to toughen up the plan. The result was the publication in September 1993 of a new plan, the so-called 'Phase 2' of the 'Programme de retour à l'équilibre'.[30] Already there were signs of the government getting cold feet, as it cut to practically nil the number of compulsory redundancies which would be allowed. However, the official line remained that the plan had government support and would be put into effect.

On 19 October, the explosion came. Air France workers protesting about the reduction in their shift allowances overwhelmed a hesitant police force at Paris Charles de Gaulle airport and invaded the runways. Passengers were held hostage and aircraft damaged, and the disorder spread to other airports. The government's resolve lasted just under a week. On 24 October, Bernard Bosson, transport minister in the cohabitation government, told Attali that the plan was being withdrawn.

Attali writes:

> Once the first shock was over, I told him: what a mistake! ... What a setback for the airline! And for the state – what an absence of authority!!²³¹

Like all memoirs, Attali's are an act of self-justification. Nonetheless, his account of the minister's reaction to his outburst has the ring of truth about it:

> I can remember him saying to me in no particular order 'risk of it [the disorder] spreading...could be an explosion...opinion polls against us...president on TV tomorrow night...'³²

It was a situation far removed from the myth of the Strong State, serenely applying the General Will.

Attali resigned and was replaced by Christian Blanc. Blanc is not an *énarque*. His first job was in business, after which he became a civil servant. Before his appointment to Air France, he had been a Prefect and the President of the RATP (the Paris transport authority). He too produced a plan for making economies; he too was opposed by strikes and disorder. He came to the conclusion that only a complete privatization of the airline could break its sense of dependency. The idea of full privatization was vetoed by the Communist Minister of Transport in the Jospin government, J.-C. Gayssot, and in September 1997, Blanc resigned. He had done better than Attali, however. Air Inter was still losing money, but Air France had made a modest profit for the first time in almost ten years.

The ownership and control of business

The situation at Air France was symptomatic of the relationship between the state and the businesses it owned, a relationship growing steadily more difficult as competitive pressure increased.

When Britain was beginning the process of privatization in the early 1980s, France, alone amongst West European countries, was moving in the opposite direction. The Socialist/Communist coalition which came to power in 1981 put through parliament in 1982 a nationalization law which created the largest public sector in any Western economy. The ideas behind this went back to an earlier tradition. During World War II, the *Conseil national de la Résistance* had promised to abolish 'the feudal baronies of the economy' and 'return to the nation the main means of production, the fruit of our common labour'.[33] De Gaulle himself had said, just after the liberation of Paris, that the private interest should always give way to the general interest, that the great sources of common wealth should be exploited for the advantage of all.[34]

Between 1944 and 1946 de Gaulle's provisional government and the governments which followed nationalized the four largest clearing banks, Renault, the coal mines, gas, electricity, the largest insurance companies, Air France, various shipping lines, and the Paris city transport system. (The armament manufacturers and the mainline railways had been nationalized before the war.) There were some further extensions of the public sector in subsequent years, notably the merger of Nord-Aviation and Sud-Aviation under state control in 1970. However, although during the 1960s and 1970s there were many state-sponsored mergers (as part of the *dirigiste* enthusiasm for big-ness) most of manufacturing industry remained outside state ownership.

It was the aim of the government which came to power in 1981 to extend nationalization to cover the largest firms in manufacturing, as well as those parts of the banking system which had escaped in 1945. First the state took full control of the two loss-making steel companies, Usinor and Sacilor, by a debt-for-equity swap. More controversially, the state acquired, by compulsion, all shares in the Compagnie Générale d'Electricité, Saint-Gobain, Pechiney-Ugine-Kuhlman, Rhône-Poulenc, and Thomson-Brandt, the owners being compensated by the issue of interest-bearing government bonds which they could either sell or keep to maturity. It negotiated the purchase of the French subsidiaries of International Telephone and Telegraph; in the case of Dassault, Matra, and Roussel Uclaf, it negotiated the purchase of a majority stake. The state was now the owner of firms in industries ranging from heavy engineering through glass-making to pharmaceuticals and consumer electronics.

The industrial firms nationalized were groups. In other words, they were clusters of companies, headed by a parent, which held shares in dozens of subsidiaries. Sometimes these subsidiaries were close to the core activity of the parent, and sometimes not. Thomson-Brandt, in its consumer electronics division, had a company which produced light-bulbs; Matra, basically a defence-electronics company, had a subsidiary which made clocks. In some cases the parent company (and now the state, as its successor) owned 100 per cent of a subsidiary whereas in other instances ownership was shared with another firm or firms; in some cases the other parent had also passed into the nationalized sector, but in other cases not, thus creating a company under joint public/private ownership.

Nor was that all. In addition to the industrial firms, the state nationalized the two large financial holding companies, Compagnie financière de Paris et des Pays Bas (more commonly known as Paribas) and Compagnie financière de Suez. These invest in other businesses, offering capital in return for a stake in the business, and earning their reward from the dividends paid to them as shareholders. They have some wholly-owned subsidiaries of their own, chiefly engaged in providing financial services such as banking and consumer credit. All these shareholdings, both large and small, now had an owner from the public sector.

The size of the public sector is not therefore as easy to measure as one might imagine. In the case of industry, INSEE (the national statistical office) reckoned in 1983 that the nationalized sector employed 23 per cent of the workforce and accounted for 31 per cent of turnover, 28 per cent of value added, 30 per cent of exports, 49 per cent of investment, and 53 per cent of fixed capital.[35] This would indicate that the nationalizations of 1981–82 doubled the size of the publicly owned industrial sector. In banking, state-owned banks now accounted for 90 per cent of all bank deposits. In all, the public sector in 1983 consisted of some 3,000 firms, employing 9 per cent of the national workforce.[36]

The industrial groups acquired in 1981–82 included many mediocre performers. Losses at Usinor and Sacilor were huge, but the difficulties were not confined to steel-making. In 1981, the last complete year before nationalization, Saint-Gobain and the CGE were modestly profitable, but Pechiney, Thomson-Brandt and Rhône-Poulenc all made losses.[37] The newly nationalized firms had been told by the Minister of Industry, Pierre Dreyfus, that they should behave as businesses. In his letter of instructions to the new chairmen, he had exhorted them to seek economic efficiency through a continuous increase in competitiveness.[38]

But what if the increase in competitiveness could be achieved by increasing the productivity of labour? By making do with fewer staff, or not replacing any who left? What then of the government's employment policy? And whether or not they were making profits, how were the nationalized firms to be financed? Only the most profitable firms can finance their investment needs entirely from their own resources.

Others must borrow, either by bank loans or by issuing bonds. Another option is to sell shares to investors, who thereby acquire a stake in the ownership of the business. But for the nationalized firms of 1982, even the profitable ones, issuing shares was obviously impossible, as the nationalization process had consisted precisely of the purchase of the shares of the former investors.

A partial solution came in 1983, with the creation of two financial instruments new to France, the *titre participatif* and the *certificat d'investissement*.[39] The *titre participatif* paid interest, like a bond, but also gave investors an additional amount related to profits (if any), like the dividends paid from profits which they might have hoped to earn as shareholders. The *certificats d'investissement* were just like shares, but with one difference. Although investors received a dividend paid from profits, they could not, unlike real shareholders, vote at the company's annual meetings. Their voting rights were exercised on their behalf by the state, so they could not vote to challenge the company's policy or dismiss its (state-appointed) directors.

Titres participatifs and *certificats d'investissement* were both attempts to square a circle, by attracting funds from private investors without conceding any control. Investors were happy to play along, but at a price. The less control investors have over the way their money is spent, the greater the risk they are required to assume. They expect to be paid for that absence of control, and firms have to tempt them with more generous remuneration to encourage them to invest. *Titres participatifs* and *certificats d'investissement* have been notoriously expensive ways of raising capital.[40]

The real difficulties for the government came over the question of the selling of subsidiaries. There were, as we have seen, thousands of them, and the chairmen of the parent companies had been told to promote 'economic efficiency'. There could be numerous sound business reasons for disposing of a subsidiary, but what if the purchaser was a private firm? Three-quarters of French manufacturing had, after all, remained in the private sector. This put the government in legal and political difficulties.

Taking the legal difficulties first, it will be recalled that the constitution of 1958 had drastically curtailed the powers of parliament. Article 34 gives a list of subjects which are in 'the domain of the law' in which only parliament can legislate. Anything which is not on the list is in 'the domain of regulation', meaning that the government can make regulations on that subject, regulations which parliament cannot challenge. Among the subjects listed in Article 34 is 'the nationalization of undertakings (*entreprises*) and the transfer of the property of undertakings from the public to the private sector'. To be precise, the constitution does not require that each sale of a subsidiary to the private sector should be the subject of a separate law; rather, it provides that a law must lay down the procedures by which such transfers are to take place. There was no such law, and a provision in the nationalization law which purported to give company chairmen the power to sell at least foreign subsidiaries on their own initiative had been declared unconstitutional by the *Conseil Constitutionnel*. The government had promised to bring forward a separate law to deal with the matter.

On 28 October 1982 the government published a bill concerning the transfer to the private sector of the property of undertakings in the public sector. The difficulty was now political. Such was the government's fear of the reaction of pro-nationalization members amongst its own supporters that the bill was never debated and remained a dead letter. This left the nationalized firms in a difficult situation, if they were to be able to dispose of subsidiaries according to ordinary commercial criteria. What they opted for, with the government's blessing, was to carry on regardless. From 1982 to 1986 some 300 companies were sold, without lawful authority. The fact that the purchasers were sometimes foreign increased the political criticism of what was happening. (The public sector was, however, bigger in 1986 than it had been four years earlier, as state-owned firms had acquired 400 subsidiaries from the private sector.)

The trade unions were vehement opponents of the illegal privatizations. The CGT obtained an order from the Commercial Court at Nanterre restraining Renault from selling two subsidiaries, Remix and Micmo-Gitanes, but too late, however, for the order was given on 10 June 1986, by which time the first cohabitation government had been in office for almost three months. The new government's privatization laws[41] retrospectively validated the illegal transfers to the private sector which had taken place under the Socialists. More importantly, the legislation included a list of 65 firms for privatization: banks, insurance companies, and manufacturing groups, some of them nationalized in 1945, others in 1982.

The legislation provided that shares in the firms to be privatized would be sold through the financial markets. 'However', Article 4 continued, 'the Minister for Economic Affairs may choose a purchaser off-market'. This is the origin of the celebrated *noyaux durs*, literally 'hard cores'. The government avoided the term, preferring 'stable groups of shareholders'. In the case of each privatized firm, the minister,

Edouard Balladur, sold small blocks of shares to companies of his choice. These might be other companies undergoing privatization, or companies from the private sector, or companies remaining, for the time being at least, in the nationalized sector. Those who bought the shares in this way acquired them subject to two conditions: that they could not be sold at all for two years, and that for three years after that they could only be sold to the privatized firm itself or to a purchaser approved by it. The shareholdings sold were usually small, perhaps two or three per cent each, but when added together they gave the privatized firm a *noyau dur* or hard core of shareholders, typically holding between them 20 to 30 per cent of the firm's capital, which they had promised not to sell no matter what happened to the price. This was a formidable protection against take-over. A 'raider' would have to acquire an enormous number of the remaining shares in order to gain control, and even then would face a troublesome minority, if not quite a blocking minority.

The *noyaux durs* created a network of shareholdings of preposterous complexity. Privatized bank A holds shares in privatized company B, which in turn holds shares in bank A, and both hold shares in privatized company C, whose shareholders include nationalized company D, and so on.[42] *Noyaux durs* are much more effective as barriers to take-over than as instruments of control over the policy of the company. Firstly, the state does not participate directly in the *noyaux durs* but only indirectly, through shareholdings held by the nationalized firms; secondly, the degree of state involvement weakens slowly, as those nationalized firms are themselves, one by one, privatized. However, the privatization programme was halted in October 1987 by a worldwide fall in share prices. Of the 65 companies listed in the 1986 law, 14 had gone into the private sector.

The first cohabitation was a long electoral campaign for the presidential election of 1988. Chirac needed to get results quickly. For Mitterrand, it was more a matter of playing a waiting game – waiting, that is, for Chirac to trip up, and taking every opportunity to portray himself as the wise voice of common sense. What was the candidate Mitterrand to say about privatization? If he promised a wave of re-nationalizations, he risked, even in France, a negative reaction, as well as questions about how he proposed to pay for them. On the other hand, if he promised to pursue the privatization programme, he was conceding that he had changed his mind and that his opponent was right.

The answer came in a television interview on 22 March 1988:

> Nationalizations and privatizations: so much upheaval in so short a time, and yet we are entering a period, between now and 31 December 1992, which will see the creation of a single internal market between the twelve...This requires [from France] such energy...that I don't think we should get into another battle about nationalizations...we also need to end...this contagion of privatizations...Neither one nor the other of these reforms is appropriate at the present time.

This smokescreen was vintage Mitterrand. From his phrase 'neither... nor (*ni...ni* in French) comes the policy known as the *ni-ni* applied in the years following Mitterrand's victory. This neat formula had got Mitterrand out of a difficulty, but was very hard to apply in practice. Inevitably, Mitterrand announced a relaxation of the *ni-ni* at a press conference on 11 September 1991. This time the smokescreen was 'unemployment', and not Europe, as in March 1988. This made possible the sale, the following summer, of a minority stake in Total, a state-owned oil company, the first and last such operation before the Socialist defeat at the legislative election of 1993, which brought the right back to power and made the last two years of Mitterrand's presidency a second cohabitation.

The new prime minister, Edouard Balladur, put through parliament a new privatization law. Many of the companies listed for privatization were part of the 'unfinished business' from 1986, but others were new; the latter included Renault, in state hands since 1944. In 1986, Chirac and Balladur had specifically ruled out the privatization of firms 'which provide a public service or manage a monopoly'.[43] In 1993, there was a very modest relaxation of this, to the extent that SEITA, an old state monopoly on the tobacco trade, was to be sold off. But the important monopolies, the utilities, were to remain in the public sector. In so far as the regulatory regime for activities such as telecommunications and electricity has changed at all in France, it has done so for the same reason that air traffic had to be deregulated – the need to implement, however reluctantly, European directives.

When the Socialists returned to power in 1997, bringing into existence a third cohabitation, they carried out their predecessors' plans to sell a minority stake in France Telecom. Yet their motive was the same as Balladur's had been in 1993, summed up by a headline in the British

Financial Times: 'Deficit, not ideology, drives French sell-off'.[44] In other words, they needed the money.

'Noyaux durs', corporate governance and foreign investors

Like that of 1986, the privatization law of 1993 gives power to sell shares off-market to chosen investors, which has created *noyaux durs*. Both the government and the firms concerned still refuse to use the term *noyau dur*. A variety of euphemisms have been found. A current one is *actionnaires de référence* (approximately 'key shareholders' or 'anchor shareholders'). *Noyaux durs* have tended to become more concentrated. In the case of Paribas, for instance, the *noyau dur* had 13 members in 1989 owning between them 15.8 per cent of the shares; by 1995 there were only 3 members, but they held 28.2 per cent of the shares.[45]

The noyaux durs of the recently privatized firms are really only a state-organized version of a technique by which French firms have long since sought to protect themselves against unwelcome outsiders. This is the *pacte d'actionnaires*, by which firms purchase shares in each other and agree to hold on to those shares no matter what may happen to the price, and no matter what may be the dividend paid. It is customary to give the *noyau dur* shareholders representation on the board of directors, with the result that there is not only an interlocking network of shareholdings but an interlocking network of directorships as well. It is true that the law limits such cross-shareholdings to 10 per cent of each firm's capital, but this provision is easily avoided. If it is desired that, in reality, company A will control more than 10 per cent of the shares of company B, then some of the shares in B will be held by A's subsidiary, C. When it comes to the shareholders' annual meeting, A's and C's representatives will vote the same way. (B, meanwhile, will arrange that its subsidiary D will hold shares in A.)

A similar device is *autocontrôle*, by which a company arranges that some shares in itself are held by its own subsidiaries. At the shareholders' meetings, the representatives of the subsidiaries will of course vote in the way the parent wants them to. The purpose of these manoeuvres is not only to prevent take-over, but more generally, to square a circle: to invite external investors into the firm without conceding any control to them. In the case of *autocontrôle*, for instance, the relative weight of an external shareholding can be driven down by swelling the firm's capital to include the 'tame' shareholdings of the subsidiaries.

The same wish to maintain control explains the popularity of *certificats d'investissement*, not only with nationalized firms but also with private ones, especially when a family is seeking to maintain its position. *Certificats d'investissement* pay a dividend, just like a share, but the shareholder's voting rights are given to someone else. In the nationalized firms, the state keeps them for itself; in private firms they are distributed among the existing shareholders, a perfect device for cementing the control of the existing owners by inflating their voting power.

Another device for doing this is the 'double vote'. Companies can adopt a rule by which those who have held shares in the company for two years can have, for every share they hold, not one vote but two. In its original version, the French legislation which provided for this possibility allowed the double vote to be restricted to French shareholders,[46] but this was tactfully modified in 1992 to include nationals of other EC states.[47] A shareholding which by value is worth, say, only 20 per cent of the company's share capital is thereby converted into 40 per cent of the votes.

Conclusion

The tactics described above are all very well if investors are undemanding, or if they are locked in France behind a wall of exchange controls and have few choices about what to do with their money. But exchange controls were abolished in 1990, and French investors do have choices. Moreover, companies which agree to participate in cross-share-holdings or in *noyaux durs* may find that they are stuck with a poorly performing asset which pays them low dividends, and as they come under increasing competitive pressure themselves they are being pushed into finding a better use for their money. It has become more difficult to find firms willing to enter the *noyaux durs* and in the most recent privatizations, it has been necessary to use the state-owned utilities such as Electricité de France to fill the gaps in them.

Globalization includes, as we have said, a worldwide competition to capture savings. French firms have increasingly turned to foreign shareholders for funds. American and British investors in particular have little patience with such traditional French devices for maintaining control as the 'double vote'. Major worldwide investors include the American and British pension funds, investing on behalf of the company pension schemes operated by many large employers in those countries. The American and British fund managers are under intense pressure to maximize their returns, if necessary by insisting on management changes in the firms in which they have invested. The introduction of such funds into France had been planned by the RPR–UDF government, but was stalled when the Socialists returned to power. It remains to be seen how long it will take before French firms find themselves having to answer not only to troublesome Anglo-Saxon fund managers but to new and equally unwelcome French counterparts, disturbing the traditional and very cosy structures of ownership and control.

Notes

1. Lavialle de Lameillère (1865), *Documents législatifs sur la télégraphie électrique en France*, quoted by Rosanvallon, P. (1990), *L'Etat en France*, Seuil, Paris, p.106.
2. *Ordonnance 45–1483 du 30 juin 1945 relative aux prix* and *Ordonnance 45–1484 du 30 juin 1945 relative à la constatation, la poursuite et la répression des infractions à la législation économique.*
3. *Loi du 19 août 1936 tendant à réprimer la hausse injustifiée des prix.* Of course, the idea had a much longer ancestry than that: fear of the revolutionary mob had led the Convention to vote a *Maximum Général* on food prices in September 1793.
4. *Salaire minimum interprofessionnel garanti*, introduced by Art 31x of the *Loi du 11 février 1950*. In 1969 the method of calculating it changed and it became the SMIC (*salaire minimum interprofessionnel de croissance*).
5. *Journal Officiel, Assemblée Nationale, Débats*, 20 June 1952.
6. Assemblée nationale debate of 6 March 1934, quoted by Lefeuvre, D. (1997), 'La Grande Distribution ou sucre de masse', in Marseille, J. (ed.), *La Révolution commerciale en France*, Le Monde Editions, Paris, p.116.
7. *Le Monde*, 20 March 1996.
8. de Montchrestien, A. (1615), *Traité de l'économie politique*, in Cole, C.W. (1939), *Colbert and a Century of French Mercantilism*, Columbia UP, New York, p.89.
9. Leclerc, E. (1985), has given his account of these events in *Ma Vie pour un combat*, Belfond. Paris. In English, Adams, W.J. (1989), relies heavily on Leclerc in *Restructuring the French Economy*, Brookings, Washington, pp.224–243.
10. Or *Commission technique des ententes et de position dominante* as it became in 1963.
11. Article 7. Similar wording had in fact been introduced into French law in 1967 (*Ordonnance du 28 septembre 1967 relative au respect de la loyauté en matière de concurrence*, Article 2.), but what had been lacking then was an effective means of enforcement.
12. The practice consists of selling a certain product very visibly, and at a loss, in the hope that customers will be tempted into the shop, where their other purchases will cover the loss.

13. This was the celebrated Loi Royer, familiarly called after the name of its promoter, Jean Royer, then Minister of Commerce. Officially the *Loi du 27 décembre 1973 d'orientation du commerce et de l'artisanat.*
14. 'La grande distribution est désarmée face à l'hostilité du pouvoir', 20 March 1996.
15. (1963), *NV Algemene Transport-en-Expeditie Onderneming van Gend en Loos v. Nederlanse administratie der belastingen*, ECR (European Court Reports) 1.
16. (1991), *Opinion on the draft agreement on a European Economic Area*, ECR I.
17. See Hartley, T. (1996), 'The European Court, Judicial Objectivity and the Constitution of the European Union', *Law Quarterly Review*, vol. 112, January, p.95.
18. Interview with M.-E. Leclerc in Gandillot, T. and Kamm, T. (1990), *Mille jours pour faire l'Europe*, Lattès, Paris, p.44.
19. The case is reported as (1985), *Cullet v. Leclerc* 2 CMLR (Common Market Law Reports) 524.
20. 'Les pétroliers accélèrent la modernisation de leurs réseaux', *Les Echos*, 5 April 1995.
21. Which forbids agreements or concerted practices that have the object or effect of preventing, restricting or distorting competition.
22. (1985), Bureau national interprofessionnel du cognac v. Clair, 2 CMLR 430.
23. (1988), Bureau national interprofessionnel du cognac v. Aubert, 4 CMLR 331.
24. The French text of the treaty uses the word *entreprise*, which like its rather inelegant English translation 'an undertaking' is intended to show that a wide range of business organizations can be caught, whether they are partnerships, limited companies, or whatever.
25. Reported as (1986), *Ministère public v. Lucas Asjès and others*, 3 CMLR 173, but generally known as the Nouvelles Frontières case.
26. Nouvelles Frontières were prosecuted for selling tickets routed via London which were cheaper than point-to-point fares available from Paris.
27. Attali, B. (1994), *Les guerres du ciel*, Fayard, Paris, p.87. Sir Leon, a British member of the Commission, was at that time responsible for competition policy. French authors, including Attali, commonly brand him an 'extreme freemarketeer' (*ultralibéral*).
28. Ibid., p.61.
29. Ibid., p.163.
30. It called for an operating surplus of five billion francs by 1995. This would have been an astonishing turnaround if it had happened, as five billion francs (£500 million or $825 million) was the operating loss for 1993.
31. Attali, p.219.
32. Ibid.
33. Quoted by Blanc, J. and Brulé, C. (1983), *Les Nationalisations françaises en 1982*, La Documentation française, Paris.
34. Speech at the Palais de Chaillot, Paris, 12 September 1944. Reprinted in de Gaulle, C. (1959), *Mémoires de guerre, lll, Le Salut*, Plon, Paris, p.343.
35. Quoted by Bancel, F. (1995), 'Le processus de privatisation; la spécificité française', in Dion, F. (ed.), *Les Privatisations en France, en Allemagne, en Grande-Bretagne et en Italie*, La Documentation française, Paris, p.26.

36. Ibid p.26.
37. Blanc and Brulé, p.32.
38. 'Lettre de mission aux administrateurs généraux', 17 February 1982, reprinted in *Cahiers français*, no. 214, p.12.
39. By virtue of the *Loi du 3 janvier 1983 sur le développement des investissements et la protection de l'épargne*, more commonly known as the *Loi Delors* after the finance minister who promoted it.
40. *Certificats d'investissement* will earn the same dividend as a share, but will usually trade at a discount to the shares, in other words, investors have to be attracted by a higher price/earnings ratio.
41. *Loi du 2 juillet 1986 autorisant le gouvernement à prendre diverses mesures d'ordre économique et social; Loi du 6 août 1986 relative aux modalités d'application des privatisations.*
42. See, for instance, the diagrams in Hamdouch, A., (1989), *L'Etat d'influence*, CNRS, Paris.
43. Balladur, E. (1986), *Vers la liberté*, La Documentation française, Paris, p.72.
44. *Financial Times*, 22 June 1993.
45. *Les Echos*, 9 Dec 1989 and 11 January 1996, quoted by L'Hélias, S. (1997), *Le Retour de l'actionnaire*, Gualino, Paris, p.54.
46. *Loi du 24 juillet 1966 sur les sociétés commerciales*, Article 175.
47. More precisely, it was in response to fear of a challenge under Article 7 of the Treaty of Rome, which forbids discrimination on grounds of nationality.

Bibliography

Adams, W. J. (1989), *Restructuring the French Economy*, Brookings, Washington.
Attali, B. (1994), *Les guerres du ciel*, Fayard, Paris.
Balladur, E. (1986), *Vers la liberté*, La Documentation française, Paris.
Blanc, J. and Brulé, C. (1983), *Les Nationalisations françaises en 1982*, La Documentation française, Paris.
Dion, F. (ed.), *Les Privatisations en France, en Allemagne, en Grande-Bretagne et en Italie*, La Documentation française, Paris.
Gandillot, T. and Kamm, T. (1990), *Mille jours pour faire l'Europe*, Lattès, Paris.
Hamdouch, A. (1989), *L'Etat d'influence*, CNRS, Paris.
Hartley, T. (1996), 'The European Court, Judicial Objectivity and the Constitution of the European Union', *Law Quarterly Review*, vol. 112, January.
L'Hélias, S. (1997), *Le Retour de l'actionnaire*, Gualino, Paris.
Marseille, J. (ed.), *La Révolution commerciale en France*, Le Monde Editions, Paris.
Rosanvallon, P. (1990), *L'Etat en France*, Seuil, Paris.

5
The Press, the PAF and the Decline of Tutelage

Jill Forbes

Introduction: *'le paysage audiovisuel français'*

At a press conference held in July 1970 President Georges Pompidou set out his conception of the role of French broadcasting and broadcasters: 'Journalists who work for the ORTF are different from journalists who work elsewhere. Whether we like it or not, the ORTF is the Voice of France. This is how it is viewed abroad and this is the way the general public think of it [...] This means that those who broadcast on television or France Inter are in some way speaking in the name of France, and what I personally ask is that they should speak in a manner worthy of that role.'[1] Coming two years after the events of May 1968 which had brought the issue of the control of broadcasting to the forefront of political concerns, these remarks were widely interpreted as a justification for censorship based on the existence of an ideological position common to both journalists and government.[2] But in the quarter of a century that has gone by since then, the French press and audio-visual media – familiarly known as the *paysage audiovisuel français* (PAF) – have undergone such radical changes that Pompidou's conception seems more irrelevant than scandalous. The direct state control of television and radio established for the purpose of wartime propaganda has been undermined, while the decentralized regime for the press and print media, set up at the Liberation, was widely flouted and has now been abandoned.[3] What is more, French politicians have ceased to view broadcasting and the press as rival centres of power that can be played off against each other, and have come to understand them as elements in a much larger economy of communications which extends from cable-laying, at one extreme, to programme production at the other. As service industries which are concerned with leisure,

91

entertainment and information and which rely on advanced technologies for their delivery, the media lie at the heart of the economies of the coming century. The political interest they excite in France is just as intense as it has ever been, and the struggle for power within the media just as keen, but the way this is done and its mode of expression have changed. It was during the 1980s, particularly under the socialist government elected in 1981, that government attitudes towards the media altered radically, but the full impact of the changes that have occurred would be difficult to understand without some knowledge of the historical context.

France as world leader

From the 1830s until the outbreak of the First World War France was a leader in the development of communications technologies and products. Indeed, one of the legacies bequeathed by the engineers and entrepreneurs of that period is the continuing national preoccupation with the communications media, whether in transport, images or sounds.[4] France was in the forefront of developments in telegraphy, photography and film, and in the mass circulation press, financed by the combination of advertising and low prices, which expanded so rapidly that by the beginning of the century *Le Petit Parisien* was the most widely distributed newspaper in the world.[5] The foundation of this phenomenal growth was the law on press freedom enacted in July 1881 which put an end to direct and indirect censorship.[6]

From 1914 onwards, however, weakened by renewed censorship and paper shortages which diminished their credibility and their quality, daily newspapers ceased to flourish. During the depression of the inter-war years Parisian newspapers became increasingly ephemeral as they became economically less viable, with the result that industrialists, whose major commercial or manufacturing interests had little to do with the media or communications industries, began to become newspaper proprietors. The textile manufacturer Jean Prouvost was one such businessman: he purchased *Paris-midi* in 1924 and *Paris Soir* in 1930, transforming the latter by means of sensational reporting and photo-journalism; in 1937 he launched *Marie-Claire* and just before the war took over a sports magazine *Match* which he relaunched as the immensely successful *Paris-Match* after the war had ended. He was later to acquire *Le Figaro* as well. Similarly, the perfume and cosmetics manufacturer François Coty tried to create a press group to support his political ambitions with the acquisition of *Le Gaulois* which he merged with *Le Figaro* (purchased in 1922) and with the launch of *L'Ami du peuple* in 1928.[7] But the interwar years also saw the development of newspapers of a different kind: the political papers (*la presse d'opinion*) which reflected the increasing polarization of views between right and left which occurred throughout the 1930s.[8] The most famous of these was *L'Humanité*, which had been founded by Jean Jaurès in 1904 but was taken over by the Communist Party after the Congrès de Tours in 1920, but there were many other similar titles.[9] The influence the so-called '*puissances d'argent*' exercised by controlling information and determining the life and death of newspapers led politicians of the left, such as Léon Blum, the Prime Minister under the 1936 Popular Front, to view a form of 'nationalization' as the best way to underpin press freedom and ensure the expression of a range of political opinions, and the experience of the Second World War strengthened this view.[10]

But while the Paris press became increasingly unstable and finan-cially insecure, the regional press flourished, and by 1939 the circula-tion of provincial dailies was equal to that of Parisian daily newspapers.[11] The strength of the non-Parisian press was a reflection of the political and cultural characteristics of France in the 1930s, a country in which, despite a highly centralized administration, political power and cul-tural habits were strongly regionalized. Indeed, cultural historians have argued that it was not until after the second world war that France achieved a 'nationalized' culture, thanks to the development of educa-tion, the improvement in communications and, above all, the spread of radio and television.[12] In contrast with Britain, for example, where the press in the 1930s contributed significantly to the 'nationalization' of culture, the newspapers in France tended to reinforce regional differ-ences and each regional newspaper had a political role to play in sup-port of local politicians whom they helped to establish regional 'fiefdoms'. Indeed, without the support of a regional newspaper politi-cal success was inconceivable.[13]

But it was the experience of the Occupation that was to prove deci-sive in the recent history of the press in France. The German invasion, followed by the division of France into an Occupied Zone in the north and Unoccupied Zone (until 1942) in the south, drove a stake through the heart of the Paris newspaper industry, but it stimulated the regional newspapers which continued to publish independently, though under increasing constraints from paper and print shortages. Some Paris titles left the capital for Lyons, where they survived with much reduced cir-culations and facilities – until the Germans invaded the south of the country, when they ceased publication.[14] In the Occupied Zone, the

Germans expropriated newspapers, as they did film production companies, and while the pro-Nazi titles continued publication but with much reduced circulations and credibility, the population increasingly turned for information towards the radio, especially the broadcasts supplied by the BBC to which De Gaulle had access.[15]

The 1944 '*Ordonnances*' and their impact

At the Liberation of 1944, therefore, the newspaper industry was fragmented into the three broad categories of the collaborationist press, the regional press and the clandestine press,[16] while radio was the only means of addressing the country as a whole. In the press *Ordonnances* issued in 1944, and which remained in force until the 1980s, the provisional government was eager to create a legislative framework which would punish newspapers and proprietors who had collaborated with the Germans by continuing to publish in the Occupied Zone and by printing pro-Nazi propaganda, and which would simultaneously protect the print media from the *puissances d'argent* which were held to have corrupted them before the war and so prepared the way for occupation and collaboration. They wished to reward those who had taken part in the Resistance and, above all, they wished to ensure the good health of the *presse d'opinion* rather than, and in many cases instead of, the widely-read, popular newspapers developed by the *puissances d'argent* in the interwar years. The idea was that every shade of Resistance opinion would be represented by a newspaper both in Paris and in the provinces,[17] and a completely new kind of editor or proprietor came into being as newspapers were attributed to individuals on the basis of their politics rather than their track records as journalists or their financial resources. These Resistance beneficiaries, among whom were Emilien Amaury, Hubert Beuve-Méry, Gaston Defferre and Pierre Lazareff, were in practice chosen by the government since, for several years, no newspaper could be launched without government authorization.[18]

The *Ordonnances* established a regime in which readers knew who owned and published newspapers, and in which the press was protected from mergers, take-overs, foreign ownership and concentration, but also one in which the state played a significant role in granting permission to publish,[19] and in nationalizing, subsidizing, and tightly controlling, companies concerned with manufacturing and selling paper (in short supply after the war), and those like Havas, Agence

France Presse and the Nouvelles Messageries de la Presse Parisienne, whose business was advertising, news-gathering and distribution.[20] But the *Ordonnances* also created a situation which weakened titles financially so that many were unable to survive in the medium term. The law made it impossible for newspapers to merge or to associate different titles, or to become involved with cognate activities, or to achieve vertical integration; nor could commercial or industrial capital be injected into newspaper businesses. Advertising rates were set annually; the government controlled allocations of paper and thus the size of newspapers; and the government fixed the cover price of titles (making no distinction between 'popular' and 'quality' publications). Productivity gains were rendered difficult by the opposition of extremely strong trade unions.

These measures reflected the widely-held view that newspapers were not ordinary commercial businesses, a view that was already prevalent before the war and was still current in the 1960s when France successfully argued within the EEC that newspapers were 'exceptional' and should not be subject to the 'free market' provisions of the Treaty of Rome.[21] Yet the effect of these measures was the opposite of that intended, since they helped to reduce the number of national daily newspapers in circulation in the 1950s and 1960s, creating *de facto* concentration. In the 1970s, the loss of advertising revenue to television and rising production costs made rationalization and modernization essential to the survival of titles, but this was fiercely opposed by the print unions, especially at *Le Parisien Libéré*, owned by Amaury, where the technicians remained on strike for two years, effectively destroying the financial viability of the paper. The failure of both the Amaury and the Prouvost groups to carry through financial rationalization allowed the Groupe Hersant to buy up their titles, thus bringing together under a single proprietor for the first time, and in defiance of the law, both national and regional daily newspapers. Even a newspaper such as *Le Monde* found that the financial structure devised at the Liberation to protect the title from mergers and take-overs acted as a significant brake on its capacity for survival. It has therefore been argued that the long-term effect of the *Ordonnances* was to reduce the economic (and ultimately the political) significance of the Paris press and to reinforce the economic buoyancy of the regional and magazine press, with the magazine sector proving particularly dynamic and entrepreneurial. By the 1980s it was here that the locus of financial power was to be found.

Television and radio

The audiovisual media were a quite different matter. As far back as the *ancien régime* the state had sought to control communications through licensing, taxes and the institution of monopolies. This tradition was reinforced by the threat of war in 1939. In July of that year Premier Daladier appointed a 'Commissioner for Information' whose task was 'to organize, co-ordinate and lead all the French information and pro-paganda services'.[22] His department rapidly evolved into the fully fledged Ministry of Information which remained in place, with changes of title, until 1974.[23] The Fourth Republic notion was that media management should be 'militant' and active and should 'provide a counterweight to the opposition view which is systematically put forward by the press'.[24] Radio had become politically significant during the war and it continued to be so in peacetime. The opposition was not allowed access to the air waves, except during elections, so that De Gaulle claimed to have been denied air time on radio and television from the time he left government in 1946 until his press conference in May 1958.[25] Indeed, it is even suggested that coverage of that celebrated press conference was provided only by the foreign media. Censorship was exercised throughout the period of wars of independence allegedly in order not to 'demoralize' the nation. But the apogee of government interference was reached in May and June 1968 when the ORTF failed to report fully or accurately the demonstrations taking place on the streets and in universities and factories.[26] This episode discredited French television in the eyes of many viewers, and its legacy was felt throughout the 1970s in the persistent calls for government to cease interfering in the presentation of news and current affairs.

The reasons for censorship and tight news management were varied. In addition to providing a counterweight to a supposedly hostile press, it was felt that radio and television offered politicians the means of direct contact with the 'masses', a need which sprang from the political culture of France and which, in turn reinforced that culture. It was not confined to one part of the political spectrum. The socialist Pierre Mendès-France, when Prime Minister, would broadcast 'Saturday night chats' which were opportunities for him to speak 'directly' to the electorate in an intimate manner.[27] De Gaulle made similar use of television – hence his nickname 'Microphone General' – and with the hindsight of history he was to write: 'I want to be linked to the people themselves, through their eyes and ears, and not just to the elites. French people must see and hear me and I must see and hear them.

I was able to use the combination of microphone and screen just when this new invention was beginning its extraordinary development. Suddenly I was given an unrivalled means of being present everywhere'.[28] The state 'monopoly' of television and radio was frequently defended as the only means of ensuring that a dignified and worthy image of the country would be widely broadcast and of avoiding the corrupting influence of commercialism.[29] The notion that radio and television should serve as means of popular education 'raising the cultural level of the masses', however patronizing it may be considered in the 1990s, was subscribed to by many media professionals in France as elsewhere and was felt to be best served by state control of the media (just as the state controlled the education system). De Gaulle's unique mixture of populism and charismatic leadership, together with his 'presidentialization' of French government, were undoubtedly assisted by his consummate exploitation of television. But these characteristics have also meant that it is easy to overstate the extent to which the French broadcasting media were exceptional in their pro-government leanings. In the 1960s and 1970s television and radio in all European countries treated politicians with a respect that would be inconceivable today.

Despite all these factors, in the years immediately following 1968 there were vociferous demands that television should reflect the diversity of political and social viewpoints. By 1981, television news and current affairs had yet to shake off their reputation for government bias, so that the Socialists were to come into office in 1981 with the strong expectation that radical reform would take place. The need for change was further strengthened by the financial crisis which struck television as the market reached maturity, and costs rose with the launch of the third channel in 1972, creating the need for new programmes. In some political quarters, especially among Giscardians, the solution appeared to be privatization – a limited form of which was, indeed, achieved in 1975, within the overall context of the state-run monopoly, by breaking up the ORTF into notionally competing companies whose licence fee revenue depended on audience figures and by allowing television channels to increase the amount of advertising screened.

'Tout ce qui est médiatique est politique'[30]

The election of Mitterrand and the socialist government in 1981 was the first change of régime for 25 years and brought with it a new set of political priorities, raising expectations that the relationship between broadcasting and government would change. However, even this process became highly politicized, with the successive establishment of no fewer than three bodies to regulate broadcasting, each of which had a slightly different political composition and was given slightly different responsibilities. On the recommendation of the Moinot Commission on the future of broadcasting, set up by the incoming government,[31] the first such body was the *Haute Autorité* (1982–6). It consisted of nine members, three nominated by the President of the Republic, three by the President of the National Assembly and three by the Senate, following the model of the *Conseil constitutionnel*. In the event, this gave the Socialists a majority which they undoubtedly used to influence appointments to key posts, in some cases against the advice of the chairwoman, the well-respected and well-connected journalist Michèle Cotta.[32] Furthermore, the powers given to the Haute Autorité were limited: the government continued to draw up the service contracts *(cahiers des charges)*, appointed the directors of TDF (the company responsible for engineering) and of INA (the *Institut national de l'audiovisuel* responsible for research, training and the archive), and distributed the revenue from the licence fee and from advertising.

After the parliamentary elections of 1986 a second body was created, as promised in the manifesto of the RPR, entitled the *Commission nationale de la communication et des libertés* (CNCL) (1986–9), with an enlarged membership of thirteen, an enhanced budget, and a revised set of tasks. Once again, the government continued to distribute the revenue from the licence fee and advertising but, in a move towards what was to become a major function of its successor, the Commission was given the task of awarding frequencies.[33] Finally, when the Socialists returned to power in 1988, this was replaced by the body which has survived, the *Conseil supérieur de l'audiovisuel* (CSA), with nine members appointed on the Conseil constitutionnel model.

The original intention was to create an organization which could ensure an 'arm's length' relationship between government and broadcasting, and the most important task of the *Haute Autorité* was therefore seen as appointing the controllers of the various television channels and ensuring fairness and impartiality in news and current affairs, especially at election times. However, the memoirs of those concerned, especially Cotta,[34] suggest that whatever their public professions of good faith, the Socialists in office were quite as determined as their predecessors that their sympathizers should occupy key posts in television, and that they exerted considerable pressure to ensure that this happened. Over the decade, however, the role of these bodies evolved in such a way that their political make-up became less and less significant,[35] so that the present functions of the CSA relate less to preventing direct political influence than to the regulation of private and privatized television companies, to the awarding of frequencies and technological standards in general, and to ensuring that companies fulfil the contracts for which their franchises were awarded.[36] This is because, when the Socialists came into office, they had to come to terms with a technological and economic revolution whose impact they had not foreseen in opposition. Despite their initial programme of nationalizations and their initial belief that France could set its own economic agenda based on the stimulation of the domestic market, they very rapidly had to confront the downsizing and delocalization attendant on globalization and the international impetus towards privatization and reduced state control. All these trends posed particular challenges to the *paysage audiovisuel français* as conceived at the Liberation – and as still subscribed to by many members of the socialist government, in particular the influential Minister of Culture, Jack Lang – and the consequent shifts were so radical that, it could be argued, the media became the laboratory for the new economics.

The inexorable spread of new technologies and consumer electronics in the 1980s brought about the demise of the Gaullist vision of a strategically managed and protected media sector. Domestic video, for example, provided an alternative way of 'importing' foreign programmes, free from state control or quotas, while satellite technology threatened to permit countries such as Luxembourg, home to the aggressive and private CLT, legally to beam 'non-French' and often American programmes into French territory from outside. Government policy was forced to evolve to keep pace. Within the space of three or four years the policy of protecting public service, state-owned television was replaced by one of aggressive privatization, while the separation of the press and the audio-visual media, considered axiomatic in the early 1980s, was replaced by a policy which believed the national interest to require the creation of large media conglomerates in France capable of rivalling in power and influence comparable European and American media groups such as Time Warner, Bertelsmann, or News International. Similarly, the practice of delaying innovations until French technology could catch up[37] or pursuing a policy of incompatible standards was replaced by support for mergers designed to render the electronics and media industries competitive in the global market.

The most obvious changes occurred in the television industry. The Socialists, who had, in opposition, strongly defended the state television 'monopoly', now moved swiftly to embrace commercial television. The pay-TV channel Canal Plus was launched by Havas in 1984, initially as a 'concession de service public' (like the utilities) and not a private company, and it was designed to offer the kind of schedules built round films, sport and news, that would be available by satellite from outside France or through cable and video within the country. This was followed, in the most spectacular policy reversal, by the creation of two commercial channels, La Cinq and TV6, both launched at great speed before the elections of spring 1986, when the Socialists anticipated they would be voted out of office. President Mitterrand, it is claimed, was more anxious to ensure that the proprietors of the commercial television channels would be politically sympathetic than that the programmes scheduled would be worthwhile, awarding the franchise for La Cinq to a consortium led by Silvio Berlusconi and the socialist Jérôme Seydoux, but paying insufficient attention to the economic viability of the channel. The Chirac government duly elected in that year went further. The CNCL it created reallocated the franchise for La Cinq, reducing Seydoux's holding and allowing the right-wing newspaper proprietor Robert Hersant, a target of socialist ire because of his newspaper acquisitions and mergers, to buy into the consortium. It also privatized the flagship first channel TF1, selling it to the Bouygues construction group in 1987.[38] All these moves appear to represent a shift of power from the state to the private sector, but this is to ignore the nature of French capitalism and the close, if indirect, influence of the state in the reconfiguration of the private sector. This influence is exercised through decisions to privatize, nationalize and franchise, or to allow take-overs and mergers, and it has been particularly evident in the 1980s and 1990s as changes of government and periods of 'cohabitation' have revealed different conceptions of the way the national interest might be secured.

'Les trois H'

This is most interestingly demonstrated in the recent history of the three major French media groups known as 'les trois H': Hersant, Havas and Hachette. Robert Hersant's career as a publisher had begun with the Pétainist *Jeunes Forces* ('organe des jeunes du Maréchal') launched in 1942, and he had quickly identified the new, postwar market for leisure and consumer publications with *Auto journal*, launched in 1950.

This was the first of an immensely successful portfolio that was to include *TV Hebdo and Paris Turf*. In 1952 his newspaper interests became more political with the acquisition of *Oise-Matin*, which served as a platform for his National Assembly election campaign of 1956, as well as the foundation of his provincial newspaper empire – which came to include such well-known titles as the socialist *Nord-Matin* (acquired in 1968), the Resistance paper *Paris-Normandie* (acquired in 1972) together with titles in the Centre region of France, in the Rhône-Alpes region, and in the overseas Departments and Territories, with *France-Antilles*. Although Hersant's ambitions did not, initially, appear different, except in scale, from those of other publisher politicians such as Jean-Jacques Servan-Schreiber or Gaston Defferre,[39] his successive take-overs, mergers and closures which in some cases resulted in monopolies, as in the Rhône-Alpes region, not only earned him the nickname 'le Papivore' (paper-eater), but they also gave rise to disquiet on the Left, who saw his burgeoning empire as an attack on freedom of the press, and among old-fashioned Gaullists who believed that his activities ran counter to the spirit if not the letter of the 1944 *Ordonnances*. Indeed, Alain Peyrefitte reported that De Gaulle, when told of Hersant's intention of launching *France-Antilles*, remarked 'Hersant n'est pas des nôtres'.[40]

The acquisition of *Le Figaro* from the Prouvost group in July 1975 marked a qualitative change in Hersant's ambitions, for this was his first national daily newspaper, and the symbolic purchase of 'the great newspaper of the bourgeoisie'. It was rapidly followed by that of *France Soir* in 1976 and *L'Aurore* in July 1978, leading to the absorption of *L'Aurore* within *Le Figaro*. It now seemed clear that Hersant was deliberately flouting the 1944 *Ordonnances* by creating a monopoly in the conservative and right-wing national press. In 1978, a first attempt to stop his expansion by legal means failed,[41] but the incoming socialist administration of 1981 was determined to try a second time. The resulting statute, enacted in October 1984, and familiarly dubbed 'the anti-Hersant law', had as its central provision that no single press group could control more than 15 per cent of national daily circulation or 15 per cent of daily provincial circulation, or, if a group owned both national and regional titles, not more than 10 per cent of total circulation. But, as a result of a ruling by the *Conseil constitutionnel*, these 'anti-trust' provisions could not be applied retrospectively – so that the legislation not only failed to damage Hersant; it also benefited his group by preventing others from creating similar conglomerates. On this occasion, the Hersant press had mounted a virulent campaign against the proposed new law and had been successful in drawing its teeth.

In August 1986, the newly elected Chirac government replaced this statute with one of its own, which for the first time recognized the changed context in which the media operated. It set a ceiling of 30 per cent of total daily newspaper circulation to be owned by any one group but, more important, abolished the regulatory framework of 1944 and recognized that the distinction between 'national' and 'regional' publications was outdated. This was not only the first time that the *de facto* unified national culture had been recognized in press and media law, but it was also the first time that the legislation indicated that the creation of large media groups might be nationally desirable.[42]

As far as the Groupe Hersant was concerned, diversification into other media and other activities had already taken place. Hersant was the first French press baron to realize economies of scale in his printing operations by opening the large Paris-Print plant at Roissy and linking it to regional printing centres which served his regional newspapers. He likewise created three advertising departments (*régies*) and a news agency; he planned to launch a popular daily newspaper, *Paris Star*; and he diversified abroad, into Spain, Belgium and, from 1990 onwards, into Eastern Europe.[43] Finally, in 1986, one year after it had been launched, the Hersant group was allowed by the new government to buy a share of the commercial TV channel *La Cinq* which it retained, alongside Berlusconi and Seydoux, until 1990. This venture was a failure, with *La Cinq* continuing to lose large sums of money (it went bankrupt in 1992) and it marked the end of Hersant's attempt to transform his 'empire de papier' into a communications conglomerate.

Whatever the public concerns aroused by the growth of Hersant's empire, it remained essentially a group based on print media whose owner, in the traditional French manner, had simultaneously pursued a career in politics. This was not so with the Havas Group whose history is much more unusual. Its origins go back to the nineteenth century, when in 1832 Charles Havas created a 'bureau d'information' specializing in translating news from abroad, with strong interests in the collection and distribution of information using the very best technologies available at the time. Its clients were newspapers and businesses but, unlike European rivals such as Reuters, Havas had a monopoly of information to provincial newspapers. Over time, through its privileged access to government sources of information, it became the means for the state to control information to the press, especially in foreign affairs. In the 1920s Havas added advertising to its portfolio of activities by merging with the *Société générale des annonces*. During the Second World War Havas was transformed into the OFI (*Office français d'information*), and at the Liberation partly transformed into the *Agence France-Presse* which took over Havas's information-gathering functions and became 'the nerve centre of the French press system, retaining extremely close links with government, at least until the end of the Fourth Republic'.[44] Havas itself remained an advertising agency which, during the 1950s, diversified into travel (Havas Voyages) and commercial radio (with a stake in RTL). In this way, it remained a means of exerting financial pressure on the information media, so that Presidents of the Republic were careful to ensure that its chairmen, who were always civil servants, were politically sympathetic.[45] In the 1970s the post was occupied by Yves Cannac, who had previously been a member of Giscard's cabinet and had helped to draft the 1974 reform of the ORTF; in the 1980s it was filled by André Rousselet, an individual of socialist sympathies, who was a long-term friend and golfing companion of François Mitterrand – for whom he had worked when Mitterrand was Minister of Information under the Fourth Republic – and who, in the early 1980s was director of Mitterrand's private office ('directeur de cabinet').

In 1984 Rousselet became the chairman of *Canal-Plus*, the pay TV channel launched by the Socialists in a first attempt to liberalize television broadcasting. After a shaky start, Canal Plus became an extremely successful operation and was floated on the stock exchange with Rousselet as its chairman. Meanwhile, after privatization in 1987, the press and audiovisual interests of Havas proceeded apace throughout the 1990s, so that by 1997 it had become a multi-media group with publishing interests via CEP Communication/ Groupe de la Cité [46] and a press arm that included *Nice Matin, Midi Libre and Centre France*, as well as trade publications, representing 40 per cent of its activity. [47]

Finally, the slow transformation of the Hachette Group exemplifies the confluence of interests which, twenty or thirty years ago, would not have appeared to have much in common. It is also an example of dramatic entrepreneurial renaissance brought about by diversification which transformed 'the most fantastic centre of indecisiveness'[48] into a major media conglomerate, the 'fourth largest in Europe'.[49]

The history of Hachette, of course, stretches back to the beginning of the nineteenth century when the company became a major publisher of books and dictionaries but also diversified into retail outlets and wholesale distribution. The latter activity continued during the Second

World War, which meant that the distribution branch was, briefly, nationalized. Hachette owns many of the most famous imprints in French publishing (Fayard, Grasset, Jean-Claude Lattès) and since its merger with Filipacchi has also owned Livre de poche. Its periodical publications are concentrated in the flourishing domain of financial and leisure publications such as *Elle* and *Elle Décoration*, *Télé 7 jours* and *TV-Hebdo*, popular weeklies like *France Dimanche* and *Ici Paris* and the financial press with *Le Nouvel Economiste*. It has also been immensely successful in franchising its titles abroad, *Elle* being the outstanding example with sixteen foreign editions.

But Hachette's transformation into a multimedia group really began in 1981 when Matra, a company specializing in aerospace and other transport technologies and in satellites and rockets, took a controlling interest in the financially ailing Hachette. Under Matra's dynamic chairman, Jean-Luc Lagardère, this was the signal for Hachette to begin to diversify, and it was well-placed to take advantage of the changing political climate of the 1980s. It first planned to launch a national daily newspaper, Oméga, but abandoned this project when it beat Maxwell in the acquisition of *Le Provençal* and its regional group, sold on the death of Gaston Defferre in 1986. It then acquired a significant holding in the radio station Europe 1 and attempted to purchase TF1 when it was privatized in 1987.[50] Having failed in this attempt, it acquired 22 per cent of the capital of La Cinq when Seydoux withdrew in 1990 and was implicated in the bankruptcy of La Cinq in 1992.

Most commentators note the eclecticism of the Groupe Lagardère Hachette. The *Financial Times*, in a profile of Jean-Luc Lagardère, observed drily: 'To argue the logic of an industrial grouping ranging from airborne missiles to *Elle* magazine is something of an intellectual challenge'.[51] Matra-Hachette's 'nine professions' – missiles, space, cars, urban transport, telecommunications, books, newspapers, distribution, broadcasting – certainly give the impression of 'un empire touche-à-tout'.[52] However, Lagardère's genius, already evident at Matra after he became managing director in 1977, lies in diversification. In the same way as he steered Matra from a company which worked exclusively in arms supply, whose only domestic client was the French government, towards high-tech sectors such as telecommunications and automated transport, he also perceived longer-term synergies in short-term disparities. He was facilitated in this by the 1988 privatization of Matra by the Chirac government elected in 1986. But the end of the cold war, and the consequent drop in defence expenditure by western governments, made diversification imperative, so that while it is true that

Matra bailed out Hachette after the débâcle of La Cinq, in the longer term Hachette may be seen to have brought to Matra the wherewithal to ensure its survival. The opportunity returned with the election of Jacques Chirac to the presidency in 1995 and the announcement of further privatizations, overturning the socialist administration's policy of 'ni ni' or maintaining the status quo, and in particular with the proposed privatization of Thomson, the electronics group partially nationalized by the Socialists in 1982 which, despite large injections of public money, had accumulated a huge deficit. In this bid Lagardère proposed to take over only Thomson CSF, the professional and defence electronics side of the firm, and to sell off the loss-making Thomson Multimédia to the Korean firm Daewoo. The logic of this proposal was that Lagardère would be allowed to forge European alliances and to enter the 'big league' of defence contractors, so ensuring independence from the United States. His rival was Alcatel (formerly CGE) which had shared the telecommunications market with Thomson since the mid-1970s: according to the so-called 'Yalta des telecoms' in 1983, Thomson had acquired the business in military components and consumer electronics while Alcatel had acquired telecommunications and office machinery. In choosing Lagardère's bid rather than that of Alcatel's, the Juppé government was said to be compensating Lagardère for the Chirac government's refusal of his bid for TF1 in 1987. But the sale, for the symbolic sum of one franc, was widely criticized as unpatriotic,[53] and was first stopped by the privatization commission and then overturned by the Jospin government elected in 1997. Finally, it was decided that Thomson would not, after all, be privatized, but that the state's holding would be reduced to 40 per cent and that a newly created company would bring together the satellite and telecommunications activities of Thomson, Alcatel and Aérospatiale.

Conclusion: protectionism under challenge

In considering the exercise of power in the French media, it is impossible to separate technology from ideology. The traditions of Colbertism and economic autarky which stretch back to the *ancien régime* were translated into the electronics and communications industries and hence to the audio-visual media. The desire to defend the national space from foreign penetration or invasion has a long history which was inevitably rendered more acute by the experience of military invasion, and in the field of media and communications it became commonplace to use technological standards as a form of protection. Thus in 1922 the SFR (*Société française radio-électrique*) opted for long-wave broadcasting so as to prevent the importation of American wireless sets; in 1948 François Mitterrand, then Minister of Information, departed from the policy followed elsewhere in Europe and adopted 819 lines as the French black and white TV standard in a move to protect French TV manufacturers; and in 1967 De Gaulle opted for the SECAM colour process which is different from that used elsewhere in Western Europe, the US and most of the world, again in the belief that the French space would be protected and that the system could be exported.[54]

In all these cases what began as a measure to protect French industry ended up weakening it. Thus France failed to sell the SECAM colour system widely and ended up with a smaller foreign market for its television tubes than might otherwise have been the case. It is also suggested that French manufacturers became less efficient owing to their domestic monopoly position.[55] In many respects, therefore, the use of standards as a form of protection had the same effect on the French media and electronics industries as the *Ordonnances* of 1944 had on the French newspaper industry, preventing diversification, vertical integration, foreign expansion and ultimately, growth. In the same way, the nationalizations carried out by the Socialists in the early 1980s were predicated on the idea that state control would shore up the national interest by protecting and stimulating French industry, but took place at a time of change in the world economy which rapidly made such ideas irrelevant.

The Thomson affair illustrates that it is now impossible to consider the press and publishing apart from the media and electronics industries, all of which continue to be considered strategic, albeit within a European rather than a purely national framework. The jostling for ownership of Thomson and the different approaches of successive governments also brought into sharp relief the conflict between a centralizing, Colbertist ideology and the imperatives of globalization. The most vociferous critic, Elie Cohen, put it this way: 'This affair is yet another chapter in the history of "the French disease"'. Privileging the ruler's fiat above the principle of the rule of law, confusing the roles of the state as shareholder, arms purchaser and economic regulator – as well as the victory of lobbyists over civil servants – illustrate that the management of public affairs has become a caricature of what it should be'.[56] The complaints rested on a number of factors: job losses and the possible exporting of jobs to Korea at a time of high unemployment, the fact that large amounts of public money invested in research into advanced digital television technologies would now be thrown away and that France would no longer compete in this apparently promising field, and, more subtly perhaps, that Daewoo was not itself a high-tech firm but one which specialized in the cheaper end of consumer electronics – so that the proposed take-over would allow it to benefit from research without having invested in it, and it would employ French nationals in a sector where value added was limited.

As long ago as 1972, Jacques Fauvet had commented that the press régime created at the Liberation had been based on two fundamental misapprehensions. The first was that newspapers could function outside the laws of a market based on profit. The second was that newspapers were not commercial and industrial businesses as well as providers of news and entertainment.[57] The converse has been true of the audiovisual media, and especially television, which has suffered, in France, from being seen exclusively as a locomotive of other industries, such as electronics, and as the plaything of politicians, but has rarely been seen as a medium of creative activity.[58] There is little evidence that this will change. Indeed, the voluminous coverage devoted to audiovisual questions in France, whether in newspapers or books,[59] testifies to the continuing fascination with the *paysage audiovisuel français* as the perfect arena for pay-offs, score-settling and for gladiatorial combats between opposing politicians and rival political parties.

Notes

1. My translation, and all subsequent translations from the French unless stated otherwise. Press conference 2nd July 1970 quoted in Bourdon, J. (1994), *Haute Fidélité: Pouvoir et télévision 1935–1994*, Seuil, Paris, p.126. The ORTF – Office de la radio-diffusion télévision française – created in 1964, ceased to exist in January 1975 when its various departments were split into separate companies. France Inter is the state radio station.
2. See the collection of essays in (1987), *Mai 68 à l'ORTF*, La Documentation française, Paris, produced by the Comité d'histoire de la télévision.
3. The French term 'la presse écrite' is used to distinguish the print media from 'la presse audiovisuelle' (an obvious solecism). Here I shall refer, indifferently, to the 'press', the 'news media' or the 'print media' as appropriate.
4. See, for a general discussion, Flichy, P. (1980), *Les Industries de l'imaginaire*, Presses universitaires de Grenoble, Grenoble.
5. See Charon, J.-M. (1991), *La Presse en France de 1945 à nos jours*, Editions du Seuil, Paris, pp.8–49 for a useful summary of the history of the press in France.
6. This is not to say, however, that news manipulation by the government ceased, particularly through the state-controlled news agency Havas.

7. See Albert, P. (1990), *La Presse française*, La Documentation française, Paris, p.165.
8. 'For a hundred and seventy years (1770–1940) every political movement and school of thought, every potential or actual statesman (Thiers, Clemenceau...) had one or more daily newspaper, corresponding to every last shade of political and ideological opinion', Charon, *La Presse en France* pp.129–30.
9. See for a list Albert, *La Presse française*, pp.160–61.
10. Charon, *La Presse en France*, pp.48–49.
11. Statistics from Albert, *La Presse française*, p.32.
12. See Williams, R. (1974), *Television: Technology and Cultural Form*, Fontana, pp.33–34.
13. Péan, P. and Christophe, N. (1997), *TF1: Un Pouvoir*, Fayard, Paris, p.66, express the view that 'no politician can exist without a newspaper', and quote a number of witnesses to illustrate the mechanisms of this support. The most recent and, no doubt, the last example was Gaston Defferre (d. 1986), Minister of the Interior in the 1981 socialist government, but for many years Mayor of Marseille and proprietor of the regional newspaper *Le Provençal*.
14. Known as 'journaux repliés' or newspapers which had been evacuated, these included *Le Figaro*, *L'Action française*, *Le Journal* and *Le Temps*.
15. See Eyk, H. (ed.) (1985), *La Guerre des ondes*, Armand Colin, Paris.
16. For this last see Bellanger, C. (1961), *La Presse clandestine 1940–44*, Armand Colin, Paris.
17. Charon, *La Presse en France*, p.130.
18. Ibid. pp.53–54.
19. For details of the *Ordonnances de 1944* see Charon, *La Presse en France*, p.54–57 and Kuhn, R. (1995), *The Media in France*, Routledge, London, pp.52–56.
20. The news agency branch of Havas was nationalized as the AFP while the NMPP was closely regulated and subsidized. Many newspapers depended on the AFP for their foreign coverage but its independence was particularly compromised during the colonial wars of the 1950s when it was often felt to be an arm of French government propaganda.
21. See Todorov, P. (1990), *La Presse française à l'heure de l'Europe*, La Documentation française, Paris, p.43.
22. Bourdon, *Haute Fidélité*, p.21.
23. For details see Bellanger, C. (1969–76), *Histoire générale de la presse française*, PUF, Paris, 5 vols., vol. 4.
24. Bourdon, *Haute Fidélité*, p.59.
25. Quoted in Péan, *TF1: Un Pouvoir*, p.23.
26. See *Mai 68 à l'ORTF*.
27. Quoted in Bourdon, *Haute Fidélité*, p.42, who stresses what Mendès-France owed to Roosevelt's example.
28. De Gaulle, C. (1994), *Mémoires d'espoir*, Plon, Paris, p.223. Of course, television was hardly interactive in the way de Gaulle implies.
29. In contrast to British television, for example, where the duopoly created by the launch of commercial television dates back to 1954. For a discussion see Mehl, D. (1990), 'Audiovisuel: le service public, naufrage d'une notion', *Médiaspouvoirs*, 19, pp.6–18.

30. 'Everything to do with the media is political', Péan, *TF1: un pouvoir*, p.315.
31. Pierre Moinot's report which, according to Bourdon, p.247, 'was above all concerned with reorganizing the past', was published as *Pour une réforme de l'audiovisuel.*
32. For details see Bourdon p.254–55.
33. See Bourdon, p.271–78.
34. Cotta, *Miroirs de Jupiter*, p.176.
35. Indeed, Bourdon suggests that Philippe Guilhaume was appointed to the post of joint Controller of Antenne 2 and FR3 in defiance of the government.
36. Programme quality became an election issue in 1986 and gave the Socialists the pretext for abolishing the CNCL. See, in particular, the collection of articles published in *La Télévision en 1987* (*Le Monde*, 1988).
37. This is, of course, not confined to the media: one of the most recent and most tragic examples is provided by the *affaire du sang contaminé,* when the director of the agency responsible for providing blood to haemophiliacs in France continued to supply HIV-infected blood to sufferers while waiting until a French-developed test for HIV blood infection was available, rather than use a foreign-developed test.
38. For an immensely detailed account see Péan, *TF1: Un Pouvoir.*
39. For details of Hersant's acquisitions see Albert, *La Presse française* p.91.
40. 'Hersant is not one of us', quoted in Peyrefitte's obituary tribute to Hersant in *Le Figaro* 23 April 1996.
41. Albert, *La Presse française*, p.91.
42. For details of this legislation and a discussion of its consequences see Kuhn, *The Media in France*, pp.56–58.
43. See Charon, *La Presse en France*, pp.218–220.
44. See Kuhn, *The Media in France*, pp.66–7, 250.
45. Ibid., p.95: '[Giscard] placed personal supporters at the head of Sofirad, Havas, Radio-Monte-Carlo and Radio Luxembourg'.
46. This Group owns the imprints Dalloz, Dunod, Masson, Nathan, Bordas, Larousse, Laffont, Plon and Belfond.
47. 'Havas est devenu une vraie "World Company…"', *CB News*, No. 467, 10–16 February 1997, pp.4–5.
48. Quoted in Guillou, B. (1984), *Les Stratégies multimédias des groupes de communication*, La Documentation française, Paris, p.102.
49. Sablon, C. (1996), *Lagardère Groupe*, Eurostaf, Paris, p.31. The others are CEP Communicaton, Prisma Presse, and EMAP. For a useful, if now dated, overview of Hachette's development, see Cauchard, D. (1993), *Hachette*, Eurostaf, Paris.
50. For an account of the battle between Bouygues and Lagardère see Péan, *TF1: Un Pouvoir* p.183–239.
51. *Financial Times*, 19 February 1993.
52. Isnard, J., 'L'Aigle à deux têtes', *Le Monde*, 18 October 1996.
53. See Cohen, E., 'Une leçon d'intelligence et de dévouement public', *Le Monde*, 18 December 1996.
54. For a discussion of the use of technological norms to protect French industry see (1979), *Les Industries culturelles*, La Documentation française, Paris, pp. 94–96, and Forbes, J. (1983), 'Everyone needs standards' in *Screen*,

vol. 24, no. 1, January–February pp.28–39. See also Brochand, C. (1996), *Economie de la télévision française*, Nathan, Paris.
55. According to Brochand, *Economie de la télévision*, p.65, by 1967 more than half of the television sets in France were already manufactured by two French companies.
56. Cohen, E., *Le Monde*, 18 December 1996.
57. Quoted in Bellanger, *Histoire générale de la presse*, vol. V, p.460.
58. One of the most recent examples is Bourdieu, P. (1996), *Sur la télévision*, Liber, Paris, which discusses television exclusively in terms of its treatment of news, current affairs and book programmes, but makes no mention of drama, series, films, documentaries, variety shows and so on.
59. Two recent examples, frequently referred to here, Péan, *TF1: Un Pouvoir* and Bourdon *Haute Fidélité: Pouvoir et télévision*, are both careful to include the word 'power' in their titles.

Bibliography

Albert, Pierre (1990), *La Presse française*, La Documentation française, Paris.
Bellanger, Claude (1969–76), *Histoire générale de la presse française*, 5 vols., Presses universitaires de France, Paris.
—— (1961), *La Presse clandestine*, Armand Colin, Paris.
Bourdon, Jérôme (1994), *Haute Fidélité: Pouvoir et télévision 1935–1994*, Editions du Seuil, Paris.
Brochand, Christian (1996), *Economie de la télévision*, Nathan, Paris.
Cauchard, Denis (1993), *Hachette*, Eurostaf, Paris.
Charon, Jean-Marie (1991), *La Presse en France de 1945 à nos jours*, Editions du Seuil, Paris.
Cohen, Elie (1992), *Le Colbertisme 'High tech'*, Hachette, Paris.
Cotta, Michèle (1986), *Les Miroirs de Jupiter*, Fayard, Paris.
Forbes, Jill (1983), 'Everyone Needs Standards', *Screen*, vol. 24, No. 1.
Guillou, Bernard (1984), *Les Stratégies multimédias des groupes de communication*, La Documentation française, Paris.
Kuhn, Raymond (1995), *The Media in France*, Routledge, London.
Lefébure, Antoine (1992), *Havas: les Arcanes du pouvoir*, Grasset, Paris.
Madezin, Barbara (1995), *Havas*, Eurostaf, Paris.
Mehl, Dominique (1990), 'Audiovisuel: le service public, naufrage d'une notion', *Médiaspouvoirs*, 19.
Moinot, Pierre (1981), *Pour une réforme de l'audiovisuel*, La Documentation française, Paris.
Péan, Pierre and Nick, Christophe (1997), *TF1: Un Pouvoir*, Fayard, Paris.
Sablon, Christine (1996), *Lagardère Groupe*, Eurostaf, Paris.
Todorov, Pierre (1990), *La Presse française à l'heure de l'Europe*, La Documentation française, Paris.

6
Education: from Confessionalism to Consumerism

Gino G. Raymond

Introduction

Of the ideas influencing the revolution of 1789, Jean-Jacques Rousseau's are those which spring most immediately to mind. The fact that there were 32 editions in France of *Du Contrat Social* between 1789 and 1799 is ample evidence of the currency his blueprint for society had gained. His prescription for the creation of a just society complemented the essay on the origins of inequality, *De l'Inégalité parmi les hommes*, in which he posited a direct link between the type of education provided for the young people of a society and the vigour of that society as a polity; a community subject to the institutions of civil government organized by the state. With the characteristic candour of an autodidact, Rousseau acknowledged his eclecticism as he looked to history to justify his assumptions, when alluding to the examples set in antiquity.[1] But in case the notion that educational provision and the development of a certain concept of society is regarded as a symbiotic relationship purely in the intellectual tradition of Jacobin republicanism, it is noteworthy that under the *ancien régime* also the conviction could be articulated that it was incumbent upon the state to provide free and compulsory schooling. This was the case when the Estates General met at Orleans in 1560, but in that instance the reason lay in the perceived need to educate France's youth on the dangers posed by Protestantism.

In short, education and a 'projet de société' go hand in hand, whether it is a society governed by the hierarchical and theocratic values of the *ancien régime*, the egalitarian and integrating vision of society emanating from the revolution of 1789, or the elastic social fabric of a postmodern community of self-legislating constituencies. What this chapter will illustrate is the manner in which the social vocation of state education in France, from its classic definition at the beginning of the Third Republic, has in fact accommodated a series of compromises which, a century after the triumph of republicanism, has brought into question the uniformizing assumptions guiding that project; assumptions superseded by concerns that redefine the mission of the Republic itself.

The handmaid of the state

The old adage that, in contrast to Anglo-Saxon systems, a minister of education in France could predict at any given time of the day exactly what the children of his country were learning, alluded to the 'single central power … controlling public administration throughout the country' described by de Tocqueville,[2] and shaped under the ancien regime by powerful civil servants like Sully, Richelieu and Colbert. Where it served the interests of the absolutist state, governments of the ancien regime intervened strategically to invest principally in technical and vocational training. In the obvious sphere of defence, good artillery schools already existed in Metz, Strasbourg and Perpignan when, in 1751, Louis XV ordered the establishment of the Ecole Royale Militaire at Château de Vincennes, in the light of military reversals suffered at the hands of the Austrians and the British. But as early as 1716, the government of the Duc d'Orléans had laid the foundation for the development of arguably the best civil engineering school in Europe, the Ecole des Ponts et Chaussées, when the supervision of construction schemes initiated by the state was confided to the Corps des Ponts et Chaussées. However, by the time of its demise, the ancien regime was as corrupt as it was centralized.[3] The practice of selling offices of state and transforming them into legacies that could be passed on from one generation to the next was a chronic impediment to the recruitment and training of talent.

While the revolution of 1789 represented an undeniable and funda-mental break with the assumptions that governed the ancien regime, there were nonetheless assumptions about the role of education which persisted and dovetailed with the debate initiated by 1789 as to whether the Revolution liberated the individual as an individual or through membership of the republican state. Rousseau's *Emile*, which appeared in 1762, had already articulated popular disenchantment with the dry scholasticism of Jesuit schools by promoting the more attractive empha-sis on the individual's 'natural' intellectual development. Conversely, and before the Jacobin statism to which the events of 1789 gave rise, La Chalotais in his essay *On National Education* elucidated the co-identity of the person as individual and citizen so characteristic of republican ideology, which led him to demand 'an education which depends upon nothing but the state, because it belongs to it in essence... because in the end the children of the state must be brought up by members of the state'.[4]

The plan for a General Organization of Public Instruction, commissioned by the Legislative Assembly which steered France's revolutionary destiny from 1791–92, proclaimed a belief in the power of education to change society while at the same time attempting to balance the rights of the state and individual freedoms. By the time the Jacobins had gained the upper hand in the Convention which replaced the Assembly in 1793, the foregoing balance was regarded as an Olympian misreading of the realities of revolution on the ground, and of the need for education to serve the popular struggle for social equality as directed by the state. Plans for free and compulsory elementary education in state schools were aborted soon after the Jacobins were toppled in the swing back to the centre represented by the Thermidorian reaction in the summer of 1794, shifting the emphasis of reform back to the kind of secondary and specialized training that the country was familiar with. The Directory which ran the country from 1795 to 1799 reverted to the idea of education as a recruiting sergeant for specialists to serve the state, and the most famous of the special schools it set up was the Ecole Polytechnique which opened its doors at the Palais Bourbon in 1795. But this change in orientation did not negate the lesson which was made explicit in the ambitions of the Jacobins, that education was the supreme instrument for replicating and universalizing the values underpinning the power of the state, whether that took the form of a national, republican or, as in Napoleon Bonaparte's case, an imperial ideology.

A pragmatist as well as an innovator, Napoleon created an imperial hierarchy but offered the possibility of social equality through education – however, in the service of the Emperor rather than the Republic. Furthermore, to create an aristocracy open to the talents, the Napoleonic *Université* controlling education resorted to the meritocratic tools which, as Bourdieu and Passeron have pointed out, were devised under the ancien regime: the *aggrégation*, a competitive state examination for teachers in the secondary sector, and the *Concours général*, the prize competition which pitted the best Parisian lycées against each other.[5] By 1808 Napoleon had in place the centralizing mechanisms designed to ensure that those who passed through the education system were, first and foremost, trained to use their talents in a way which suited the state, and that those who taught them did not depart from the educational orthodoxy that made them faithful civil servants. The *Grand-Maître* of *l'Université* was appointed by the Head of State, and the regional academies he supervised projected his authority down to the level of the commune, delivering standardized curricula and a national system of examinations recognizable today, regulating entry into teaching or other avenues of state service: the *baccalauréat*, the *licence* and the *doctorat*. Furthermore, the ethos of the educators found a central point for its dissemination with the creation of the *Ecole Normale*.

The final collapse of the Napoleonic regime in 1815 and the more enduring restoration of the monarchy certainly compromised the secular nature of the national system erected under Napoleon. During the decade that followed, religious congregations like the Christian Brothers gained control of hundreds of schools, and the extent of Church influence in education was signalled by the appointment of Abbé Freyssinous to the ministry of education. When the Bourbon restoration gave way to the Orleanist regime in 1830, the charter which founded the legitimacy of Louis-Philippe's reign further established the co-identity of *l'école libre* with religious schools by giving church groups greater freedom to open schools. Moreover, the Guizot law of 1833 appeared to bow to the authority of the church by restoring clerical influence in the realm of moral education in state primary schools. The brief republican summer of 1848 which brought down the Orleanist regime was soon superseded by the conservative reaction that gave rise to the Falloux law of 1850, reinforcing the role of the church in secondary as well as primary education.

If one looks back more critically, however, one finds that the foregoing compromises were more calculating than craven. Napoleon's readmission of religious teaching orders into primary education, like his peace with the papacy enshrined in the Concordat of 1801, was designed to buttress rather than undermine the power of his state. As, in the latter case, Napoleon wished to reinforce his state by pacifying Catholic opinion in France, so with the teaching orders he used the resources they represented in the service of his regime by placing the schools they ran under the supervision of state inspectors. Even at the height of Catholic royalist reaction after the Bourbon restoration, the centralizing and secular state pattern rationalized under Napoleon continued to operate, and before the demise of that regime control of local school committees by bishops was removed. During the Orleanist regime that followed, at the same time as the Guizot law was giving greater freedom to the clergy to involve themselves in education, the right of the state to inspect all schools was maintained and *l'Université* consolidated its position as the centralized framework for the regulation of the education system. The concessions to the Church included in the legislation framed by Guizot and Falloux operated in a wider frame of reference than the simple contest between spiritual and secular authority. For Guizot particularly, educational provision at primary level was deplorably limited, barely better than in England and considerably behind what had been achieved in Prussia. All other considerations aside, the impetus given to *l'école libre* before the advent of the Third Republic supplemented the state's ability to respond to the economic changes of the nineteenth century, particularly the increasing need for skilled labour, and to respond to the political changes driven by the aspirations of newly emerging social classes.

The Third Republic model: secular mission or secular compromise?

The collapse of the Second Empire precipitated by the Franco-Prussian War, and the proclamation of a Third Republic on 4 September 1870, removed the most anachronistic cleavages, whether monarchical or imperial, that divided France against itself and obstructed the realization of an egalitarian, republican 'projet de société' that had been almost continuously deferred for a century. However, the fact that almost four years elapsed before the constitutional laws framing the Third Republic were passed was indicative of the uncertainty that persisted regarding the shape of the new polity that would emerge, and in particular the entrenched nature of the residual Catholic and monarchical opposition to the Republic. In the light of this domestic opposition, and with such vivid memories of the recent military catastrophe visited on the integrity of the French state by the Prussians, it was no wonder that the triumphant Republicans of the 1880s envisaged education as a bulwark supporting the state. In retrospect, some of the expectations of state education seem naive or extreme, such as the creation of 'school battalions' of eleven to twelve-year-old boys whose parade-ground drill and exercises with wooden rifles at school would imbue them with a sense of duty regarding the defence of the Republic.[6] But the underlying ethos was clear: republican schools would provide an instruction in patriotism through the medium of state-directed moral and civic instruction. The ideology driving this ambition had been succinctly articulated by Léon Gambetta, who posited an interlocking relationship between individual rights and national unity, with the former being fulfilled in the latter. State education was the crucial instrument in the pursuit of this goal, because the vocation of the school would be to teach the pupil 'what his dignity is, what solidarity links him to those around him; it must show him that he has a rank in the commune, in the department, in the nation; it must remind him above all that there is a moral being to whom all must be given, all must be sacrificed, life, future, family, and that this being is France'.[7]

Framed in terms such as Gambetta's, the republican project clearly emerges as a secular faith that can accommodate no rival in the way it is translated through the education system. The triumph of Gambetta's 'Opportunist' republicans in the 1880s was evoked by the ubiquitous expression of republican culture with myths, rites and rituals: statues with heroic republican themes investing every public space, every town hall inscribed with the three defining values of the Revolution and replete with busts of Marianne personifying the Republic – and, most symbolically, the adoption in 1880 of Bastille Day on July 14 as the national holiday celebrating the republican ideal. It was during his first period as premier that Jules Ferry began to push through the legislative changes that would make education the vehicle for carrying forward the republican transformation of society, driven by the three fundamental principles of 'gratuité, obligation, neutralité confessionnelle' (non fee-paying, compulsory and secular). The first founding principle was laid by the law passed on 16 June 1881 abolishing fees in state primary schools, and this was followed in 1882 by legislation placing the obligation on parents to educate their children to this level. The third founding principle, however, was the most contentious: *laïcité*, or secularism. In the debates in parliament leading up to the passage of the necessary legislation on 23 March 1882, the numerous arguments deployed by the pro-Catholic lobby in favour of religious education in state schools essentially pointed to the question which, a century later, is once more proving to be the underlying issue at the heart of the education debate in France: can the republican state be neutral? As the duc de Broglie remarked, if state education is to observe a 'neutralité confessionnelle' within its schools, on what basis then would a moral education rest? In response to the advocates of an accommodation in the state school curriculum with the religion of most of its pupils, Ferry articulated the doctrine that would take concrete form a quarter of a century later with the formal separation of church and state in 1905. By invoking the independence of civil society vis-à-vis religion, Ferry married the notions of *laïcité*, individual freedom of conscience and equality, and made them synonymous with a republican project for society to be advanced through the civic education dispensed in state schools.

But while the debate between the dogmatists on either side of the secular/spiritual divide could appear averse to any compromise, Ferry himself was not, and the pattern set by the Third for subsequent Republics was the paradox of a profession of faith in *laïcité* coupled with increasing generosity to *l'école libre* or, in reality, church schools. The regime set up by Ferry was itself generous to church schools, allowing them the freedom to set up as long as, according to the decree of 1887, academic inspections revealed nothing contrary to the constitution of the state, its laws and public decency. While examinations and examination passes were accredited by the state, at the local level the financial help offered to the children of poor families who opted for private schools could continue as long as it was provided in equal measure to poor children going to state schools. This concession to the availability of public money for the indirect funding of private schools would become broader and more direct with the passage of time in the life of the Third Republic. The *loi Astier*, passed in 1919, allowed local authorities not only to recognize but also to subsidize directly private technical colleges. If, during the Third Republic, anticlericalism became a means of rallying the left rather than countering a genuine threat to the Republic, during the short-lived Fourth Republic the rallying cry seemed to fall on increasingly deaf ears. The *décret Poinso-Chapuis* in 1947 allowed public funds to subsidize the endeavours of those organizations helping to educate the children of families in difficulty. But since, as its opponents argued, state education was free, the subsidy would in reality be destined for private education. But the failure of this opposition was further underlined by the *loi Marie* of 1951, which extended the availability of state bursaries to students in private schools.

The practical considerations underlying the implementation of educational policy meant that for Ferry and his successors, once the dominance of the republican state was established, the main concern was to lay the foundations of a modern education system for all French children, and to that end *l'école libre* was allowed the means to function as a kind of *supplétif*, or auxiliary; a brand of pragmatism not entirely dissimilar to the kind which informed the way the regimes following the

Bourbon restoration profited from the Catholic church's input into education. However, it is under the Fifth Republic that the role of *l'école libre* has been afforded the means to grow and assert itself, not as a *supplétif*, but as a full partner in *l'éducation nationale*, and in so doing to highlight the challenge to the universalist ideology of Ferry's triumphant republicanism.

From 'service supplétif' to 'partenaire égale'

The Debré law of 1959 marked a fundamental shift in the attitude of the French state to private education through the way the relationship between the two was rethought. The new contractual relationship offered to private schools, which tied, in considerable detail, the nature of the educational provision in them and its assessment to the state model, at the same time recognized formally the specific nature, or 'caractère propre' (i.e. confessional) of these establishments in a way which not only underwrote their independence passively through the notion of 'liberté respectée' but which now strengthened it through the notion of 'liberté assistée'. In reality, this was signified by the state assuming the salary and social security costs for teachers in those schools, in what appeared to be a direct contradiction of the provisions in the law of 1886 stipulating that only a secular teaching body could dispense state-funded education.

The precedent set by the state's recognition of the 'caractère propre' of confessional schools showed its full implications in the *loi Guermeur* of 1977. This legislation allowed the heads of church schools, with the sanction of local education authorities, to select staff according to criteria other than their state-recognized qualifications, even though their status was aligned with that of teachers in the state sector. By the same token, and in defence of its 'caractère propre', a confessional school could refuse to employ a teacher approved by the local authority.[8] It was little surprise, therefore, that by the beginning of the 1980s the Catholic bureaucracy charged with promoting church education (*Secrétariat général de l'enseignement catholique*) could argue that confessional schools constituted an authentic national education service and was an equal partner with the state system. But the fortunes of two ministers of education during the ensuing decade, one Socialist and one Gaullist, showed the extent to which a simple interpretation of this evolution as a triumph of the confessionalists underestimated the breadth of the implications for the culture of republicanism and its classic cleavages.

The anticlerical traditions of socialist republicans had been revived by François Mitterrand's victory in the presidential election of 1981, and particularly the 90th of his 110 propositions for France offering, finally, the realization of a unified and secular education system for France, a 'grand service public unifié et laïque'. Although Mitterrand had committed himself to the principle of change through conviction rather than constraint ('convaincre et non contraindre') there were three clear sticking points, the first two of which would offend the confessionalists and the third of which would offend the secularists: the assimilation of private schools in receipt of state aid into the 'carte scolaire' (i.e. the programme for the opening and closing of classes and parental choice) characterizing the state system; giving the teachers in them a civil service status similar to their counterparts in the state system; and finding a new formula to continue the local funding of private schools effectively under contract ('sous contrat d'association') to provide educational services.[9] Alain Savary, the minister entrusted with this mission, attempted to placate the confessionalists with the argument that 'national' did not mean uniform, and he devised a new formula for reconciling the state and the private sector, within the embrace of an EIP (*établissement d'intérêt public*), literally an establishment serving the public interest which bound local authorities and state and private schools in a geographical area into a contractual relationship. Savary's innovations failed to convince, and the confessionalists were the first to mobilize and to mobilize massively, culminating in the demonstration in the streets of Paris on 24 June 1984 by over one million people in defence of what they called the freedom of education. Arguing that he did not want the nation to be divided, on 12 July President Mitterrand announced that the proposed legislation putting the Savary reforms into effect was being withdrawn.

The very successful campaign to protect *l'école libre* was not simply a victory by the confessionalists over atavistic socialist reflexes; the freedom being defended had taken on an altogether more pervasive and flexible meaning. The minister for higher education during the first period of cohabitation between a centre-right government and a socialist president, Alain Devaquet, was charged by Prime Minister Jacques Chirac with the task of opening the doors of the higher education system to the wind of change which had brought a new, economically liberal-minded majority to power. In his general policy statement of 9 April 1986, Chirac expressed his belief that France's 74 universities could open up more positively to the wider world if they adopted notions of competition and sought to emulate the best practice

found outside the academic world. A key instrument for the achievement of this change would be the attribution of greater autonomy to
the universities in the way they recruited students and, ultimately,
rewarded their efforts with the award of degrees. Between the articulation of Devaquet's proposed reforms in July 1986 and the start of the
new academic year, a mobilization of students and teachers had
occurred which resulted in half a million of them coming out onto the
streets in opposition to the plans on 27 November, in Paris and 50
other French towns, in the biggest student demonstration since May
1968. That same evening, the committee co-ordinating the actions of
school students and university students hatched the plan for a demonstration in Paris on 4 December, in order to increase pressure on the
government to withdraw the proposed legislation. In the intervening
week conciliatory noises began to emerge from the government, which
had failed wholly to predict the scale of the opposition, in the direction of student leaders, but no accommodation was reached in time
to halt the demonstration planned for 4 December. The half-million
students who gathered in Paris began their demonstration in a festive
atmosphere, but by the end of the day violent confrontations occurred
with the police which continued into the following day and resulted
in the death of a student. Faced with open misgivings on the part of
senior members of his cabinet over the price worth paying for persever-
ing with the reforms, on 8 December Jacques Chirac announced the
withdrawal of the proposed legislation.

As Isabelle Thomas, a prominent student leader, explained at the
time, although the student movement was independent of the political
parties, it was not apolitical.[10] What for the government was enhanced
autonomy for universities was interpreted by the students as the introduction of selection. What the government judged to be an assimilation of the freedom of the market-place into higher education was
perceived by the students as an erosion of their freedom to exercise
an automatic right to higher education once the *baccalauréat* had been
successfully negotiated. The opposition that both Savary and Devaquet
encountered, though generated by different reasons, reflected a change
in mentality among those both serving the education system and
those served by it: the emergence of a preference for 'éducation' as
opposed to the classic notion of 'instruction' – that is, predicated on
the formal transmission of an established culture,[11] including a shared
understanding of the relationship between the citizen and the state
in France. The young had shown the extent to which France has
evolved into a postmodern society and the tension that this evolution

creates with classic, hierarchical republican structures, causes and cleavages.

The victory for the defenders of Ferry's principle of 'neutralité scolaire' in 1994, when attempts to revise the *loi Falloux* were judged unconstitutional by the Conseil constitutionnel, was inevitably perceived by their sympathizers as a victory for the secular Republic. But as some of the anxieties expressed on the right of the political spectrum showed, the underlying tension was generated by a post-ideological conflict over resources rather than the old opposition between the secular and the religious. The law itself, promoted by the comte de Falloux and passed in 1850, was designed to protect education from falling completely into the hands of the state by limiting the investment of public funds into the extension of private schools to 10 per cent of the budget for these establishments. The defeat of the Socialists in the legislative elections of 1993 resulted in a new centre-right government with a new minister for education, François Bayrou, openly sympathetic to private education. Bayrou's backing for proposed legislation removing the ceiling to public investment in private schools alerted the 'neutralistes' to the possibility that, in view of the diversity of funding that would become available to private schools (state and local government, parent associations, sponsors and others), private schools would find themselves in an exceptionally privileged position vis-à-vis state schools in the battle for resources. But as some members of the centre-right majority in the National Assembly discovered, the enthusiasm of their grass-roots supporters for the principle of removing the ceiling was tempered by a growing fear of what such a reform of the *loi Falloux* might mean in terms of the pressures on local budgets. The report of the Vedel commission, charged with reporting on the state of funding for private education and what the proposed changes might cost, revealed a pattern of funding that was far from simple and in many cases broke the provisions of the *loi Falloux* through hidden subsidies that sometimes amounted up to 40 per cent of the budget of a private school. The massive demonstration planned by the neutralists for 16 January 1994 was, in a sense, handed the victory before the event when, on 13 January, the Conseil constitutionnel effectively halted the revision of the *loi Falloux*.

At the point when the battle between the confessionalists and the neutralists was reaching a climax, the left-leaning weekly, *Le Nouvel Observateur*, decided to investigate the phenomenon of *l'école privée* in secular France, and particularly the real nature of the expectations of those who resorted to it.[12] Not surprisingly, in the light of the generosity

122 Structures of Power in Modern France

of the proposals for reform and the succession of reforms that had preceded it, the understanding of the term 'privée' had to be rethought. If private schools meant those that were financially independent, then the use of the term had to be revised, since such establishments educated barely 100,000 young French people. The truth is that *l'école privée* exists under contract to the secular state, because in return for its adoption of the same curriculum as the state sector, the state undertakes to remunerate its teachers on the same basis as their counterparts in public service, and in the private *collèges* and *lycées* (middle and upper schools or junior high and senior high), to subsidize the education of the pupils, together with the local authorities, on the basis of the same capitation as exists in the state sector. By the mid-1990s private schools relied on state funding to educate approximately one-sixth of all school pupils in France.

As for the specific character which set *l'école privée* apart, its religious (overwhelmingly Catholic) vocation, *Le Nouvel Observateur* found that only between 10 to 15 per cent of parents subscribed to this as a reason for sending their children to these schools. Private schools were attractive above all to parents with a clear educational strategy for their offspring. The children of small business people, artisans and managers were proportionally twice as numerous as they would be in a state school. Conversely, the children of manual workers were under-represented by half. The disadvantage of less exceptionally qualified teachers (notably fewer *agrégés*, for example, than in state schools) was more than offset, for ambitious parents, by the availability of teachers in private schools, the smaller school and class sizes, higher pass rates at the *baccalauréat*, and, inevitably related to the foregoing advantages, the fact that private schools could in effect select their pupils. In the pursuit of success, or the avoidance of failure, surveys showed that by the mid-1990s one-third of all school-age children in France had at some point or other had experience of 'l'école privée'. Paradoxically, for the majority of parents using it, 'l'école privée' had become an option offering what the state sector could not offer, but largely subsidized by the state, characterized by a spiritual vocation largely devoid of relevance to the pupils, offering the same programmes as the state schools but without the integrating, egalitarian republican ethos on which they are founded.

The end of ideology

It was a telling historical coincidence that the most profound challenge to the perception articulated by Ferry and his followers, that the school was a crucible in which the constituent parts of a secular and egalitarian society would cohere, occurred in 1989, the year marking the bicentenary of the Revolution. In September of that year the principal of the Collège Gabriel-Havez in Creil decided to exclude three Muslim girls for insisting on wearing their Islamic headscarves in class, on the grounds that this represented a resort to ostentatious religious apparel and therefore contravened the confessional neutrality of the school. The issue of the *foulard islamique* provoked an intense debate between those who insisted on the role of the school as a *lieu d'émancipation*, a crucial site for the creation of a free and secular society, and those who challenged the right of the state to suppress *différence* in pursuit of a founding principle of republican ideology. One of the many ironies of the situation was the conflict between those who supported the school authorities in terms of a republican libertarian tradition and those young people in the school system who interpreted the enjoyment of liberty in a quite different way, and who saw in the act an authoritarian infringement of the right of their schoolfriends to define themselves as they chose by wearing what they chose. In spite of the support given to state school principals by the ministry regarding the principle at stake, in reality the state had started to beat a slow retreat. The notion of *laïcité* was undergoing a profound reappraisal; by the time of the next 'cohabitation' between a left-wing president and a centre-right government, that traditionally homogenizing principle had become a supple mechanism for 'la gestion des pluralismes', or the management of plural interests.

The perspective the affair of the *foulard islamique* threw on the attitude of the young indicated the underlying determination of many of them to distance themselves from the conventional vehicles for the pursuit of political power. This suspicion of traditional structures of power was strengthened by a scandal which emerged in July 1998 due to the forced resignation of the director of the body created to manage the insurance regime covering students, the MNEF (*Mutuelle nationale des étudiants de France*). This was a regime set up in 1948 at the behest of the French students' union, UNEF (*l'Union nationale des étudiants de France*) with a specific brief and funding from the national insurance system (*Caisse nationale d'assurance maladie*) to cover the health and welfare needs of students. The 1998 report of the Commission charged with regulating this type of *mutuelle* revealed a network of undeclared financial dealings and political links that pointed, in part, to senior members of the Socialist majority in the National Assembly. An ensuing investigation by the newspaper *Le Monde*[13] highlighted the extent to which representatives of the student body in France had become embroiled in the ideological battle to determine who would govern the state. By 1979 a clear line had been formed among the student representatives (partly motivated by the 'anti-Stalinism' resulting from the break-up of the common programme for government between the Socialists and the Communists) which hitched their union and the MNEF to the political bandwagon that would convey François Mitterrand to power. The possibility of holding concurrent responsibilities in the UNEF as well as the MNEF facilitated the development of a tacit political line that, in the reconstituted and rechristened UNEF-ID (*indépendance et démocratie*) in 1980, allied it to the Socialist cause and turned it into a 'kindergarten' for the party, providing it with a new generation of workers, advisers and deputies in the Assembly.

As Isabelle Thomas said of the protest movement against the Devaquet reforms, the refusal of the student protesters to subscribe to party political vehicles in pursuit of their objectives did not mean that they were apolitical, but rather that they rejected the notion that change could only be pursued through the traditional institutional means offered by the Republic. In the years since their defence of the right to university education unrestricted by further selection after the baccalauréat, young people have shown an increasing willingness to pursue their own 'projet de société', but by circumventing the means postulated in the republican political culture which it was once the mission of the education system to dispense. And nowhere has this been more obvious than in the mobilization against racism in France, where even the presence of political parties with a revolutionary tradition, like the Socialists and the Communists, has been tolerated rather than welcomed in the big rallies such as the one in Strasbourg in the spring of 1997.[14]

Conclusion

The problem now is that, *faute de mieux*, education in France operates according to a Third Republic blueprint, designed to serve the establishment of a secular Republic, but one whose principal assumptions have been overtaken to a significant extent by social change. The education system in France no longer offers a credible 'projet de société', or at best it offers one whose stock is clearly diminishing. The young in particular, are no longer attracted by it. They bypass it, as they bypass the political parties, in order to pursue their own visions of society. Ironically, and as non-French observers or users of the education system (especially at tertiary level) have discovered, negotiating the realities of an ostensibly egalitarian system in far too many cases offers its users an education in how to play the system in a very unfraternal and inegalitarian manner. Resort to the *système D* (*débrouillardise*, or managing to get round the system) reinforces the sentiment, not unknown under the *ancien régime*, that the isolated individual is engaged in a perpetual struggle against the Leviathan state.[15]

The constant factor identifiable in the battles waged by Claude Allègre, the education minister appointed under the new Socialist government that came to power in 1997, whether tackling the lax regime governing the provision of in-service training for teachers or the remuneration of their supplementary hours, or facing the demands of parents for more resources for schools in deprived municipalities like Seine Saint-Denis, is an underlying acceptance that the dynamic for change can no longer be driven by the all-powerful state, but by what academic observers are already used to calling the user-customer.[16]

One of the initiatives launched in the great education debate was the *colloque national* that took place in Lyon at the end of April 1998. It was notable for the way it solicited the views of the users of the system in the attempt to analyze its shortcomings and ways of rectifying them. In one of the most comprehensive consumer surveys ever organized in France, four million questionnaires were sent out to students and their teachers in order to provide the raw material for the colloquium to debate. Illustrative of the fundamental change that is occurring, the preliminary findings focused on the desire of students to have better personal contact with teachers, in a system that burdened them less academically en bloc, and was more inclined to follow their progress individually. In short, customer care rather than mass instruction. One could argue that the adaptation currently being made to the specific identity of young people in the education system as clients completes the adjustment identified as lacking by Antoine Prost prior to the events of May 1968, to accommodate the fact that the youth of France had a specific sociopolitical identity of its own.[17]

As the heirs of Gambetta and Ferry attempt to offer a vision of French society for the 21st century that both integrates and liberates, a discourse has emerged that defines itself more in terms of what it is not rather than what it is: 'ni gauche ni droite'. Leading figures of the Socialist establishment underline the progress made in dumping the statist orthodoxies of previous generations, and while education remains a core consideration in the shaping of a new society, it must be an education divested of the desire to compartmentalize students and instruct them didactically, but invested instead with the will to enable students to liberate their own sense of initiative.[18] Thus, while on the one hand *l'école républicaine* must become a neutralist facilitator serving the emergence of individual potentialities and destinies, on the other the conviction abides that France can only fulfil itself when serving a 'grand dessein'. For Jack Lang, the way of squaring the circle, of having a state-directed national vision that is also neutralist and individualist, is to rethink the common home which constitutes it, *la République*. Through measures like the automatic inclusion of young people on electoral registers once they reach the age of 18, these young people (mostly still school students) would become the co-authors of their destiny with those who manage the structures of power in the Republic.

In what appears to be an extension of the pedagogy which posits that the conscious activity of learning is most fruitful when conveyed subconsciously as the enjoyment of leisure, Lang and others edge towards a *projet de société* that relies on a virtual *République* as the vehicle to take it forward; an egalitarian and communitarian conveyance that offers security without the sensation of constraint. Whether this *République relookée* retains the essence of its original vocation depends on its ability to contain the very real frictions generated by the sectional conflicts of interest within it.

Notes

1. Rousseau, Jean-Jacques (1975), *De l'Inégalité parmi les hommes*, in *Du Contrat social et autres oeuvres politiques*, Classiques Garnier, Paris. His references to Sparta and Athens were arguably conditioned by an awareness that Aristophanes saw education as a civic duty for the youth of the aristocracy, and that for Aristotle education and the political organization of the state were objectives that should cohere and not conflict.
2. de Tocqueville, A (1955), *The Old Regime and the French Revolution*, trans. S. Gilbert, Doubleday, New York, p.57.
3. For a detailed and fascinating insight into the burden this corruption placed on the ancien regime, see Doyle, W. (1996), *Venality: the Sale of Offices in Eighteenth-Century France*, Clarendon Press, Oxford.
4. In Bendix, R. (1964), *Nation-Building and Citizenship*, Anchor Books, Garden City, N.Y.
5. Bourdieu, P. and Passeron, J.-C. (1970), *La Reproduction*, Editions de Minuit, Paris, p.182.
6. Agulhon, M. (1993), *The French Republic 1879–1992*, Blackwell, Oxford, p.44.

7. Gambetta, L. (1881–1885), *Discours et plaidoyers politiques de Gambetta*, Chamuel, Paris, 3 vols., II, p.254. Quoted in Zeldin, T. (1979), *France 1848–1945: Politics and Anger*, OUP, Oxford, p.251.
8. Roger Labrusse notes the case of a teacher in a church primary school who was sacked from her post after remarrying. The court of appeal found that the employer had not abused its powers since it was acting to preserve the 'caractère propre' of the school due to the fact that the Catholic Church did not recognize divorce. In Labrusse, R. (1997), *La question scolaire en France*, PUF, Paris, p.79.
9. Favier, P. and Martin-Roland (1991), M. *La Décennie Mitterrand: les épreuves*, Seuil, Paris, pp.101–2.
10. Ibid., p.599.
11. Judge, H., Lemosse, M., Paine, L. and Sedlack, M. (1994), *The University and the Teachers: France, the United States, England*, Triangle Books, Wallingford, p.244.
12. Fohr, A., Raynaert, F., Péretié, O. and Jullien, C.-F., 'La vérité sur l'école privée', *Le Nouvel Observateur*, 13–19 January 1994.
13. Delberghe, M., 'Une participation active à la saga mitterrandienne', *Le Monde*, 28 July 1998.
14. Schneider, R. and Carton, D., 'Strasbourg: le rude message de la rue', *Le Nouvel Observateur*, 3–9 April 1997.
15. Corbett, A. (1996), 'Secular, free and compulsory', in Corbett, A., and Moon, B. (eds), *Education in France: Continuity and Change in the Mitterrand Years*, Routledge, London, pp.4–21, p.14.
16. Ballion, R. (1996), 'A changing focus of power', in Corbett and Moon, pp.189–196, p.189.
17. Prost, A. (1968), *Histoire de l'enseignement en France, 1800–1967*, Armand Colin, Paris, p.482.
18. Lang, J., 'Cap à gauche, cap vers l'audace', *Le Monde*, 18 August 1998.

Bibliography

Agulhon, M. (1993), *The French Republic 1879–1992*, Blackwell, Oxford.
Albertini, P. (1992) *L'Ecole en France*, Hachette, Paris.
Anderson, R. D. (1975), *Education in France 1848–1870*, Clarendon Press, Oxford.
Bendix, R. (1964), *Nation-Building and Citizenship*, Anchor Books, Garden City, N. Y.
Bourdieu, P. (1984), *Homo Academicus*, Polity Press, Cambridge.
—— and Passeron, J.-C. (1970), *La Reproduction*, Editions de Minuit, Paris.
Corbett, A., and Moon, B. (eds), *Education in France: Continuity and Change in the Mitterrand Years*, Routledge, London.
Doyle, W. (1996), *Venality: the Sale of Offices in Eighteenth-Century France*, Clarendon Press, Oxford.
Favier, P. and Martin-Roland (1991), M. *La Décennie Mitterrand: les épreuves*, Seuil, Paris.
Ferry, J. (1996), *La république des citoyens*, Imprimerie Nationale, Paris.
Green, A. (1990), *Education and State Formation*, St. Martin's Press, New York.
Judge, H., Lemosse, M., Paine, L. and Sedlack, M. (1994), *The University and the Teachers: France, the United States, England*, Triangle Books, Wallingford.

Labrusse, R. (1997), *La question scolaire en France*, PUF, Paris.

Lelièvre, C. (1996), *L'école "à la française" en danger?* Nathan, Paris.

Maury, L. (1996), *Les origines de l'école laïque en France*, PUF, Paris.

Organization for Economic Cooperation and Development (1994), *Review of National Policies for Education: France*, OECD, Paris.

Prost, A. (1968), *Histoire de l'enseignement en France, 1800–1967*, Armand Colin, Paris.

——, A. (1991), *Education, société et politique. Une histoire de l'enseignement en France de 1945 à nos jours*, Seuil, Paris.

Robert, A. (1993), *Système éducatif et réformes: de 1944 à nos jours*, Nathan, Paris.

Rousseau, Jean-Jacques (1975), *Du Contrat social et autres oeuvres politiques*, Classiques Garnier, Paris.

de Tocqueville, A (1955), *The Old Regime and the French Revolution*, Doubleday, New York.

Zeldin, T. (1979), *France 1848–1945: Politics and Anger*, OUP, Oxford.

7
The State and Religion: Rethinking *Laïcité*

Georges Salemohamed

Introduction

The French state owes much of its development and many of its principal characteristics to its relations with organized religion. Three religions – Catholicism, Protestantism and Judaism – are historically important from this point of view. A fourth, Islam, appeared on the scene some thirty years ago. Of the first three, only Catholicism has had fundamentally problematical relations with the state. These touched on the nature of the state and the place of the Catholic church within it. Was the Catholic church in post-revolutionary France to lose the political influence and administrative privileges it enjoyed in the *ancien régime*? This question dominated a long period of conflict between Catholics or Catholicism and the state which started with the French Revolution of 1789 and found its institutional solution with the Law of Separation of church and state in 1905.

The 1905 separation law is a landmark in modern French history, the culmination of a long process of secularization leading to a body of doctrine which today functions as the ethos of the republican state. It is by reference to this secularist doctrine that Islam in France now, and the behaviour of Moslems in French society, are frequently condemned on the assumption that they constitute a danger to the integrity of that society. To a great extent, therefore, Islam at present occupies a position vis-à-vis the state not so long vacated by Catholicism.

The case of Protestantism and of Judaism offers a contrast to that of Catholicism and Islam. Neither Protestants nor Jews who embraced secularism wholeheartedly have experienced the same incompatibility between their religion and the state as most Catholics in the past and as some Moslems today. However, as opposed to Protestants who suffered no serious consequences as a result of their commitment to a secular republic, Jews have frequently been victims of oppression conducted in the assumed higher interests of the French state or of the French nation. The two great examples are the Dreyfus affair in the 1890s and Jewish persecution and betrayal by the Vichy régime under Marshal Pétain in occupied France during the Second World War. Both examples demonstrate the existence of a sometimes virulent antisemitism in the past which is now in decline. Even so, a certain insensitivity still remains about Jewish feelings and Jewish contributions to the construction of the modern French state. They were much in evidence between 1988 and 1992 in President Mitterrand's habit of laying a wreath every year on Marshall Pétain's tomb, a practice which, faced with criticism, he subsequently abandoned.

The Jewish example illustrates the difficulties of separating cultural and social from political considerations when looking at the relationship between religion and the state. This is especially true in the case of Islam, where racism plays perhaps an important part, in addition to problems which have to do with the social integration of a community that has developed out of recent immigration into France. Catholics, of course, were never faced with the same problems as Jews and Moslems in this respect. Theirs was always, from 1789, a problem to do with acceptance of, and adaptation to, a model of governance which threatened to alter the balance between religion and politics in favour of the latter. But as this model began to take shape within a new legal-institutional framework which seemed permanent, it became clear to Catholics that participation in the newly created political process was an imperative. Another imperative, not unrelated to the first, was control of the education system, subsequently to develop into the idea that the church should have its own parallel system. Both education and political participation were directed towards maintaining the influence of Catholicism in society against the competing claims of a state which even before 1905 seemed launched on the path to supremacy over the church. Both, through solving a number of problems to do with the place of the Catholic church in the modern world, led to the full integration of Catholics and of Catholicism into the modern republican polity. It was a difficult process which, as will be seen later with Islam, set the terms for the future accommodation of other religions with the state.

Catholic integration into the political process

To understand how difficult that process was it is useful to look at the tortuous path secularization took before church–state relations were finally settled by the Separation Law of 1905. The state which resulted from this was the polar opposite of what it was in the *ancien régime*. But this was the outcome of a long struggle which, some argue, was only finally resolved with the Vatican Council in 1962.

Early on in the *ancien régime*, France was a theocracy in which papal control over the state characterized the relationship between monarchy and Catholicism. France was, in fact, the leading papal theocracy, 'the eldest daughter of the Church'. But by the time the Revolution came, theocracy was already in decline and, with it, the church's power over the state, even though the church continued to occupy a prominent place in the institutions. This diminished status was the work of Gallicanism.

As a philosophy, Gallicanism remained faithful to Catholic doctrines, but asserted the church of France's independence from the holy see. It thus assumed a great deal of political importance, since it was largely an attempt to reduce the power of papal intervention in state affairs. It thereby established for the first time the principle of a separation of the temporal power belonging to the sovereign from the spiritual power exercised by the church.

The first instinct of the Revolution of 1789 was to adopt the Gallicanist formula in its Civil Constitution of the Clergy of 1790. Papal opposition to it – and the opposition of much of the French clergy as a consequence of opposition to the Revolution itself – led to a Separation Law in 1794. This in turn gave way to a return to Gallicanism under Napoleon Bonaparte, whose Concordat of 1801– 1802 with Rome lasted until 1905.

These three attempts in post-revolutionary France, all designed to alter existing arrangements governing church–state relations, must be seen against a background of institutional instability and social turmoil. These led to a quick succession of régimes – two republics, two empires, two restored monarchies – each with a different vision of the place of the church in society and politics. Given these conditions, nothing could be considered permanent – neither the institutional arrangement set up for the state nor, within this, the place assigned to the church. The result was a France divided in two – 'les deux Frances' – between Catholics and anti-Catholics, which meant the estrangement of Catholics from all but the most counter-revolutionary politics, usually associated with nostalgia for a return to the *ancien régime*.

Reacting to a situation in which faith alone seemed to fix the boundaries of what was acceptable or desirable politically, some Catholics in
the middle of the 19th century articulated different conceptions of the
relevance of religion to politics from those upheld by the church. Once
the Third Republic, set up in 1875, had survived the débâcle of the
Boulangiste failed coup d'état of 1889, followed by the right-wing
trauma generated by the Dreyfus Affair in 1895, and looked safe, these
conceptions began to gain ground. Ultimately, despite other difficulties
on the way – the rise of right-wing authoritarianism in the shape of the
Action Française, which lasted well into the late 1930s, and church collaboration with Pétain during the war – they succeeded in effecting the
reconciliation of Catholicism with democracy.

Democracy in fact – or rather, opposition to it – was central to the
arguments of those who objected to any possible disassociation of religion from politics and therefore to the removal of church influence in
state affairs. For long the church had encouraged the mediaeval idea
that both society and politics had their source in religion. The ideal
institutions were therefore not those created by human beings but
those handed down through divine dispensation. Hence the condemnation of the democratic institutions which the Revolution sought to
establish. They made the divine unnecessary, something which the
antireligious stance of the Revolution seemed to confirm.

Three principal movements – Liberal Catholicism, Social Catholicism
and Christian Democracy – were responsible for changing Catholic
attitudes on this subject. All three aimed at working for a compromise
between Catholicism and republican democratic politics. Social Catholicism in particular became important, because it married its political
vision with a social philosophy which brought it close to some republican parties, especially those inspired by Socialism.[1]

All three experienced great difficulties that were due mostly to doc-
trinal opposition from the Vatican. For example, one of the leaders of
Liberal Catholicism, Lamennais, was condemned in 1832 for juxtapos-
ing belief in God and freedom as a human right. Similarly, Social
Catholicism came under fire later on for subsuming religion under its
prescription of a secular politics which combined the pursuit of democracy with that of social justice. The only relief from papal opposition
came in 1891 with Leo XIII's encyclical *Rerum Novarum*, which for the
first time enjoined Catholic "ralliement" with the Republic. This lasted
until Pope Leo XIII died and was succeeded by the more intransigent
Pope Pius V, who fell out with the Republic in 1904 and precipitated
the Separation Law of 1905.

Despite all these difficulties, Social Catholicism and Christian Democracy – but not Liberal Catholicism – continued to develop. The first gave rise to a number of lay catholic organizations in the world of work, in agriculture and education. Some of them, like the JOC (*Jeunesse Ouvrière Chrétienne*) or JAC (*Jeunesse Agricole Chrétienne*) are still in existence to this day. They provided the cadres for representative organizations such as trade unions – the CFTC, which became the CFDT in 1964, is one good example – which gave the social philosophy of Catholicism a voice in the industrial and agricultural fields. The second gave rise to the idea that a Catholic party need not be antirepublican, counter-revolutionary, authoritarian and monarchist. Christian Democracy never produced a party until after the Second World War. When it did, in the shape of the MRP (*Mouvement Républicain Populaire*) this became the second largest party in France. Politically, organizations like the JOC and the MRP bridged the gap between Socialism and Marxism on the left, both militantly atheistic and secular, and right-wing parties which tended before to have a monopoly of the Catholic vote. Today that vote is more evenly distributed, testifying to the complete political integration into the republican state of Catholicism. The disappearance of the MRP after 1958 in the wake of a triumphant Gaullism was an early sign of this.

Education and civic identity

Whereas political organization and participation were the means by which Catholics achieved political integration and accommodation with the Republic, education became for both, and specially for the Republicans, the ground for social cohesion. At first, education provided a battlefield where Republicans and Catholics fought out their respective visions of society. An important point of contention was control of the education system. A church monopoly dating back to the Middle Ages, control of education became an important issue as post-revolutionary France progressed towards the Third Republic. Secularization of the system secured it for the state in 1882, significantly before the state itself was secularized in 1905.

Some Republicans had always opposed church control of education. As early as 1793 the Revolution's Declaration of Human Rights defined education as having a universal social mission. Later, in the Third Republic, Gambetta, reiterated this point of view in blunter terms: 'for me, it's a political, and, I would add, a social necessity',[2] whereas, for Jules Ferry, the architect of the 1882 law, state ascendancy in educational matters was meant to induce 'love for the Republic'.[3] However, what the Republicans dreamt of had already taken place to an extent when they came to power after 1875. By then, education, primary and secondary, had already passed into state hands, although the church still exerted an influence on the system through compulsory religious teaching. This was due to the *loi Falloux* of 1850 which sought both to increase church influence in public sector education and give it the right to organize its own parallel education system. The Falloux law is notable for having legalized 'l'enseignement libre', that is, a private sector education which became, for a long time, a Catholic church preserve. Its importance – although curiously it has never been abrogated – is that it made the move for secularization even more urgent.

The Ferry legislation established three principles which remain those of the French educational system to this day: it is a secular system and it provides a free but compulsory education. Beyond these three formal principles, the system is dedicated to dispensing a 'neutral education'. Neutrality in the context of the time meant prohibition of religious instruction in state schools. It entailed the replacement of religion by a universal – that is, a rational – moral system which purported to unify, in contrast to religion, considered to be divisive. The prevalence of philosophy teaching in French schools up to recently has its origin in this search for a republican rationale. It provided an intellectual basis to secularism as a doctrine and underpinned a form of civic pedagogy which was able to appeal to all faiths because it took a neutral standpoint in relation to religion.

All in all, the battle for a republican state education was one waged on the conviction that education was vital to the construction of a new civic identity, hitherto determined by religion. The intention, following both secularization laws, of the state and of education, was, gradually, to integrate a population divided not only by religion but also by regional cultures and dialects. It is important to mention this. We then see how, as the church lost its hold on the educational system, other specific traits of that system emerged: its rigorous centralization and its imposition of a rigid syllabus throughout the whole country, both designed to ensure uniformity throughout. Everything was thus done in the interest of forging unity out of diversity. Religion was at first a major obstacle to this, but by no means the only one.

What the French society's experience with religion before and after secularization illustrates is the uniqueness of the French republican state which resulted largely from the tension between the two. Alone amongst comparable societies, this state preceded and created a nation and a national identity, both of which everywhere else preceded the formation of the state. However, the success of this republican model of integration, as it is often called, has depended on a certain sacrifice of principle to expediency. The existence of private schools subsidized by the state is the best-known example. For a long time after secularization Catholics campaigned for state subsidies to Catholic schools. The issue was one of many dividing left-wing from right-wing parties and governments. The left has always been opposed to state subsidies but has had to find accommodation with them in the end.

Subsidies to private schools, not all of them Catholic, would appear to have become a permanent feature of the French education system. When in 1984 the Socialist government tried to bring a measure of unity to public and private education without affecting subsidies or religious teaching, a perceived threat to the viability of private schools brought a million protesters out in the streets. The Savary bill was buried. But this was nothing compared to the situation in 1959 when a law for the first time sought to give subsidies to private schools. Then 11 million people are reported to have signed a petition opposing the law. The strength of feeling over private education has waned with the years. Catholics now send their children without hesitation to state schools and non-Catholics to private schools. Those who protested against the threat to subsidies in 1984 were not all Catholics and the secularist principles of state education are now acknowledged by Catholics and non-Catholics alike.

Secularization as a doctrine[4]

One of the most important results of Catholic integration into the republican model has been the development of a secularist doctrine which amounts to more than the mere statement of secularization as the separation of church and state. It is important to make a distinction between the two, that is, between a secular state and secularism as doctrine.

Secularization simply refers to two distinct spheres of influence and power. One, touching on the private area of individual belief, belongs to the church, though not exclusively. The other, the collective area of policy-making and legislation, belongs to the state. This does not mean, however, that the state cannot legislate on issues which go against moral principles upheld by the church or that the church cannot seek to influence state action. In 1979 the state legalized abortion, despite some furious opposition from the church which all but accused it of murder. By contrast, more recently, in 1996, the church opposed the state strongly on the subject of the rights of immigrants and refugees, some churchmen going as far as to defy the state in giving a number of such people shelter in church buildings, and protesting against their deportation. Neither event affected the *modus vivendi* reached by the two institutions, even though the state had its own way in the end in both instances.

This peaceful coexistence between them acknowledges the primacy of the state in organizing social life. The church and religion are conceded a role in society, but it is a reduced role. The church more or less occupies the position of a pressure group in the state, alongside other pressure groups which include other religions and churches. The French constitution of 1958 gives this idea of parity of treatment official sanction when it describes the French Republic as 'indivisible, secular, democratic and social' (article 2) and goes on to assert the equality before the law of all citizens 'without distinction of origin, race or religion'. Catholicism is no longer, as it once was, the 'religion of the French' but rather one faith amongst others. The state's posture is one of neutrality towards them all.

This idea does no more than confirm the principle of neutrality already enshrined in the settlement over secular education. It is a principle which is at the very heart of modern secularism. Secularism now is different from what it was in the period preceding the Third Republic and immediately after 1905. Then, Catholic intransigence fed by dreams of a return to a clericalist state made secularism a synonym for irreligiousness. It now stands for toleration of all religions and, thus, for pluralism. With these three features, neutrality, equality, toleration, along with pluralism which they all entail, it lays the modern French state's claim to a long tradition of human rights inaugurated by the 1789 Revolution.

It is an important tradition. When some of the principles underlying it were first articulated in the Universal Declaration of Human Rights (1793), they were opposed by the church on the grounds that they gave precedence to human over divine rights. Divine rights then, politically, meant the divine rights of the monarchy which the Revolution had overthrown. In addition, the notion of human rights was a child of Enlightenment philosophy which opposed reason to faith and was thus considered either hostile or indifferent to religion. This reason–faith dualism is no longer sustainable in the modern world.[5] The result is that the republican state is fully embraced by Catholics and, with it, the main ideas of the 1789 Revolution. Secularism, in other words, as well as secularization no longer divides Catholics from the rest.

One important consequence of this is that over and above what it establishes as the proper role of religion in society, secularism nowadays represents a general consent over some basic principles of democracy as they apply to the French state. This state is said to be one and indivisible. It, rather than religion, as was the case before the Revolution, confers citizenship and rights. Of these the most fundamental are freedom and equality, and with regard to religion, the right of the individual to protection against compulsory fusion into groups or organizations.

Islam and the secular state

There are an estimated four million Moslems in France, which would make Islam the second religion after Catholicism. There are in fact fewer Moslems than this, because figures in this area of research are often extrapolated from the number of immigrants or of people of immigrant origin living in France – mostly North African – on the assumption that the vast majority of them are Moslem. There are other similar eccentricities in surveys on the size of the Moslem population in France. Although not intending to do so, they give support to the popular notion of a sizeable Moslem community not quite attuned to life in a secular state.

The idea of an inherent incompatibility between Islam and secularism arose in 1989 when three Moslem girls attended classes at a lyceé in Creil wearing headscarves. The headscarf is an item of conventional Moslem clothing for women. The schoolgirls' refusal to remove theirs very quickly turned into an issue of national importance, raising fears about the future of French secularism. At first adopting a liberal line, the then Minister of Education, Lionel Jospin, finally under pressure, sought the advice of the Council of state and ruled that demonstrating one's belief through external symbols like the headscarf – the 'foulard' – was permissible on school premises if the intention was not to provoke. His successor in 1993, François Bayrou, adopted the same view but hinted that the headscarf was provocative. More recently, in 1996, he has sought to solve the problem by putting forward a bill in parliament that seeks to ban religious symbols altogether from schools.

Bayrou's bill, seven years after the 'foulard' affair first broke out, is puzzling in that, since then, only two hundred or so Moslem girls have followed suit. It was customary at one time to prohibit religious symbols altogether from classrooms. With the decline of the conflict between Catholicism and the state the question of religious symbols lost its importance. The 'foulard' affair, which is indicative of a new tension between religion – that is, Islam – and the state, has brought it back. The 'foulard' now represents for many people much of what they find threatening in Islam. Its implications are still hotly debated, especially in intellectual journals where proponents of toleration are often pitted against hard-line secularists.[6]

The role of intellectuals in the 'foulard' affair is easily explained. In as much as there is a republican state with an elaborate secularist doctrine, it is the work of intellectuals, past and present. There might not even have been an affair had it not been for a long contribution by a number of intellectuals, including the philosopher Alain Finkielkraut, who – in the periodical *Nouvel Observateur*[7] – attacked both the girls and Islam. In a tone which has been described as recalling the 'J'accuse' letter of Zola in the Dreyfus affair, the philosophers argued that any concession on the wearing of the 'foulard' would be capitulation of the republican school to foreign powers and thus betrayal of the republican state which, in conformity with the secularist doctrine, they identified with democracy.

Political arguments on the issue have on the whole adopted the philosophers' standpoint. They often echo past criticisms of the role of religious faith as a determinant of loyalty to the state. At one time most Catholics were presumed to be 'ultramontane' in their allegiance: that is, they were thought to favour a situation in which the power of the state was subsumed under the episcopal authority of Rome. Similarly today, Moslems in general are said to look beyond the frontiers of France in order to bestow their allegiance either on the not infrequently theocratically inclined states of their own or their parents' origin or else on some worldwide Islamic movement.

The image which Islam as a religion has acquired lies at the root of these feelings, which are of fear arising from Islamic militancy throughout the world. Islam is characterized by its opponents as fundamentally hostile to the distinction between spiritual and temporal power, between religious and political systems. Although Moslems protest that this is based on misinterpretation, the image persists. It gained currency in the late 1980s – coinciding more or less with the beginning of the 'foulard' affair – through terrorist acts perpetrated in France and elsewhere by fanatical Moslems, often under orders from Iran. Iran and its leader, the theocratic Ayatolla Khomenei, came then to represent for many people what Islam stood for: a religion bent on conquest, violent and antidemocratic – a religion, in short, which makes politics in all instances serve its particular interests.

This negative picture of Islam has been reinforced recently in 1996 by the activities of fundamentalists in Algeria in their struggle for political power and by more foreign-inspired terrorist attacks in France. They fuel existing suspicions about the links between Moslems in France and their coreligionists abroad, especially in Algeria. These suspicions are difficult to challenge, since everything else seems, on the surface, to support the view of Islam in France as an outpost of a pan-Islamic movement. For example, the building of mosques and their running costs are frequently financed from outside sources. The same is true of most Imams who, for want of qualified French Moslems, tend to be foreign nationals on the payrolls of Moslem countries. Both these have led to the charge that mosques, along with a network of informal meeting-places for Moslems which are supposed to function as places for prayer, often double up as nurseries for Islamic militants. Suspicions about the activities, real or assumed, of Islamic militancy are so strong that even an innocuous practice like the pilgrimage to Mecca, which a few Moslems from France undertake, is sometimes treated as if it too formed part of a general Islamic conspiracy instigated from abroad.

This idea of foreign intrusion, already at work in the numerous protests that have attended the building of mosques in certain areas, resurfaced in the 'foulard' episode when Islamic culture itself came under scrutiny. Those who condemned the schoolgirls by invoking French secularism, aside from invoking the principle of a secular division between religion and the state, did so on the basis that the girls infringed another important secularist principle considered fundamental to Western democracy and even ethics: equality. From this standpoint, the 'foulard', according to its opponents, did not just stand for the unconscious representation of female subjugation in Islamic culture; it also appeared to proclaim and even to justify it. This, amongst other things, is what critics of the whole episode meant when they spoke of provocation. The term also referred to the fact that the girls, in full knowledge of the secular conditions under which school life operates, persisted nevertheless in challenging them. It also, finally, signified the aggressive affirmation of a distinctiveness, of a tenacious clinging to a cultural identity, some of whose oddities Westerners find anathema.

One of these is female circumcision. There is no evidence that this is practised on any significant scale in France. Another is the religious practice of the ritual slaughter of animals for food. Both, though cultural, raise strong ethical objections. They must be placed alongside other cases where the objections are less sincere but still touch on culture, although in the more usual sense. Thus, for example, the construction of mosques is often opposed on the grounds of their incompatibility with the French architectural landscape in towns and cities. In fact, mosques or 'mosquées cathédrales', as they are sometimes called, are objected to more because they tend to give visibility to – signifying the acceptance, if not the permanence – both of a foreign culture and a foreign community. In many instances, this is the reason why even enlightened local councils yield to pressure and refuse to give permission for the construction of mosques.

Viewed in terms of community identity and distinctiveness of culture, the 'foulard' affair then brings to light issues which at certain levels are indistinguishable from those to do with the integration of non-European immigrants into a European culture. The secularist reaction to the wearing of the headscarf indicates the conditions under which this integration should take place. They centre largely on the need to conform to the Jacobin tradition of an unmediated relation of the individual with civil society, a relation initiated from above by the state and not from below by the community. French secularism as a doctrine is militantly anti-multiculturalist, because its proponents have always argued that natural communities, religious or otherwise, dissolve the individual into an organic whole, fuse him with it and therefore diminish his freedom. Even when it is conceded that community identity has a place it is always with the proviso that national identity comes first.

This tradition harks back to the Le Chapelier law of 1791 which prohibited the existence of professional bodies standing between the citizen and the state. It retarded the development in particular of trade unions. The law is no longer operative, but the tradition remains. It buttresses the permanency of a centralized and interventionist state, notwithstanding the decentralization measures of the mid-1980s. It also accounts for the existence of a culture of state dependency which atomizes the citizen and discourages the formation of voluntary groups.

In societies which welcome multiculturalism, voluntary associations – often, but not always, organized within ethnic communities – negotiate integration through regular contacts with other informal organisms and access to public bodies and public authorities. Their relative absence in France throws the burden on the state which responds either with laws tightening up an existing practice – Bayrou's bill – or with new laws, or else by insisting that certain rights which in multi-cultural societies are conducive to integration be denied to non-citizens. Thus France has always refused to allow even long-standing residents who are non-citizens the right to vote at municipal elections. Similarly, to mention a fairly mundane example, the state will not pay for the appointment of Moslem military or prison 'chaplains' if they do not have French citizenship.

Apart from a well-entrenched legalistic tradition in France which makes ad hoc treatment difficult, there is another reason why the state does not attend to all the specific conditions and requirements of each religion. It is feared that this would, in certain circumstances, violate the principle of secularist equality. Here, equality takes on a second meaning within the secularist doctrine: it refers to the equal treatment of all officially recognized religions. Some observers have noted that this leaves intact historic privileges enjoyed by Catholicism. Even so, the state has shown some flexibility and a readiness to modify some of the provisions of laws relating to the constitution of religious bodies and their entitlement to state subsidies. Two laws are relevant in this respect. There is the 1901 law on cultural associations, which include schools. This stipulates that no such associations, if they receive public subsidies, are to be run by religious organizations. There is also the law of 1905 under which registered religious faiths may receive financial help from public authorities – for example, to carry out repairs to buildings – as long as they do not extend their activities beyond what can legitimately be classed as religious. Islamic religious activities, because of their different nature, cannot sustain this division. Islamic associations pursuing religious aims are therefore allowed to register under the 1901 law which, curiously, does not prohibit groups from having religious objectives.

In addition to registration, the 1901 law allows Islamic associations to benefit from subsidies for the construction of religious buildings. Islam, however, is not the only religion to benefit from legislative rein-terpretations of this kind, through which the state seeks to introduce a degree of flexibility. Other beneficiaries, the Protestants in particular, were in fact the first to stimulate changes in the two laws mentioned. Islam is thus merely reaping the advantages from precedents set for other religions. Moslems see in this a prima facie case for legal changes to cater for their special needs, subject to the benefits brought about by them, especially financial, being made available to other reli-gions as well.

The end of the republican model?

The 'foulard' affair is often seen by Moslems as an example of where the equality principle operates at a different level to penalize them. The distinction, according to them, between provocative and non-provocative religious insignia has no other effect than to sanction the wearing of religious insignia by people of other faiths while prohibiting Moslems from wearing theirs. Some Moslems also insist that the 'foulard', far from being provocative, is not, as is often assumed, an aggressive expression of ethnic identity or of separateness, but rather a way of negotiating integration. On this argument, the girls wear the 'foulard' only to satisfy a family sense of dress ethics and as a way of ensuring that the family allows them to continue their studies.[8]

Whereas the 'foulard', therefore, symbolizes for its opponents a challenge to the ethos of secularism, it symbolizes the reverse for those who justify its use for more positive reasons. However, not all secularists condemn the wearing of the 'foulard'. There are those who argue that prohibition violates an equally important principle of secularism: toleration. Does this signify, as is sometimes asserted, a fracture within secularism? There are at any rate two views now about the place of secularism in the modern age. There are, on the one hand, those who look back to the past, to the law of separation, and view any assertion of religious differences as dangerous. They look up to the state as educator and unifier. They see it as the instrument that holds society together and in doing so must of necessity oppose particularistic tendencies with the danger they bring of social divisiveness. There is, on the other hand, an emerging category of secularists who direct their attention to society, who look forward to multiculturalism as a welcome and inevitable consequence of population movements. Whereas the former can be said to be monists, the latter are pluralists. They accept that the society constructed by the republican state can be other than what it is without threatening the state.

Both types of secularists are in earnest about their desire for complete Moslem integration. The pluralists, however, are those whose recommendations are more directed towards the search for accommodation with Islam. Islam is not as institutionalized a religion as Catholicism. It does not have an institutionalized priesthood. The Imams are not priests but wise men, steeped in the religious knowledge and doctrines of Islam, who lead prayers. They are not, unlike Catholic priests, under the jurisdiction of a higher authority. The main recommendation, espoused by the pluralists, is that Islam in France be organized on a consistorial basis, similar to the Jewish faith, so as to provide the state with an official Moslem interlocutor. Allied to this is the suggested creation of a Ministry of Religion so as to provide all religions with one single authority to deal with their affairs. At present, Islam, depending on the nature of its dealings with the state, has to be in contact with three different ministries, including the Ministry of Education.

There will remain problems. Some of them are shared by many religions. One of them is school timetabling, the practice in schools of not having classes on Wednesday afternoon, holding them instead on Saturday morning. The origin of this was to enable Catholic pupils to receive religious instruction on Wednesday afternoon. Today even Catholic parents who wish for a long family weekend away from home object to it, as do Jewish parents who would prefer not to send their children to school on the day of the Sabbath which, to complicate matters, is on a Friday for Moslems.[9]

There are technical problems of adjustment and harmonization such as these, but also, for Islam, a number of cultural-social problems in matters to do with such things as polygamy, the institution of dowry, or divorce on request by the male partner. Strange as it may appear, the technical problems may be more difficult to solve. For example, how is it possible to ensure that examination dates do not coincide with religious festivals when there are at least three religions to consider? The difficulty is greater with respect to Islam, because the Islamic religious calendar is lunar and festival dates vary from year to year. In these two cases the technical problems derive from the specificity of Islam as a religion. In others – polygamy, divorce, etc. – they derive from purely cultural practices which enjoy legal status in some Islamic countries. Significantly, these are easier to solve because they are problems more of perception than of fact as they relate to Moslems in France. They certainly do not constitute the norm of cultural practices characterizing the social life of Moslems living in France.

In fact, from a cultural point of view, which also includes political culture, there is evidence of a substantial and inevitable, though gradual, integration of the Moslem population. Politically, this can be seen in the increasing number of local councillors with a Moslem background. There were some 500 in 1989. Although current figures are not available, there are undoubtedly more now. The political representation of Moslems is likely to go on increasing in future. More important than this is the attitude of young Moslems towards society and religion. A survey of young North Africans in 1995 showed a majority identifying themselves more with French culture than with the culture of their parents' country of origin. A substantial number are either opposed or indifferent to Islamic fundamentalism (43 per cent) as opposed to those who are strongly or moderately for (21 per cent).[10] This still leaves far too many young Moslems whose declared propensity for extreme religious views must give cause for concern, except that the same survey also finds the great majority of them looking to education and work as a means of social integration.

In the face of all this evidence – one could also mention that intermarriage is on the increase, as well as the number of Moslems taking up French citizenship – the explanation for the 'foulard' affair may lie elsewhere than in the assumed resistance of Moslems to integration. Is the strength of emotion generated by the 'foulard' amongst secularists as well as the split it reveals amongst the latter the symptom of a more general malaise about the state itself? Can the state of republican integration, the overarching expression of social stability which harmonizes particular interests through political, economic and social intervention, survive the new conditions ushered in by globalization and the gradual march towards European supranationality? If it is true, as some argue, that the great strikes of winter 1995 and 1996 confirm a long trend towards the general dislocation of the state apparatus,[11] then it may well be that the 'foulard' affair was its first symptom.

Notes

1. For a succinct analysis of the historical development of all these movements and doctrines see Soltau, R.H. (1959), *French Political Thought in the Nineteenth Century*, Russel & Russel, New York.
2. Mégrine, B. (1963), *La Question Scolaire*, PUF, Paris, p.41.
3. Ibid., p.43.
4. Costa-Lascoux, J. (1996), *Les Trois Ages de la Laïcité*, Hachette, Paris. See the introduction for a brief account of changes that have taken place in the notion of *laïcité* (secularization).
5. It is sometimes argued that secularism is in fact a kind of faith appealing to reason rather than to God or the church. This view is much in line with what is called the humanization of the divine in Ferry, L. (1996), *L'Homme-Dieu*, Grasset, Paris.
6. Compare Finkielkraut, A. with Wieviorka, M. (1995), in *Pouvoirs*, no. 75, pp.53–71.
7. *Le Nouvel Observateur*, 2 November 1989.
8. In fact very few even wear the headscarf. They are more preoccupied with being allowed to wear jeans by their parents. See Roze, A. (1995), *La France Arc-en-Ciel*, Julliard, Paris.

9. See Costa-Lascoux, chapter 3, for other examples.
10. SOFRES (1995), p.165–166.
11. See Touraine, A. (1996), *Le Grand Refus*, Fayard, Paris, p.39; and also Cesari, J. (1994), *Etre Musulman en France*, Karthala, Paris, p.258, who forecasts the end of the 'spécificité française'.

Bibliography

Barbier, M. (1987), *Religion et Politique dans la Pensée Moderne*, Presses Universitaires de Nancy, Nancy.
Bauberot, J. (1994), *Religions et Laïcité dans l'Europe des Douze*, Syros, Paris.
Cesari, J. (1994), *Etre Musulman en France*, Karthala, Paris.
Costa-Lascoux, J. (1996), *Les Trois Ages de la Laïcité*, Hachette, Paris.
Ferry, L. (1996), *L'Homme-Dieu*, Grasset, Paris.
Gaspard, F. and Khosrokhavar, F. (1995), *Le Foulard et la République*, La Découverte, Paris.
Le Goff, J. and Rémond, R. (1992), *Histoire de la France Religieuse*, vol. 4, Seuil, Paris.
Mégrine, B. (1963), *La Question Scolaire*, PUF, Paris.
Mestiri, E. (1990), *L'Immigration*, La Découverte, Paris.
Morsy, M. (1993), *Demain, L'Islam en France*, Mame, Paris.
Pouvoirs, No. 75 (1995), *La Laïcité*, Seuil, Paris.
Soltau, R. H. (1959), *French Political Thought in the Nineteenth Century*, Russel & Russel, New York.
Roze, A. (1995), *La France Arc-en-Ciel*, Julliard, Paris.
SOFRES (1995), *L'Etat de l'Opinion*, Seuil, Paris.
Touraine, A. (ed.) (1996), *Le Grand Refus*, Fayard, Paris.

8
Language and Power
Dennis Ager

Introduction: French – an affair of state

Presidents Charles De Gaulle, Georges Pompidou, François Mitterrand and Jacques Chirac were all greatly interested, but in rather special ways, in matters affecting the French language. De Gaulle set up the *Haut Comité de la Langue Française* in plush offices under the Prime Minister and charged it in 1966 with overseeing the 'defence' and the 'expansion' of the language, in France and abroad. Pompidou made sure that things happened in language matters – the ministerial circular at last giving effect to the 1951 Deixonne law on regional languages saw the light of day in 1969; the *Agence de Coopération Culturelle et Technique*, supporting international 'Francophonie', was created in 1970, even though much of the push for this came from Quebec; terminology commissions, agreeing the French versions of American terms which are then made legally binding in official documents and in the industry, were set up in specific ministries as from 1970; the Bas-Lauriol law, protecting the consumer from the non-use of French, even though it formally dates from 1975, was set in motion while Pompidou was still alive. Under Mitterrand, the *Haut Comité* and associated government language organizations were reorganized in 1984 and again in 1989; international summit meetings of French-speaking countries eventually started in 1986 and have taken place every two years since. Even though the Toubon Act of 1994 actually got on the statute book under Prime Minister Edouard Balladur and before Chirac won the 1995 Presidentials, since becoming President Chirac has retained many of the language agencies and reinforced the 'Francophonie' summit meetings.

Contemporary French language policy

Many 'Anglo-Saxon' commentators find this level of interest and all
this policy activity amazing. What on earth have the Presidency and
the Prime Minister's office got to do with language? Why do the
French set up a 'Ministry of Purity', fine the Body Shop for selling
goods labelled in English, or the Metz-based branch of the Georgia
Institute of Technology in Atlanta for using English on its Web site?[1]
What link is there between such petty matters (the fines are only £130
or so) and the major purposes of the State? French language policy on
the eve of the new millennium has three clearly defined objectives:
'assurer la présence et le rayonnement du français, langue de la
République; conserver au français son rôle de langue de communication internationale; préserver la diversité culturelle et linguistique dans
le monde par la promotion du plurilinguisme'.[2]

The 'défense' and 'expansion' of the early Gaullist policy have been
modified over the years to become 'présence' and 'rayonnement',
while the second and third aims, expressed in rather defeatist terms as
'conserver' and 'préserver', represent a sharper focus and an awareness
of the existence of other languages which had not been present in any
earlier formulation. Within France, the aim is to reinforce the status
and prestige of French as the official language and to make sure it is
used everywhere. Its spread is to be encouraged not only within but
also outside France. Preserving its role as a language of international
communication, although seemingly aimed at international activities
such as trade or diplomacy, is in fact also aimed at the many international bodies ranging from the United Nations and the European
Council to the Olympic Games, many of which are tempted to adopt
one language only as the easiest way of communicating with their
many members. The protection of the world's cultural and linguistic
diversity seems at first sight a rather strange aim in a policy for French:
but the purpose is as much negative as positive, and the phrase also
hides an attack on English, or rather American, influence, seen as promoting globalization and monoculturalism.

Legislating for French

Ensuring that French is widely used and its use encouraged is
not merely symbolic policy: it has led to specific recent legislation 'with teeth'. Nor is the policy something of little or no wider

interest: parliamentary debates in 1994 spread over four days and provoked considerable press and public interest. A 1992 amendment to
the Constitution had already established that French was the language
of the Republic – or rather that the language of the Republic was
French, since Belgium, Switzerland, Quebec and some others objected
to such high-handedness. Balladur as prime minister, in order to reinforce this official status, instructed ministers that the use of good
French should play a part in the annual appraisals and in the promotion patterns of civil servants. The 1994 Toubon Act then made it compulsory, for the civil service and all those dealing with government
agencies (since the Constitutional Council considered that the Act
should not apply to private citizens) to use French in domains such as
education, advertising, internal communication in workplaces, the
media, and the congress industry.[3]

These domains were chosen deliberately to ensure that French had
high status in France. Apart from education, which is the direct responsibility of the government, the domains are those in which government
action can often only be indirect, but which are so visible in the life of
the country that language use in them is immediately obvious to the
population. Of them all, it is probably in the media that this Act
(together with the associated Carignon Act on the proportion of French-
language productions to be broadcast) has had most effect, and where
self-censorship is most likely to have multiplier effects over and above
what is actually required. This, indeed, has been the effect in Quebec,
which acted as the model for much of this legislation and where the
aim of giving status and prestige to French had stronger motives.

'*Rayonnement*'(spreading language use) is of central concern to education, where the policy involves not merely that French is the medium
of education, but also that the 'quality' of French is maintained.
Spreading the language outside metropolitan France has been more difficult to legislate for since the end of colonialism, and since some of the
remaining Pacific *TOM* (*Territoires d'Outre-Mer*: New Caledonia,
Polynesia, Wallis and Futuna, Antarctic Territories) have dared on occasions to raise the spectre of local autonomy. The *DOM* (*Départements
d'Outre-Mer*: Guadeloupe, Guyane, Martinique, Réunion) however have
no choice as to their official language, and Creole has no public role in
them. Policy here is a matter of encouraging the use of French in places
like Mauritius and Louisiana, but on occasion extends to more political
actions like supporting Quebec's independence, or even supporting the
former regime in Rwanda and Zaïre because they were a bulwark against
the Ugandan-trained and Anglophone incomers. There are of course

more mundane aspects: encouraging the development of Web browsers which can recognize the accented characters of French, instituting the *Semaine de la Langue française* or the *Journée de la Francophonie*.

The policy is implemented through the *Délégation Générale à la Langue Française,* working to an advisory *Conseil Supérieur* now attached to the Ministry of Culture, which is mainly concerned with the first aim. It reports each year to Parliament on its activities and on the general position of French, and has an overall brief on language matters in all ministries, particularly with the Ministry of Education. The second and third aims are also pursued by the Ministry of Foreign Affairs and the Ministry for Co-operation, as well as a special group chaired by the President (*Haut Conseil de la Francophonie*). Recently, the French Academy has become linked more closely with these agencies. The Francophone summit meetings and the associated permanent organization, somewhat like the Commonwealth, are supported by the international Agency for Francophonie, likely to be headed by a major international figure of the stature of Boutros Boutros Ghali, former Secretary-General of the United Nations. Surrounding these public bodies is a group of language defence organizations, five of which have semi-official status in that they can act as the injured party if offences against the French language are committed.

The continuity of language policy

To speak of de Gaulle, Pompidou, Mitterrand and Chirac makes it seem that such views and policies concerning language are creations of the late twentieth century. Nothing could be farther from the truth for the first objective, at any rate. It is commonly agreed that French was born in 842 AD as the result of a political act, and that the elevation of *francien* from the status of dialect to that of language was an exercise in the use of State power: 'throughout its history, the linguistic unification of France has been linked to its political unification and to the progress of centralization'.[4] Such unification and centralization, indeed, associated with the abolition of any vestige of multilingualism in France, represented not merely one aim of French power among others but, at this stage, the sole aim and purpose of the State. The opponents that were successively attacked were the Latin of the law and of royal administration, leading to the first period of French international glory in the twelfth and thirteenth century crusades; and the regional languages and dialects of feudalism, destroyed by François ler who first declared

French as, in effect, an official language in 1539. True, throughout the seventeenth century the state's efforts were supported by less immediately political forces: growing economic power, international trading and the start of overseas empires, the increasing importance of new social groups in towns. But state influence in the definition of taste and acceptability, and in the creation of the French classical linguistic model, was central and reinforced by the power of the royal Court, and the French Academy would have had as short an existence as Jonathan Swift's London coffee house a century later had Richelieu not ensured its survival and given it the clear role of making French suitable for government as well as for the arts and sciences. This second period of glory for French saw it used in diplomacy, literature, philosophy and generally as the means of communication for the European elite.

As in the earlier periods under the monarchy, the Revolution of 1789 was very clear about the purpose of language: to unify the country, to convey the aims and values of the revolutionaries, and to spread to all, in France and abroad, the notions expressed in the Declaration of the Rights of Man and Citizen. Although Napoleon's rule saw no linguistic legislation, and the expansion of the language marked time then and later in the nineteenth century as nationalist aspirations used local languages as their symbol and as the former supremacy of French in the diplomatic world slowly gave way to English, the educational policy of the later nineteenth century saw to it that French built on Napoleonic administrative centralization to bring the language to every corner of the country. Indeed, the application of linguistic policy (*tout en français*) to the colonial empire was absolute and occasionally brutal. Decolonization, voluntary as in 1960, and much less so as in Vietnam in 1954 and Algeria in 1962, has not been followed by the disappearance of French, even in these countries, and indeed Vietnam (although not Algeria) now attends the international summits of organized 'Francophonie'.[5] These summits group some 40 countries or administrative regions including Europeans (Belgium, Switzerland), North Americans (Quebec, New Brunswick, Canada itself) and Africans (Tunisia and Egypt, and most if not all the former *Afrique Equatoriale* and *Occidentale* countries, together with Mauritius and others). Interestingly, neither the *DOM* nor the *TOM* are separately represented.

French and France: an indissoluble link

Why has it been necessary to insist on the use of French? Why has there been a battle, and why has the battle continued for so long? French language policy objectives are supported by very clear reasoning:

> La langue française est au coeur de notre culture et de notre patri-
> moine, un patrimoine que nous partageons avec l'ensemble de la
> communauté francophone. Instrument essentiel de la cohésion
> sociale, elle est aussi l'un des vecteurs majeurs du rayonnement de
> notre pays. L'action du Gouvernement doit viser à lui conserver ce
> rôle.[6]

The first phrase is a very clear statement of linguistic determinism, widely known in linguistics as the Sapir-Whorf hypothesis, and of which the strongest form is that language and society are indissolubly linked. What is claimed is that social reality can only be conceptualized through the linguistic forms developed within that society: in effect, that 'France' only exists when seen through French. French identity is the French language, with all the meanings that only that language can convey; so any break-up of French necessarily means that French society and its specific meaning has broken up as well. From the Revolution and through the nineteenth century one source for possible break-up was clear, and still tortures the central power: fragmentation of territory (*la balkanisation*) is seen as fragmentation of ideas and identity and is symbolized by the possible fragmentation of language use, whether this means using languages other than French, allowing French itself to break down into different dialects, or being corrupted from within by poor or inaccurate usage. Regionalism hence possesses a powerful symbol in regional languages, even in regional dialects and even in local accents, and the conclusion of the Barère Report of 1794 is ingrained in the hearts of those who believe in the central importance of language to French identity: 'federalism and superstition speak Breton, emigration and hatred for the Republic speak German, the counterrevolution speaks Italian and fanaticism speaks Basque'. Since the Revolution, possible break-up is thought to come from different directions as well: social divisions within France, misunderstanding or lack of knowledge of cultural inheritance (the *patrimoine*) and, the danger most talked about recently, from abroad in the shape of pressures from English.

Motivations for language policy have been examined elsewhere and characterized as identity, image and insecurity.[7] The feeling of insecurity (that French is in danger and could suffer since it is not strong enough to withstand external attack) is reinforced by pride in French identity and the conviction that French reflects this in some unique way. Image (the image of French to others, particularly abroad) is as strong a motive: it is not quite the *mission civilisatrice* of old, but occasionally perilously close.

Sharpening the weapon: standardizing French

The instrument of power and the weapon of war, if it is to be deployed by the state, must be forged and sharpened by the state. French needed to be standardized, elaborated and taught. Many languages have become standardized through the collective unconscious need of the community for an unambiguous linguistic coinage, but French took the path – in which it was not alone in Europe – of establishing a State-supported organization to oversee the process. Indeed Cardinal Richelieu, well before the Revolution, was very aware of the value of what became the *Académie Française* when he approved its establishment in 1635: it was to give certainty and rules to French, and the Academy has been very conscious of its role since. It has occasionally seemed to some like a collection of sleepy old men, meeting once a week for a couple of hours to fine-tune the definition of a rarely-used word, and it is for this reason that it had been to an extent bypassed by such up-to-date inventions as the terminology commissions dealing with Americanized computer terminology. But Academy Secretary Maurice Druon acidly pointed out in 1994 that the Academy might well have avoided the embarrassment the government had to endure when the Constitutional Council decided that the Toubon Law had gone too far in trying to insist that the whole population had to use this official terminology. His point has been so well taken by the government that the revamped commissions and their processes now present their conclusions only with the advice of, and indeed under the umbrella of, the Academy itself.[8]

The use of official channels to standardize language has continued apace, although with varied success. Three examples: in 1990, an attempt was made to refine spelling to bring it into line with changes in pronunciation and with linguistic research – no different from what had happened in the Academy's 1694 dictionary, or in the various tidying-up operations it had been involved in since.[9] Sexism in language was tackled by an ad-hoc Terminology Committee set up by (and in) the Ministry of Women's Rights, which made some very minor proposals in 1986.[10] Thirdly, the Ministry of Education has continued to publish

Tolérances to advise panels of examiners on the forms which can be accepted in public examinations.

Using the weapon

The purpose of a standard language is to facilitate communication. But communication always has a purpose and an aim, and one of the most widespread of these is to act as the medium of power relationships, as any advertiser, priest or politician knows full well. Powerful politicians use powerful language, and consciously play on the terms they use, as many discourse analysts have shown.[11] Political language is essentially dramatic and emotive language, in which the play of the characters represented by the *je* of the speaker, the *vous* of the addressee and the *il(s)* of the political enemy play out the structure of dramatic rhetoric (the rhythm, progression and culminations/crescendos of the meaning) against the background of the setting. This 'setting' consists of the aim of the text, its intended audience, what is not said in language but relies on the common universe of understanding of speaker and hearer. Standardization of the means of conveying denotational and connotational meaning is fundamental to political language: not merely has the audience to understand and react to what is said, but to the implications of the whole text. Use of the common currency and awareness of shared perceptions is essential, but what makes a particular message memorable is the deliberate selection of elements and the striking use of the unusual. The resonance of imagery, of expressions like *le quarteron des Généraux, la hargne et la grogne* by de Gaulle; *la force tranquille* by Mitterrand; *une France apaisée* in the most recent appeals of Chirac for social cohesion, may contribute much to the power of such leaders, who rely on both the discourse of politics and on their own individual interpretation of this for their symbolic power.

Even a rapid analysis of a sample paragraph of President Jacques Chirac's 1997 New Year broadcast to the French population shows how techniques – such as repetition, variation in the length of sentences, rhythm as shown in the crescendo of the paragraph or the development of a point, the careful choice of some terms rather than others, and 'spin', or the slant given to some points – can give an impression of vigour and power and convey authority. As the *Figaro* commentator pointed out in presenting the text of the broadcast in that newspaper, Chirac was positive and quick to convey his optimism and his ambition, to condemn the *'immobilisme'* and *'conservatisme'* of the past, but to stress the concept of reform and the necessity of reforming in a context of responsible dialogue and calm:

> Nous devons devenir un pays capable d'anticiper et de conduire, dans la sérénité, les nécessaires évolutions de la société. Il n'y a pas de dialogue social sans respect de l'autre. Mais il n'y a pas de vrai dialogue social sans culture de la responsabilité. Ne pas porter atteinte à l'intérêt général au nom d'intérêts particuliers. Ne pas tout attendre de l'Etat. Accepter le principe de la réforme à condition qu'elle soit juste et concertée. En France, chaque jour, des accords entre partenaires sociaux sont conclus qui font avancer les choses. Et j'y suis très attentif car le progrès social et la cohésion nationale en dépendent.

The fact that there is a close relationship between the use of prestigious language and the powerful is hardly news, and hardly specific to France. But perhaps the awareness of the relationship, and the deliberate attempt to ensure that the weapon is finely tuned and deployed, is.

So it would seem that not merely has French official policy not changed since the Revolution and the laws of 1794 (and possibly not much since 842) but that the official policy of defence and promotion, reflecting pretty closely the views of the majority of the country as various opinion polls have shown, demonstrates such continuity and unanimity in policy that there is no room for any form of conflict at all. But conflict on language matters there is, and in this field as in others officialdom is unlikely to find society at peace or even at ease with itself.

Rejecting the symbol of dominance

Standard languages represent, like the coinage, the society which has unconsciously but collectively fashioned and adopted them. In this, they reflect the inbuilt ideology of their society. The usage made of the standard language by particular politicians and parties reflects their ideological choices, but only from what is available to them.[12] To return for a moment to the extract from the Chirac speech, we should consider the meaning of the cliché words and phrases it includes: *dialogue social*, *intérêt général* and *intérêt particulier*, *la réforme*, *partenaires sociaux*, *cohésion nationale*. How far these concepts and clichés reflect the assumptions of the French political scene can be seen from any attempt to translate them into English: while 'reform' might have the same connotations in the Chiraquian world as it did in British Prime Minister John Major's and thus represent a political slant, the same cannot be said of 'social dialogue', 'social partners' or 'national cohesion'. Such concepts are either excluded from British political discourse or have specific political connotations: they are used by Blair but not by Major. Indeed, the word 'society' itself was banned for avowed Thatcherites. The French terms could have been used in any Mitterrand speech during his Presidency: they form part of French political discourse in the same way that '*nous*' and '*la France*' are synonymous in the same discourse, irrespective of party. It is clear that the vocabulary from which the President drew implies a number of concepts which together form an accepted universe of French political discourse within which the political debate can take place.

Standard French in both written and spoken forms has long acted as a symbol of Parisian dominance, of the power of the ruling social classes, and hence of the traditional view of the identity of France. It is hardly surprising that this symbol of legitimacy and authority has, equally traditionally, been attacked by regionalists. What seems to be happening more and more in recent years has been its rejection by social outsiders, its weakness in the face of economic change, and its undermining by two main groups who have difficulties with the traditional 'hexagon', or concept of France: the young on the one hand and immigrants on the other. The rejection, too, has seemed in recent times to be both somewhat more successful than it used to be and to be to a degree more violent.

French is not monolithic anyway

Standard French, like any other standard language, is in any case under attack from social varieties of many sorts. Working-class accents and language use, described in acute detail in Anglo-Saxon sociolinguistics by such researchers as Labov in New York and Trudgill in Norwich,[13] can be just as powerful as standard language, if not more so, in expressing the reality which is lived in city centres, or, in France, in the suburbs. There are very few such studies of French class usage, or indeed of the usage of other social groups such as women, or of language as determined by sociolinguistic contexts or functions such as dyadic interaction, agreement, persuasion or denial. But it is undeniable that such varieties exist, and that most French people have available a linguistic repertoire which includes standard French and a range of other varieties.[14] The linguistic repertoire is consciously deployed to fit the circumstances, so challenges to authorized language may come from many social categories and social settings. The aristocracy, the beau monde or the intellectuals have been accused of speaking *hexagonal* or *bcbg* (*bon chic bon genre*) in order to underline their elitism, administrators of using officialese or *langue de bois* to give themselves dignity, advertisers and the media of consciously distorting language by such creations as *Roule cool* or *je positivise*, while women have been variously accused of attacks on standard French by excessive use of adjectives and adverbs, over-use of some types of adjectives (*mignon, sidéré*), or failures to adopt the traditional masculine norms of interruption in triadic conversations in order to assert their gender.

Rejection by youth

The difference between the language of the young and that of older generations reflects similar needs to specify antisocial difference.[15] In France, 1968 was a watershed year for lack of intergenerational comprehension, in language as elsewhere. Now, thirty years later, the language of fifteen-year-olds is two generations on from that time, so it is hardly surprising that slang, vocabulary and language use should mark this. One proof of rejection is the growing difference between spoken language and the written code: the popularity of the annual French spelling and dictation competitions merely underscores the fact that for most French people nowadays spelling is more like an intellectual game than reality. Pronunciation quirks like the growing use of the final *-e* where it is not traditional are fast becoming the trademarks of the young (particularly women). Words for the older generation hardly indicate love and respect: *les croulants, les son-et-lumière, les PPH* (*passeront pas l'hiver*). But the young seem to be prepared to take the adaptation of French much further than before: truncation, particularly of final syllables, is often taken to extremes which render simple comprehension difficult: *dégueulasse > dégueu > deg, santiagos > santiags > tiags*. Truncation is added to by the addition of a final *-o* or *-oche*, and the resultant form is widespread: *séropo, plastoche*. Strange formulations often adopt, but then adapt anglicisms: *looké*. Backwards slang (*verlan*), an adaptation of French with a long and respectable history, seems to have been taken over by the young increasingly since 1968, and leads to a whole variety of words which reinforce the aim of any antisocial type (to be incomprehensible except to fellow-members of the in-group) and to do so to an extent which creates almost a new language. Examples include (*crasseux* > *crado* >) *docra*, (*putain*) *tainpu*, (*pompes*) *pépons*. Older post-1968 generations are familiar with (*flic* > *keufli*) *keuf*, (*métro*) *tromé*, (*pourri*) *ripoux*, or (*arabe*) *beur* (and later *beurette*), but these changes and adaptations seem mild compared to present flights of fancy.

To a certain extent, changes like these are normal and to be expected in any language. Slang, popular and even vulgar language have their own characteristics, and they are not new to French. But rejection of the standard by young people seems to be stronger now than at many times in the past, and is perhaps associated with a new desire to rely less on established authority and more on inner resources.[16] It is perhaps excessive to see the inability to use correct French as reflecting a rejection of society at large, but the crisis of French in education is stronger now than previously. An educational system in which 55 per cent of the population has experienced at least one educational handicap; in which adult illiteracy can be traced back, for 75 per cent of cases, to such a difficulty, and in which social exclusion often derives from a vicious circle of such problems at an early age, has seemingly led to a situation in which violence in schools is now endemic. This violence at school is both symbolic and real: 'the school is the reason why children are considered failures or successes... Rupture with schools is frequent',[17] and has led to numerous political initiatives, reports and surveys. Actions have even included the drafting of national servicemen to support the teachers in difficult schools from 1992, and the creation of additional teaching posts, although many of these were abolished in subsequent budget cuts.

The connection between violence and educational achievement should not be stressed too much. The concern over standards expressed in the French press during the early 1980s was motivated mainly by the arrival at the secondary stage of pupils who would previously have dropped out of education at an earlier point or simply not entered it. One precise survey of an aspect of education, comparing achievement in spelling between 1877 and 1987, makes the points that the requirements of the past are not those of today, and that simple beliefs that things are getting worse, supported by anecdotal evidence, are insufficient to prove the point.[18] It may be that French education has not moved sufficiently far away from its traditional bias towards skills which relate little to today's real requirements. For the authors of this study, it may well be time to review the content of education, starting with the heavy burden of an impossible spelling system which it takes eight years to acquire, rather than to blame youth for rejecting such a burden, and with it, much of education.

Rejection by immigrants

Immigrants to France since 1945 and during the *trente glorieuses* brought their own languages and the general expectation was either that they would return home when they had served the economic need or that they would assimilate to France and French as the regional language users had done.[19] But not all immigrants have complied, and the growth of borrowings into French, and of new linguistic codes using the syntax of Arabic or Portuguese is well attested in second-generation immigrant youth. Words directly borrowed are frequent, not solely among such young immigrants themselves: *toubib* has a long history, while *ralouf, klebs, khomar, barka!, ballak!* (pig, dog, donkey, enough!, watch out! in Arabic) are more recent. Mixtures of French and Arabic abound (*tu fous le dawa* (jinx), *misquine* (miserable person), *tu es kho-kho* (worthless), *on va faire une doura* (tour). The growth of *verlan* as well as of a more colourful style of French has been attributed to the new generations adopting the tradition of language play, among many Africans in particular.

As with the growth of antisocial forms by young people generally, immigrant groups seem to be developing new linguistic forms whose aim is to create a new group language, a new 'we-code' which rejects the standard language of authority. This code is associated with the growth of new cultures of youth and deprivation, reflects the circumstances of mixed-race and mixed-cultural generations, and establishes the credibility of a new type of group identity – that of the local community rather than that of the wider collectivity, the State. Citizenship, and loyalty to all the population, is replaced by gang membership, and loyalty only to those one is physically near and with whom one shares limited and obvious links such as age or neighbourhood.

Rejection by the new technologies

The extent to which new technologies not created in France – the Internet, the mass media – have been felt as insidious attempts by the awful Americans to destroy French culture can be gauged from a number of indicators as well as almost any newspaper: the creation of the Terminology Commissions in 1970, the fact that most of their suggestions have concentrated on 'translating' technical anglicisms, the mission statement for the new commissions which gives as their aim 'to give French the means to continue to be present in science, technology and economic life in France and abroad',[20] and simply the changes in everyday vocabulary everyone is aware of because of the presence of new devices: *cliquer, CD-ROM, Internet, surfer, Web*. These examples do not mean that French is not fighting back: a computer is everywhere an *'ordinateur'*; *'informatique'* and its associated word family is a real *trouvaille* for French, underlining the information-ordering and symbol-manipulation capacities of the computer over its simple numerical functions and thus anticipating the real value of such machines. *'Logiciel'* is a far more significant term than 'software', *'toile'* and *'hyper-toile'* are trying to replace 'Web', *'courriel'* replaces 'e-mail'. Borrowings from British or American English exist in a number of fields, of course, often adapted from the original: *self, mini*, the *-er* of *supporter, container* or *challenger*, the *-ing* of *shampooing*.

Why such new vocabulary should be created, and why it should be essentially American is open to debate. It is not just that the technology comes from the United States. One explanation is that the French have been so conditioned by the purists and by the draconian education that they receive that they are incapable of creating new vocabulary from indigenous sources. Another is that the French have rejected the traditional humanism of the French approach to life, its balance and moderation, in favour of a wholesale love of the new and the different, and a search for the exotic and the *inédit*. The conclusion is that the French have rejected standard French in their love of the new, and some believe that such a rejection will inevitably lead to the disappearance of French and its replacement by American English. Another reason alleges an Anglo-Saxon conspiracy in devising character sets like ASCII which has no room for the accented letters of French. But the whole debate could be spurious, in the sense that when the government calls for an international convention to protect languages like French, with their accents, from reduction to the simplicity of the ASCII code forms, it simply does not understand that this is fully possible but implies that some of the standard codes have to be devoted to this rather than to such standard non-alphabetic usages as 'escape', 'line' or 'form feed', a solution which disadvantages French users. The consequence is that the commentators have created an unnecessary fuss, since the total number of new words in French is small, and they only account for about two per cent of running text, even in journalism. Whatever the outcome of the debate, there is no doubt that the words that have flooded into French from external sources are very visible on the streets, and that the net effect of the wave is to change both the sound and the feel of the language.

Rejection by the regions

A study by INSEE and INED in 1992[21] found that some 16 per cent of the population had usually been addressed as children by their parents in a language other than French, but that 95 per cent of them spoke to their own children in French. These figures include all languages, and the most spoken regional language – the dialect(s) of German spoken in Alsace – affects only 0.6 per cent of the total French population. Because the regional languages themselves were suffering internal changes such as the absorption of French vocabulary, the study concluded that 'the retreat of regional or immigrant languages in the face of pressure from French seems even greater than the numbers indicate'. But the debates of 1994 on the Toubon Bill were dominated by the regionalists, all of whom were concerned about the dangers insistence on the use of French held for the identity and character of their region. They were worried, among other things, by the strange defence of French which claimed it was in danger of suppression by greater political and economic forces when it had itself been responsible for ferociously suppressing regional languages on exactly the same grounds. Regionalism is by no means dead in France, and violent opposition to the Jacobin State takes forms other than the linguistic and the symbolic: the damage caused by Corsican separatists in 1995 amounted to 40 killed and £40 million pounds' worth of damage.

Corsica is the most obvious example of a French 'region' not content to lose its own identity in that of the Republic, but Breton activists are still in prison and Alsace still speaks of the *'Français de l'intérieur'*, while the Basque country harbours activitists from Spain on both sides and the role of Barcelona as a regional centre for the Catalan-speaking area is thought, admittedly only by some, to outweigh that of Paris. There have even been protests in Savoy, citing France's incomplete implementation of the 1860 Treaty transferring the region to France from Italy as a reason for regional autonomy.

The Corsican situation is different from that of the metropolitan regions. Corsican was not one of the four languages mentioned in the 1951 Deixonne Act (Basque, Breton, Catalan, Occitan), and had to wait until 1974 before it was accepted as being different from Italian. But by 1992 it had 11,749 students learning the language in primary and 5,183 in secondary education – third among the regions (over 100,000 students in Alsace, 70,000 approximately in Occitan),[22] even if these were only some 28 per cent of children at school. Indeed, the educational scene in Corsica is notably worse than that of the mainland: only some two-thirds of 18-year olds are still in education at that age, and over 40 per cent of Corsicans are without school qualifications at *Bac* level or higher (against about a third in metropolitan France). There have been constant demands for greater recognition of the Corsican language, and of the existence of a Corsican people, for over a century, all received by the legal system with a refusal to accept the existence of any such particular group or community.

As with the other regions, Corsica's problems are not limited to linguistic indifference from Paris. The French desert still produces economic difficulties, which for Corsica are rendered greater by its distance from France, its lack of industry and the lack of attraction its constant terrorist attacks have caused for the tourist trade. The political situation is tense but characterized by the schisms and splits among the many groups supporting independence, autonomy or greater freedom from France. These groups, who started the present wave of attacks in 1975, demonstrate their opinions less in debate than by the methods of the two other nearby islands, Sardinia and Sicily: the bomb and the bullet. *Plasticages* (use of plastic explosives like Semtex) traditionally attack the tax-gatherer, although occasionally other targets are found. Assassinations have taken place of servants of the State (most shockingly, in 1998, the Prefect) but also, and more frequently of late, of members of other independence groups in actions which are more reminiscent of the vendetta than of any systematic attempt to free the island from the oppressor. These attacks constitute a major challenge to the authority of Paris.

Conclusion

It was realized, even before the French Revolution, with the Edicts of Villers-Cotterêts in 1539, that the French language would be a major weapon in the creation of France. French was a fundamental asset in the creation of the country from a series of disparate fiefdoms, and modern France is rooted in a particular sort of language and in an attitude towards this language which sees it as indissoluble from the fundamental values: liberty and democracy, equality and justice, fraternity and French identity. But how can these fundamental values change and adapt themselves to new realities? Is it inevitable that national identity as established at a particular point of time can tolerate no changes, that it leads inevitably to *conservatisme* and *immobilisme*? Is any change to standard French an attack on French itself? Can *le hot-dog* destroy not merely *la cuisine bourgeoise*, but *la bourgeoisie française* itself as well? Linguistic control based on attempts to preserve and maintain the past, on continuity above all, has generally not been effective, and is considered by most linguists to be as worthwhile as Canute's attempts to stem the tide. But the example of Quebec, whose language laws since 1977 have restored self-confidence and pride among French-speakers in North America, give pause for thought, and the influence of international 'Francophonie' and of the importance of the retention of classical French for this reinforces the claim to maintain and preserve French as it is.

The new realities contain some old pressures (from regional fragmentation, for example) and some new ones: from social divisions, from immigration, from economic instability caused by globalization and pressure external to France. Both old and new may provoke the need for change, and the change may be accompanied by violent rejection of previous 'stability'. The violence is likely to be based on identities just as strong as those which have carried French through the centuries: on Islam, on the growth of a youth culture, on the growth in international importance of French-speakers outside France. But in rejecting the bad, the conservative, immutable language with its inherent difficulties and resistance to change, such violence may also throw out the baby with the bathwater. If traditional French, with all its difficulties and all its burden of inherited meaning, is to be rejected, then the political advantage of those who hold power now through its use will be reduced. A new political class will be needed, and policies based on retaining its international role may disappear. If Europe and Africa are important for the future of French, then French is important for the future role of France in each region. And France without French as it now is, and attitudes towards French as it now is, could be so different from contemporary France as to make the country nothing more than a pleasant holiday destination for the Anglo-Saxons.

Indeed, while maintaining present-day standard French may mean retaining the more extreme views on French identity, not far from those of Le Pen, rejecting present-day standard French may mean accepting growing US influence in fields like culture as well as economics and trade. It may lead to an adoption of the Anglo-Saxon solution of the cultural mosaic of communities and separate groups, reversing the whole history of individualism started in the Revolution and replacing it by the growth of particularisms. Rejecting present-day French may also mean rejecting the international role of French, the absorption of France into the European Community, and the end of the *pré carré* or zone of French influence in Africa, the three legs of the tripod on which the future of France rests.

Notes

1. 'In the Ministry of Purity' is the title of an article in The Times of 5 June 1992, in which Andy Martin describes the work of the Academy, the Larousse dictionaries and the Délégation Générale à la Langue Française. The fine was imposed on the Georgia Institute in 1996.
2. '... to ensure that French is widely used and its use encouraged everywhere, since it is the language of the Republic; to maintain the role of French as a language of international communication; to protect the world's cultural and linguistic diversity by promoting multilingualism'. In *Brèves*, 5, 1996.
3. See Ager, D. (1996), *Language Policy in Britain and France*, Cassell Academic, London.
4. Szulmajster-Czelnikier, A. (1996), 'Des Serments de Strasbourg à la loi Toubon: le français comme affaire d'état', *Regards sur l'Actualité*, vol. 221, mai, pp.39–54, p.40.
5. See Ager, D. (1996), *Francophonie in the 1990s. Problems and Opportunities*, Multilingual Matters, Clevedon.
6. 'French is at the heart of our culture and of our heritage, a heritage which we share with the whole of the French-speaking community. As an essential instrument of social cohesion, it is also one of the major factors in the influence our country exerts. The Government's actions must aim at maintaining this role for it'. In *Brèves*, 5, 1996.
7. Ager, *Language Policy in Britain and France*.
8. Décret 96-602 of 3 July 1996.
9. Baddeley, S. (1993), 'The 1990 French spelling reforms: an example to be followed?', *Journal of the Simplified Spelling Society*, vol. 2, pp.3–5.
10. Evans, H. (1987), 'The government and linguistic change in France: the case of feminisation', *Association for the Study of Modern and Contemporary France Review*, vol. 31, pp.20–26.
11. Bréchon, P. (ed.) (1994), *Le discours politique en France*, Documentation Française, Paris; Gaffney, J. (1993), 'Language and Style in Politics', Sanders, C. (ed.), *French Today. Language in its Social Context*, CUP, Cambridge, pp.185–198.
12. Boudon, R. (1986), *L'idéologie. L'origine des idées reçues*, Fayard, Paris.
13. See Chambers, J.K. (1995), *Sociolinguistic Theory*, Blackwell, Oxford, for a discussion of such sociolinguistic variation.
14. Ager, D. (1990), *Sociolinguistics and Contemporary French*, CUP, Cambridge; Offord, M. (1990), *Varieties of Contemporary French*, Macmillan, London.
15. George, K. (1986), 'The language of French adolescents', *Modern Languages*, vol. 67, pp.137–141; and (1993), 'Alternative French', Sanders, C. (ed.), *French Today. Language in its Social Context*, CUP, Cambridge, pp.155–171.
16. Roncière, M.C. de la (1987), *Jeunes d'aujourd'hui. Regards sur les 13–25 ans en France*, Documentation Française, Paris, p.80.
17. Borkowski, J.-L. and Dumoulin, D. (1994), 'Illettrisme et précarisation', Ferréol, G. (ed.), *Intégration et exclusion dans la société française contemporaine*, Presses Universitaires de Lille, Lille, pp.219–249.
18. Chervel, A. and Manesse, D. (1989), *La Dictée: les Français et l'orthographe*, Calmann-Lévy, Paris.

19. Ager, D. (1993), 'Identity, community and language policies in France', Ager, D., Muskens, G. and Wright, S. (eds), *Language Education for Intercultural Communication*, Multilingual Matters, Clevedon, pp.71–90.
20. *Brèves*, 1996.
21. INED (Institut national des études démographiques), 1993.
22. Ager, *Language Policy in Britain and France*, p.69.

Bibliography

Ager, D. E. (1990), *Sociolinguistics and contemporary French*, Cambridge University Press, Cambridge.

—— (1993), 'Identity, community and language policies in France', Ager, D., Muskens, G. and Wright, S. (eds), *Language education for intercultural communication*, Multilingual Matters, Clevedon.

—— (1996), *Francophonie in the 1990s. Problems and Opportunities*, Multilingual Matters, Clevedon.

—— (1996), *Language Policy in Britain and France*, Cassell Academic, London.

Baddeley, S. (1993), 'The 1990 French spelling reforms: an example to be followed?', *Journal of the Simplified Spelling Society*, vol. 2.

Bréchon, P. (ed.) (1994), *Le discours politique en France*, Etudes de la Documentation Française, Documentation Française, Paris.

Brèves (Lettre du Conseil Supérieur et de la Délégation Générale à la Langue Française). Quarterly, 1991–1996.

Borkowski, J.-L. and Dumoulin, D. (1994), 'Illettrisme et précarisation', Ferréol, G. (ed.), *Intégration et exclusion dans la société française contemporaine*, Presses Universitaires de Lille, Lille.

Boudon, R. (1986), *L'idéologie. L'origine des idées reçues*, Fayard, Paris.

Chambers, J. K. (1995), *Sociolinguistic theory*, Blackwell, Oxford.

Chervel, A. and Manesse, D. (1989), *La Dictée: les Français et l'orthographe*, Calmann Lévy, Paris.

Evans, H. (1987), 'The Government and linguistic change in France: the case of feminisation', *Association for the Study of Modern and Contemporary France Review*, vol. 31.

Gaffney, J. (1993), 'Language and style in politics', Sanders, C. (ed.), *French Today. Language in its social context*, Cambridge University Press, Cambridge.

George, K. (1986), 'The language of French adolescents', *Modern Languages*, vol. 67.

—— (1993), 'Alternative French', Sanders, C. (ed.), *French Today. Language in its social context*, Cambridge University Press, Cambridge.

INED (1993), 'L'unification linguistique de la France', *Population et Sociétés*, 285, décembre.

Offord, M. (1990), *Varieties of contemporary French*, Macmillan, London.

Ministère des Affaires Etrangères (1996), *Une politique pour le français*, Ministère des Affaires Etrangères, Paris.

Roncière, M.-C. de la (1987), *Jeunes d'aujourd'hui. Regards sur les 13–25 ans en France*, Documentation Française, Paris.

Szulmajster-Czelnikier, A. (1996), 'Des Serments de Strasbourg à la loi Toubon: le français comme affaire d'Etat', *Regards sur l'Actualité*, vol. 221, mai.

9
Decentralizing or Deconstructing the Republic?

Gino G. Raymond

Introduction

The breadth of the work undertaken during the decade and a half since the decentralization process was launched in 1982 is impressive. Forty major pieces of legislation were drafted and 300 decrees were formulated in order to facilitate the process of redistributing administrative prerogatives and responsibilities across a hierarchy of structures that remained, contrary to some expectations, remarkably stable: more than 36,000 communes, 100 departments in France and overseas, and 26 regions. The economic data shows that local authorities deploy significant weight in the national economy. In terms of the response to France's infrastructural needs, by 1997 they were responsible for 25 per cent of all public expenditure. The burden of responsibility that was shifted to the departments and the communes in the sphere of social security resulted in the disbursement of over FF90 billion in 1996, and in the sphere of education, the regions and departments spent over FF200 billion during the preceding decade upgrading the facilities in establishments for secondary education.[1] But the notion that decentralization was necessary for the political health of the Republic, as well as a more efficient administration of its affairs, was not an idea that hatched in 1982.

Alarm at the concentration of power at the centre was voiced from the inception of the Fifth Republic. The need to shift from a position of republican centralism was perceived by some commentators as vital, if France was to progress from a situation where change only occurred in the face of crises generated by overflowing resentment at the inadequacies of sclerotic administrative structures and political immobilism.[2]

A year after the voters of France had approved the constitution of the Fifth Republic by referendum, there was some loosening of the structures of administration. The decrees passed in 1959–1960 divided metropolitan France into 22 regional administrative areas, paving the way for the creation in 1964 of the *Commission de développement économique régional* (CODER), which for the first time gave the regions representation in a public body. However, the reforms proposed by Gaston Defferre after the Socialists came to power in 1981 gave much bolder expression to ideas that had been very tentatively signalled by the preceding administration. But one could argue that the much trumpeted scale of the ambition to decentralize was matched inversely by the change in the rationale behind it, as great democratizing intentions gave way to modernizing ones. Although there was an undeniable transfer of resources and competencies from the centre to the localities, the net gain was more measurable in terms of regional efficiency and competitiveness in a supra-national context, rather than sweeping democratization in a national context. In the process, choices and contradictions were exposed that deconstructed assumptions about the extent to which localized structures could mediate in the relationship between sectional interests and the state and pointed to the challenge, emanating from the parish pump and supranational bodies, of rethinking the Republic.

Legislative steps to decentralization

The great innovation of the Defferre reforms of 1982 was the impetus they gave to the emergence of the region as an independent component in the administrative and political architecture of France, with prerogatives of its own. Although the legislation did not bring any geographic modifications to the 26 regions already in existence (including those in the four overseas departments, *départements d'outre-mer*), the new administrative and financial independence given to them meant that they had progressed to a position where they were subject to the supervision of the state rather than its *a priori* tutelage. This independence was strengthened by the transfer of executive power from both regional and departmental prefects to the elected chairpersons of the departmental and regional councils (i.e. the *conseil général* and the *conseil régional*). The third major reform was to upgrade the legal and political status of the regions by making them *collectivités territoriales*, thereby giving them more representative legitimacy and 'clout' than they had enjoyed as *établissements public régionaux* after regional councils were created in the legislation of July 1972. This representative legitimacy was underpinned by the fact that thereafter regional councils would be elected by universal suffrage.[3]

There followed a series of legislative measures during the next decade and a half that were aimed at reinforcing the efficacy and accountability of decentralized administrative structures, but whose partial success, as we shall examine later, sometimes added a new dimension to the problematic relationship between the centre and the periphery in the exercise of power. The laws passed in January and July 1983 further established the respective competencies of the local authorities and the state. In 1986 the election of regional councillors by universal suffrage finally took place, and by proportional representation, as established by legislation in 1985. In January 1988 measures aimed at the 'amélioration de la décentralisation' highlighted the economic prerogatives of local authorities and in particular the financial control that could be exercised at regional level, and at the end of that year legislation defined the scope of responsibility at local authority level for the guaranteed minimum income for those in dire need (RMI, *revenu minimum d'insertion*). Legislation passed in January 1990 governing the financing of political activities was followed by measures in 1992 which, among other things, underlined the principle of 'déconcentration', defining and delimiting the prerogatives and resources attributed to the different levels of civil administration in France.[4] To complement the deconcentration (which had already made considerable ground, notably in the areas of education and training, since 1985), legislation was passed in January 1993 aimed at ensuring greater transparency in the work of local authorities. In February 1995 more powers were transferred from the state to the regions in the determination of public transport policy, and in 1996 a stability pact was drawn up between the state and the local authorities, covering the three years 1996–1998, and identifying the increases in the transfer of funds from the state to the localities that would be needed to underwrite their expenditure.

From greater democracy to greater modernization

Prior to his election to the presidency, François Mitterrand had made clear his belief that although France had needed the exercise of strong and centralized power in order to cohere as a nation, it would need decentralized powers in order not to unravel.[5] Long years in opposition at national level had meant that the only experience of government left open to the Socialists had been at local level, and this had given many of their senior politicians who also held local mandates (such as Pierre Mauroy as mayor of Lille and Gaston Defferre as mayor of Marseille) considerable familiarity with the controls and bottlenecks encountered in dealings with centralized structures of administration. It is not surprising, therefore, that the programme of decentralization should be, as Prime Minister Mauroy put it, 'la grande affaire du septennat'. However, as Cabinet discussion of Defferre's proposals reveal, the Socialists also had a Jacobin attachment to the indivisibility of the Republic that could inject numerous caveats into the debate. Jack Lang, for example, reacted vigorously against the transfer of funds from the Ministry of Culture to the local authorities because a truly national policy for developing the cultural life of the nation had not yet been elaborated. As for Defferre's plans to abolish that classic representative of centralized power in the provinces, the *préfet*, this was not constitutionally possible. They would, however, find a new guise as 'commissaires de la République', and they found an advocate for the retention of their fundamental role in the shape of President Mitterrand.[6]

As the earlier outline of the principal phases in the legislative process of decentralization suggested, the process was not immune from short-term political considerations and a degree of ideological atavism. While there was a pragmatic reason for the deferment of the elections to the regional councils until 1986 – namely, the declining prospects for the Socialists at the polls – there was also a debate within the administration centred on the underlying principles at stake. There were those who believed (including President Mitterrand himself), that the primacy of the department, as the principal level of government between the municipality and the state, should not be compromised. Instead, and to the disappointment of those in favour of developing regional awareness in France, it was the credibility of the regions which was compromised when the decision was taken to use departmental boundaries to form the outlines for the constituencies in the regional elections. In legal terms, the regions were conceived with a less enduring guarantee of their perennity than the other levels of local authority thrown up by the Jacobin paradigm. Whereas the other entities were acknowledged in clause 72 of the constitution, the regions were created by ordinary legislation and consequently could be redefined in their organization and function by ordinary legislation. In practical terms, the other major disadvantage suffered by the regions vis-à-vis the departments and the municipalities was that, while the regions received specific new grants transferred from the centre, they did not enjoy the block grant, or DGF (*Dotation Globale de Fonctionnement*) accorded to the other levels of local authority, nor therefore the corresponding degree of financial autonomy.

By July 1984, however, and in the light of three difficult years that had coincided with a downturn in the world economy, the new Socialist prime minister, Laurent Fabius, decided that the best way of restoring confidence in an administration that had started with a great reformist wave of democratization (whether in the control of the nation's assets or the exercise of the nation's voice), was to demonstrate its skill at modernization.[7] In the ensuing years the regions demonstrated their ability to adapt to horizons that proved more modest than those hoped for by the ardent advocates of decentralization.

Since the 1970s contractual agreements had existed between the state and local governments that were aimed at ensuring the compatibility of investments made at the centre and the periphery in order to serve urban districts (*communautés urbaines*), and medium-sized cities and rural areas (*contrats villes moyennes* and *contrats de pays*). However, the *Contrats de Plan Etat-Régions* which emerged from the Defferre reforms appeared to represent a qualitative leap forward, establishing planning contracts between the state and the regions that would mark a major advance from the *dirigisme* of old. The law of 29 March 1982 gave the regions formal responsibility for economic development within their boundaries, and complemented the structures already in place: the *Commissariat Général du Plan* (CGP) which had conducted national planning since 1946; and the *Délégation à l'Aménagement du Territoire et à l'Action Régionale* (DATAR) which had conducted regional policy since 1963. The planning reform adopted on 29 July 1982 underlined the vocation of the regions to elaborate regional plans, to make their input to the elaboration of the national plan and ultimately to participate in its implementation through *contrats de plan*. An ordinance on 21 January 1983 specified the rules governing these contracts and the first generation of them came into effect in 1984.

By the time the first generation of *contrats* came to an end in 1988, it became possible to begin an assessment of the distance between the expectations and the fulfilment of these decentralizing measures. Although the budgets for the regions climbed spectacularly (three times greater than Departmental budgets during the decade 1982–1991), the modest starting point and the regions' limited scope for initiative meant that, for example, it was not until 1987 that they could recruit their own civil servants. Financial instruments available to the regional authorities allowed them to intervene in the economic life of the regions to the extent that they could allocate grants to firms to enhance their activity in the area (*prime régionale à la création de l'emploi*) and provide a grant per employee (*prime régionale à l'emploi*). Less direct financial aid could be offered in the form of subsidized accommodation, long-term loans and loan guarantees. But these measures did not constitute the means to design regional policy. A closer look at what was perceived as a more genuine exercise in regional management, namely the provision of training, showed that in spite of the lead taken by regional representatives, the control of programme design and implementation remained largely in the hands of the state's professionals.[8]

The difficulty faced by the regions in taking the lead away from the departments and communes as economic actors in the planning process lay also in the fact that pre-existing relationships and priorities left limited openings for them. The organization of many businesses at departmental or municipal level did not make the attractions of regional initiatives obvious. Moreover, the promotion of major development policies by large cities and the concentration of economic activity around them inevitably took the limelight away from region-wide programmes. Yet in spite of the constraints they faced, the regions showed that there were areas where they could operate very efficiently as agents of local government and not just as agents of the state, by using the resources available at the state level for the pursuit of regional objectives. This success was most notable in education, where the regions could employ free of charge (as envisaged in the legislation of 1982–83) the administrative and technical infrastructure provided by the state. Thus, if the decision was taken to build a secondary school, they could exploit the state education offices at the regional level (*rectorats*), and the DDE (*Direction Départementale de l'Equipement*).

On a more general level, by the early 1990s, instead of pushing against a narrow legal framework governing economic intervention, the regions learned to pursue other avenues in order to exert their influence. The use of direct grants to firms declined, but initiatives to improve the business environment in which they operated increased. More specifically, the regions proved their efficiency as agents of modernization in the impetus given to the development of high-technology industries and projects. Using the 'general powers' available to them, in the early 1990s regions like the Languedoc-Roussillon launched initiatives such as the *Multipole technologique régional*, aimed at linking up high-tech industries and research in eight centres, which quickly established itself as the major economic project in the region. The input of regional councils could be even more direct, as in the creation of a science park in order to lay the foundation for the *Caen/Basse Normandie technopole*. In Lorraine also, the launch of the Metz 2000 science park owed much to the activity of the regional council. By investing in these projects the regional councils were tapping into the potent symbolism of modern technologies that were environmentally friendly, socially useful and which often inspired correspondingly innovative architecture to house them; all factors particularly appealing to middle-class electorates.

The prospect of economic renewal, in light of the somewhat mythified example of Silicon Valley, changed the orientation and the scale of the ambition of the Provence-Alpes-Côtes d'Azur region, which by 1987 had jettisoned the use of direct grants to encourage industry, opting instead for a development strategy based on new technology spread across six regional science parks. The *route des hautes technologies*, or high-tech highway connecting these endeavours through infrastructure installations like telecommunications networks, was to be funded in a way that illustrated the resourcefulness of regional councils vis-à-vis a new and major player; the European Union. In the case of the scheme conceived by Provence-Alpes-Côte d'Azur, the FF1.75 billion budget was to be spread over five years and jointly funded by the region, the state and the European Union.

While the political history of France militated against French regions developing the same kind of regional corporatism as exists in Italy or Germany (where, it could be argued, it is the regions rather than the state that become responsible for the regulation of economic interests), French regions have nonetheless shown themselves extremely adept at exploiting their relationship with the EU. In a sense, this is a logical result of the fact that regionalization and European integration have gone hand in hand.[9] As the dialogue between the EU's central institutions and the regions develops, so too do the sub-national structures that frame those exchanges. But as the case of the United Kingdom's regions demonstrates, the former does not necessarily drive the latter, and consequently the dialogue does not always bear much fruit in terms of resources. In conspicuous contrast to their UK neighbours, the French regions were among the first to open offices in Brussels, and within a decade of Defferre's reforms, 17 of the 22 French metropolitan regional authorities enjoyed permanent representation there, forming a considerable French regional lobby.

Even though the tension between 'departmentalists' and 'regionalists' suggested some ambiguity in governing circles concerning the new role of the regions in the hierarchy of competencies within France, Defferre's reforms were clearly supportive of the regions in their attempts to incorporate French interests into European policy-making processes. For example, one of the provisions of the Defferre law of 2 March 1982 empowered French regions to subscribe to agreements to collaborate on projects of mutual interest with local authorities in neighbouring countries. Moreover, the planning contracts between the regions and the French state not only allowed the regions an input in the national plan but also made them partners with the state in the definition of France's relationship to Europe. For example, the 1989–1992 national plan incorporated elements of France's response to the challenges that would emerge from the creation of the Single European Market by aligning regional and national efforts in pursuit of complementary objectives. Thus, in 1990 the national planning agency DATAR began to provide training sessions for local administrators on EU structural funds, as part of the broad aim of securing some kind of convergence between French investment strategies and EU regional funding priorities. This state support for the regions led to notable trilateral planning contracts that brought the EU into partnership with the other two parties and secured its input, for instance, into the Integrated Mediterranean Programme – bringing together the regions of Aquitaine, Corsica, Languedoc-Roussillon, Midi-Pyrénées, Provence-Alpes-Côte-d'Azur, plus the Departments of Drôme and Ardèche, who together put forward infrastructure projects that were sanctioned by the European Commission and resulted in the disbursement of FF9 billion of European money between 1986 and 1989 to help finance those projects.[10]

The Single European Act of 1986 undoubtedly strengthened the resolve of French governments to help the regions to become winners in the competitive arena of the Single European Market outside the national boundaries. The potential material gain was signalled by the meeting of the European Council in 1988, which determined that structural funds available to the regions should double over the five ensuing years and eventually account for 25 per cent of the EU budget. The response in Paris was to deploy national resources available to DATAR to support those regional federations, such as the Grand Sud and the Grand Est, endeavouring to enhance their competitiveness vis-à-vis the other powerful regions of Europe. Further support from the centre came in 1992 when another tranche of territorial administrative reforms strengthened the coordinating powers of the regional prefect and reinforced his hierarchical superiority with regard to his departmental counterpart, thereby reducing the prospect of friction between local authorities that might hinder the success of inter-regional co-operation.

The regions themselves have demonstrated an ability to exploit the gap between the French state and the European Union by tapping into funds which as individual regions of a nation-state they would not be allowed to bid for, with or without the support of the national government. Since 1986, regions like Rhône-Alpes and Alsace have been able to bid for EU funds dedicated to transfrontier projects in which the French participants have figured as members of a 'Euro-region'. In 1990 Alsace joined an Upper Rhine region (also including two German Länder and two Swiss cantons) to bid for EU funding for 30 projects under the INTERREG programme aimed at equipping border regions for the advent of the Single European Market three years later.

Implicit, however, in the foregoing overview of the success of the regions in France is that in general, the thrust of their activities has depended crucially on conformity with an agenda set by the centre, underpinned by an ethos emanating from the centre of modernization rather than democratization. The impetus given to new technologies has dovetailed with the need perceived at the centre to promote them where they did not exist, or to encourage their growth in areas where they would compensate for the decline in traditional industries. It could be argued that the new developments like the provision of state field services, allied to initiatives taken by local Chambers of Commerce and regional public–private partnerships, became a way of promoting national policies by securing co-financing at the local level.[11] One example of this is the success of structures aimed at boosting French exports, but at the regional level. Thus regions like Brittany and Alsace, figuring among the least developed industrially or most in need of new products for new markets, have developed their own structures, predominantly funded by the regions, for enhancing their contribution to the national balance of payments surplus.

On the European stage, and in spite of the success of cross-frontier co-operation with foreign regions, it remains the case that the crucial relationship within the Union, in juridical and practical terms, is that between Brussels and the nation-states. In contrast to German Länder and Belgian local authorities, French regions do not have the weight that enable the former to play a formal role at the national level in the formulation of EU policy. As the support given to regions through French decentralization suggests, the priority was to make them more effective champions for France in the European sphere. Ironically, the increase in the disbursement of EU structural funds makes the centralized state even more unavoidable, since normally bids for these resources have to be supported by national governments. More broadly, it is at present difficult to imagine that the effective participation of French regional authorities in the EU regional policy process can avoid entailing more, rather than less, *concertation* with the national planning agency DATAR and the Ministry for Planning.

Pressures from the locality and from Europe

Some of the transfers of funds and initiatives to the localities were undeniably substantial and effected considerable change. There had already been two waves of decentralizing measures before January 1985, when responsibility for maintaining and constructing *lycées* (upper, or high schools) was transferred to regional councils, and the corresponding responsibility for *collèges* (lower, or junior high schools) was transferred to departmental councils. This built on the enhanced authority given to the rectors in the 25 academies of metropolitan France, assistant rectors in 96 departments and individual school principals, at the expense of the central bureaucracy. At *collège* level particularly, scope was created for more innovative teaching and greater responsiveness to the input of the host community. This was achieved in spite of some opposition by teaching unions, whose own organization had grown to mirror the centralized structures with which they negotiated traditionally, and who were concerned at the prospect of local interference by non-specialists. Notwithstanding these misgivings by the profession, by 1992 local and regional authorities were paying 19.1 per cent of the total costs of French education.[12]

It may be argued that the rise in investment, particularly in the fabric of schools, was accelerated by the decentralization of this responsibility, but by the end of the decade a resurgence of conflicts in the sphere of education pointed to an underlying problem that could only be resolved at the national level. In the spring of 1998 the long campaign for more resources, human and material, waged by the parents and teachers in the deprived urban area of Seine-Saint-Denis resulted in the offer of a round table with them and the presidents of the departmental and regional councils, from the minister of education, Claude Allègre. While for the representatives of the local authorities the concern was to identify the bottlenecks upstream that constrained their downstream activities, for the *lycée* students anxiety stemmed from the fear that the deconcentration of competencies might result in the attribution of a 'bac au rabais', a cut-price school leaving certificate from one area of a decentralized education system without the means to do otherwise.[13]

While there are individual voices at local level which accuse central government of rowing back on decentralization,[14] there is a more widespread feeling that decentralization has become a means of diffusing responsibility rather than genuine empowerment, using local authorities as a lighting conductor, to take the heat off central government for things which it can no longer afford to do. As the continuing and vexed question of local taxation illustrates, and in particular the *taxe professionnelle* or business rate, decentralization was not matched by a radical reform of revenue raising, leaving many local representatives with the impression that the burden of assuming the cost of social and economic dysfunctions like homelessness and unemployment was simply shifted downwards to them.[15]

As for the voters at local level, the regional elections of March 1998 suggested that the prospect of participating in the operation of decentralized structures has yet to be appreciated fully as an exercise in greater democratization. Notwithstanding the many headlines devoted to the success of the left and the implosion of the centre-right, not least the willingness of five leading UDF figures to reach compromises with the Front National in order to be elected to the presidency of their respective regional councils, underlying trends showed that the elections had not gained in credibility vis-à-vis the electorate. An abstention rate of 42 per cent confirmed the downward trend of the preceding decade and reinforced the belief of some commentators that the 'crisis of representation' in France was deepening.[16] This abstentionism, allied to the rise of extreme left parties as well as the far right, strengthened the argument (which emerged with the defeat of the centre-right majority at the legislative elections in 1997) that many of the electors were using their vote to express their lack of faith in government, a 'vote sanction'. Furthermore, polling in the run-up to the elections showed that those sectors of the electorate that would be most affected by the exercise of regional competencies covering issues like transport and education were the ones who felt most alienated from the process.[17]

On the European front, while central government has supported French regions in the pursuit of objectives like European structural funds, in a manner compatible with national priorities, new levels of regional co-operation are emerging which are weightier than the obvious bilateral or trilateral cross-frontier ones. In 1987 the Assembly of European Regions (ARE) was born out of the old Council of European Regions and became an umbrella for a number of interregional organizations identifying common interests which were not necessarily contiguous, and possessing the clear vocation of reinforcing the political representation of the regions concerned within the European Union and the Council of Europe. Of the nine founding interregional organizations in the ARE, some were notable for the spread of interests represented: the Association of European Border Regions (AEBR); the Conference of Peripheral Maritime Regions (CRPM); and the Community of Traditional Industrial Regions (RETI).

On a Europe-wide level, the creation of the single market has created policy areas where Paris will not be able to steer the French regions or conduct a strictly national policy. Working hours, employment protection, vocational and professional training, trading standards, health and safety at work and consumer protection are merely some of the areas where the framing of pan-European policy by Brussels can be expected to reduce the scope for both local and national initiatives. This reduced freedom of action, however, constitutes one aspect of a greater historic compromise made by the French state in order to transform the structures of power in Europe, illustrated by its agreement to adopt the single European currency in 1999 and thereby renouncing one of the most potent and age-old symbols of national sovereignty: the right to strike its own coin.

Conclusion: rethinking the Republic

Bottom-up and top-down pressures are causing some people engaged in managing the structures of the Republic to wonder whether the time has come to rethink the centrality of a unified and hierarchized Republic and to think of structures that respond to needs, specifically by breaking the homology between prerogatives of power and their geographic and administrative definitions. If French citizens are ever more numerous in refusing to endure the 'imperium' of a state that purports to embody the general interest, how can that state pretend to embody the community of its citizens?[18] In European terms, we are seeing, for example, the creation of inter-regional entities responding to needs that cannot be accommodated by the old-fashioned nation-state but are driven by the sectoral imperatives generated when two or more regions share the same transnational interests.

Within France there is the new entity, the 'pays', recognized in the legislation passed in February 1995, which is neither a region or a department, but recognizes a coherent community of interest that may transgress these administrative boundaries.[19] It may seem ironical, given the layers of responsibilities and legal competencies that exist already, and the sometimes problematical nature of the relationships between them, that these inter-relationships should become potentially even more complex with the advent of the 'pays'. However, as the demonstrations by the half-million or so high school students in the streets of Paris in October 1998 illustrated, it is not so much the desire to see the state rolled back which is at the heart of the malaise in France but, as Marie-France Toinet argues, the lack of 'gouvernement': 'gouvernement' meaning leaders with the imagination and public-spiritedness to respond to the needs of their electorate and challenge the near-universal assumption that civil society should replace the state, arguing instead through the elaboration of appropriate policies that the state has its place, and a role that only it can fill.[20] As one of the most recent and comprehensive surveys of social change in France has highlighted, the transition from homogenizing concepts like 'classe ouvrière' to individuating ones like 'archipel des employés', has heightened the need for newer and more adaptable structures to protect the constituent parts of the social archipelago. Should those structures not be developed, the prospect then begins to grow of a political economy generated by a social psychology of victimization opening the door to populisms that polarize blame on other individuals or representative groups, rather than on deficient structures.[21]

In the short term, the challenge lies in ensuring that the ambiguities implicit in some of the decentralizing measures do not defeat their original intentions. The initiative granted to local representatives in 1992 to launch referenda on issues within the remit of local authorities was extended to the inhabitants themselves in 1995 (provided it was supported by 20 per cent of registered voters), with a view to making referenda a genuine part of the representative process, as opposed to the negationist act that referenda often prove to be owing to their operation as palliatives for the underlying impotence of voters. But more important is the need to prevent the local structures which act as counterweights to central power becoming feudal tributaries to a 'monarchical' concentration of power at the centre. And any attempt to neutralize this risk has to address the issue of the famous 'cumul des mandats' (the acquisition of a series of different political mandates by the same individuals participating on different representative bodies), if local representation is to facilitate a more genuinely collegial exercise of power for the benefit of the locality, as opposed to providing opportunities for actors to reintegrate local priorities into a national hierarchy of power struggles.[22]

The uncertainties expressed at local level that have accompanied the process of decentralization convey the sometimes justified suspicion that powers and responsibilities have been devolved for pragmatic, even self-serving reasons by the structures of power at the heart of the Republic. At the same time, those pressures for change at local level and at the supranational level have engaged the Republic in a process of evolution which, although it may not yet consign the centralized Republican blueprint to history, has made the governing elite in France conscious of the reality that a regression to the old rigidities that characterized the structures of power at the beginning of the Fifth Republic would be neither compatible with the pursuit of cohesion within France nor likely to further convergence with its partners in Europe.

Notes

1. Figures quoted in Boeuf, Jean-Luc (1997), *Quinze ans de décentralisation*, La documentation française, Paris.
2. The seminal text on this being Crozier, M (1963), *The Bureaucratic Phenomenon*, Chicago University Press, Chicago.
3. But the commitment to this change was tempered by the equivocations which resulted in the continual deferment of these elections until March 1986, meaning in reality that the regions remained *établissements publics* until that date, since the legislation stipulated that the regions could not be constituted as *collectivités territoriales* until the councils had been convened after election by universal suffrage.
4. Legislation passed in May 1991 placed Corsica in a category of its own, transforming it from a region with a special status into a unique type of local authority.
5. Mitterrand, F (1980), *Ici et Maintenant*, Fayard, Paris.
6. 'There must be those who represent the unity of the state... If decentralization displaces the apparatus of the state, we will be subject to the accusation of undermining its unity'. In Favier, P. and Martin-Rolland, M. (1990), *La décennie Mitterrand: Les ruptures*, Seuil, Paris, p.146. My translation, and all subsequent quotations originally in French.
7. As Fabius announced in his first prime ministerial speech before the National Assembly on 24 July 1984: 'To modernize and to rally, those are the priorities of the government I lead'. In Favier, P. and Martin-Rolland, M (1991), *La décennie Mitterrand: Les épreuves*, Seuil, Paris, p.172.
8. See Michel, H. (1994), 'Décideurs ou régulateurs? Le cas des élus régionaux chargés de la formation professionnelle en Bretagne' in Fontaine, J. and Le Bart, C. (eds), *Le métier politique*, L'Harmattan, Paris.
9. Mazey, S. (1995), 'French Regions and the European Union' in Loughlin, J. and Mazey, S. (eds), *The End of the French Unitary State?* Frank Cass, London, pp.132–157, p.132.

10. Ibid. p.136.
11. Le Galès, P. (1995), 'Regional Economic Policies: An Alternative to French Economic Dirigisme?' in Loughlin, J. and Mazey, S. (eds), *The End of the French Unitary State?* Frank Cass, London, pp.72–91, p.83.
12. Ministère de l'Education Nationale (1993), *Repères*, p.231.
13. Blanchard, S. and Gurrey, B., 'M. Allègre annonce une table ronde sur la Seine-Saint-Denis', *Le Monde*, 2 April 1998.
14. Jean Puech, chairman of the departmental council of Aveyron and spokesperson for the other council leaders, spelled out the dangers they foresaw to the process of genuine decentralization prior to their congress in Rouen on 14–15 October 1998, and to which the minister for decentralization, Emile Zuccarelli, was invited. In Puech's view, departmental councils had come up against a technostructure that had never been able fully to accept the Defferre reforms and that now, through, for example, the policy being elaborated on green taxes, the 'nationalization' of the policy on water, and the centralized management of the structural funds allocated by the European Union, was, he believed, recentralizing the administration in France. See 'Départements: le coup de gueule', in *L'Express*, 15–21 October 1998, p.8.
15. Delevoye, Jean-Paul, President of the association of mayors of France, 'Imaginons un autre partenariat entre les collectivités locales et l'Etat', *La Gazette des communes, des départements, des régions*, Paris, 18 November 1996. Delevoye, like many others involved in managing the consequences of decentralization, is not convinced that the process has yet succeeded in establishing 'both conceptually and institutionally the compatibility of national unity and equality on the one hand with local liberty on the other'. As is confidently asserted in Schmidt, V.A. (1990), *Democratizing France. The Political and Administrative History of Decentralization*, Cambridge University Press, Cambridge, p.392.
16. Le Gall, G. (1998), 'Cantonales et régionales: quand 1998 confirme 1997', *Revue Politique et Parlementaire*, no. 993, March/April, pp.5–23.
17. Mechet, P. (1998), 'L'opinion et les régionales de 1998: de la distance à l'indignation', *Revue Politique et Parlementaire*, no. 993, March/April, pp.61–67.
18. Picq, J. (1995), 'Il faut sortir d'une vision jacobine au profit d'une vision décentralisatrice de l'Etat lui-même', *Pouvoirs locaux*, revue trimestrielle de l'Institut de la Décentralisation, no. 24, March, pp.41–44.
19. Loi d'orientation pour l'aménagement et le développement du territoire, 4 February 1995, article 22: 'Where a territory represents a coherent geographical, cultural, economic or social entity...it may constitute a *pays*'. My translation. The principal elements of this legislation are summarized in Boeuf, p.72.
20. Toinet, Marie-France (1996), 'The Limits of Malaise in France', in Keeler, John T.S. and Schain, Martin A., *Chirac's Challenge: Liberalization, Europeanization, and Malaise in France*, Macmillan, Basingstoke, pp.279–298.
21. Rosanvallon, P. et al. (1998), *France: les révolutions invisibles*, Calmann-Lévy, Paris.
22. de Lara, P. (1996), 'La démocratie à l'épreuve de la décentralisation', in *La décentralisation en France*. Editions de la Découverte/Institut de la Décentralisation, Paris, pp.47–51.

Bibliography

Blanc, J. and Rémond, B. (1990), *Les collectivités locales*, Presses de Sciences-Po et Dalloz, Paris.

Boeuf, Jean-Luc (1997), *Quinze ans de décentralisation*, La documentation française, Paris.

Crozier, M. (1963), *The Bureaucratic Phenomenon*, Chicago University Press, Chicago.

Delcamp, A. (1995), *Les collectivités décentralisées de l'Union européenne*, La documentation française, Paris.

Editions de la Découverte (1996), *La décentralisation en France*, Paris.

Favier, P. and Martin-Rolland, M. (1990), *La décennie Mitterrand: Les ruptures*, Seuil, Paris.

—— (1991), *La décennie Mitterrand: Les épreuves*, Seuil, Paris.

Fontaine, J. and Le Bart, C. (eds) (1994), *Le métier politique*, L'Harmattan, Paris.

Le Gall, G. (1998), 'Cantonales et régionales: quand 1998 confirme 1997', *Revue Politique et Parlementaire*, no. 993, March/April.

Keeler, John T. S. and Schain, Martin A. (1996), *Chirac's Challenge: Liberalization, Europeanization, and Malaise in France*, Macmillan, Basingstoke.

Loughlin, J. and Mazey, S. (eds) (1995), *The End of the French Unitary State?* Frank Cass, London.

Mechet, P. (1998), 'L'opinion et les régionales de 1998: de la distance à l'indignation', *Revue Politique et Parlementaire*, no. 993, March/April.

Ministère de l'Education Nationale (1993), *Repères*, Paris.

Mitterrand, F. (1980), *Ici et Maintenant*, Fayard, Paris.

Némon, Jean-Claude and Wachter, Serge (1993), *Entre l'Europe et la décentralisation: les institutions territoriales françaises*, Editions de l'Aube, Paris.

Picq, J. (1995), 'Il faut sortir d'une vision jacobine au profit d'une vision décentralisatrice de l'Etat lui-même', *Pouvoirs locaux*, revue trimestrielle de l'Institut de la Décentralisation, no. 24, March.

Rosanvallon, P. et al. (1998), *France: les révolutions invisibles*, Calmann-Lévy, Paris.

Schmidt, V. A. (1990), *Democratizing France. The Political and Administrative History of Decentralization*, Cambridge University Press, Cambridge.

Index